1977

book may be kept

FOURTEEN DA

arged for each day the bo

WILLIAM FAULKNER
The Abstract and the Actual

WILLIAM FAULKNER

The Abstract and the Actual

PANTHEA REID BROUGHTON

LOUISIANA STATE UNIVERSITY PRESS

Baton Rouge

ISBN 0-8071-0083-8
Library of Congress Catalog Card Number 74-77324
Copyright © 1974 by Louisiana State University Press
All rights reserved
Manufactured in the United States of America

Designed by Dwight Agner. Set in 10/13 Fototronic
Elegante. Printed and bound by Benson Printing
Company, Nashville, Tennessee.

Acknowledgment is made to Mrs. Jill Faulkner Summers and to the Alderman
Library, University of Virginia, for permission to quote from the manuscript
and the typescript of "As I Lay Dying."

Acknowledgment is made to the University Press of Virginia for permission
to quote from *Faulkner in the University: Class Conferences at the University of Virginia,
1957–1958*, ed. Frederick L. Gwynn and Joseph L. Blotner.

Acknowledgment is also made to Random House, Inc., for permission to quote
from the following copyrighted works of William Faulkner: *Absalom, Absalom!;
A Fable; As I Lay Dying; Appendix to "The Sound and the Fury"; Collected Stories
of William Faulkner; Essays, Speeches, and Public Letters; Flags in the Dust; Go Down,
Moses; The Hamlet; Intruder in the Dust; Knight's Gambit; Lion in the Garden: Interviews
with William Faulkner, 1926–1962; The Mansion; Requiem for a Nun; The Reivers;
Sanctuary; The Town; The Unvanquished;* and *The Wild Palms.*

Published with the assistance of the Council on Research, Louisiana State
University.

To
WELDON THORNTON
JOSEPH K. DAVIS
and
CARL FOSTER

Contents

Preface

IT MAY BE an index of our alienation that we are so abstracted from our own existences that we need to read fiction to understand ourselves. If so, it is surely a further indication of alienation to admit that we have to read criticism to understand our fiction; but I, for one, resist that argument. Existence requires an art to order it and to render it comprehensible; as that existence becomes more and more complex, so too does its art, so that the art itself may demand further ordering and explanation. A particularly rough and irregular terrain can, after all, be comprehended more readily with a map, and a map can be better understood if a key to it is provided.

This analogy may startle or perhaps outrage some readers who would insist that literature is too richly concrete to be called an abstraction or compared to a map. I agree that literature is incomparably fuller in its particularity than a map is, yet I would suggest that, compared to existence itself, literature is indeed simple and abstract. The works of artist and map maker are dissimilar then, not because one is concrete, one abstract, but because to some extent one is used one way, one another; the map is utilitarian and teleological; literature is aesthetic and existential. That is, one consults a map with a specific end in mind. "How do I make my way through this wilderness?" To the man lost in the woods, it makes little difference whether the map is hand-painted on parchment or mass-produced by an oil company; all that matters is readability and accuracy. But then, what serious reader really cares whether he reads an autographed first edition or a worn paperback? The physical artifact is not the work of art. The work of art is something else: a new experience, a new understanding, an expansion; the reader or viewer or listener turns to it whether or not he feels lost. He does so in order that he may experience life more completely. The experience itself is then primarily an end, not a means. In these terms, art is nonteleological.

These terms, however, have their limitations; for to insist that literature is nonteleological is to define *teleological* only in the very limited sense of aiming toward a specific end. Propaganda, of course, like a map, is teleological in that limited sense; it is valuable not in itself but only as a means toward an end. A war story may be written in order to inspire patriotism and stimulate enlistment; with such limited, utilitarian aims, it is not literature. Literature and the other arts, however, are hardly (despite Oscar Wilde) useless or aimless. I would contend instead that the arts are utilitarian and teleological in an ultimate sense. Their ends are certainly not specific and limited, but rather general and existential. Even though they are not approached as means to specific ends, the arts are profoundly, ultimately useful in that they enable man to discover and comprehend life, to imagine a more complete existence, and, perhaps, to venture toward making it actual.

To the traveler, a map simplifies and renders comprehensible the terrain; to the reader, literature focuses and renders comprehensible life itself. It too may rescue man from the wilderness. Art exists, then, not for art's sake but for life's. Wallace Stevens writes that "what makes the poet the potent figure that he is, or was, or ought to be, is that he creates the world to which we turn incessantly and without knowing it and that he gives to life the supreme fictions without which we are unable to conceive of it." [1] Without art, life would be literally inconceivable. Surely, then, the poet's function is in the highest sense utilitarian. With such an understanding of the function of art, it is not presumptuous to say that the critic too may create work which is utilitarian in an existential sense; that is, criticism, also, may assist in the rescue of mankind and serve as a means to an ultimate end.

All too often, however, criticism seems to ignore life and address itself to issues which might be described in William Faulkner's terms as mere "picayune splitting of abstract hairs" (AA, 271). Such criticism takes art out of life and leaves its reader in what Mark Spilka calls "aesthetic suspension." Spilka explains that in imitating the objectivity of the positivists "we [modern critics] have reduced the reading process to an experience of isolated forms [,but] we *must* connect these forms with human contexts." [2] Spilka is suggesting a revision or expansion of New Critical methods so that criticism would not reduce but rather expand its province. Rather than ignoring context, criticism might then be capable of shaping it and therefore of changing "the quality of American culture." [3] Such criticism would be intrinsically valuable, ultimately existential.

Unfortunately, however, the vast accumulation of critical studies extant today rarely attains such existential import. In an age when printed material proliferates while man seems to possess neither the time, inclination, nor even ability to read it, the publication of yet another critical study must be justified, especially when the book deals with a writer such as William

1 Wallace Stevens, *The Necessary Angel: Essays on Reality and the Imagination* (New York: Vintage Books, n.d.), 31.
2 Mark Spilka, "The Necessary Stylist: A New Critical Revision," *Modern Fiction Studies*, VI (Winter, 1960–61), 297.
3 *Ibid.*

Faulkner about whom so much has already been written. My justifications are familiar ones: this book will be different; this one is needed; at least my intentions are that this study will serve in some small way to interrelate life and art.

More specifically, I feel that a study of abstractions has enormous philosophical and aesthetic implications which have been as yet inadequately explored. If other ages have been overfond of the abstraction, ours is overly hostile to it. Faulkner, however, is neither fond nor hostile. He makes the misuse of abstractions a seminal theme throughout his fiction, yet he understands that abstractions need not be so misused. Any number of his characters rely upon abstractions in autistic attempts to falsify existence. Faulkner depicts the absurdity and defeatism inherent in such attempts, but he does not assume (as so many of his contemporaries did) that the abstraction itself is at fault, for his fiction includes further examples of the ways in which abstractions may enhance rather than diminish existence. Furthermore, Faulkner seems intuitively to have understood that art itself is an abstraction. At a time when aestheticians were equating abstractness in art with incompetence, Faulkner relied freely on abstract terminology and was willing to risk a style which was often abstract, baroque, grandiose. Faulkner's understanding of the existential and aesthetic functions of abstractions is, then, more balanced, complex, and sophisticated than that of, say, Ernest Hemingway who insisted that abstractions were obscene, their use in art immoral.

My intention is to establish just how ubiquitous is Faulkner's concern with abstractions, how insightful and consistent is his judgment. The discussion is organized by theme rather than source. It is indexed by theme and by character; titles are indexed only when the work as a whole is discussed. I quote extensively from the fiction and group together selections of incidents, or characters, or comments according to their similarities, my assumption being that congruence is most significant when it emerges from diversity. This approach, to avoid redundancy and tedium, de-emphasizes context. Even though I may not review context at any length, I trust that I have not violated it.

This study is necessarily abstract and philosophical,[4] but I should like to insist and to illustrate that the abstract may be relevant. Literature, after all, even in its concrete particularity, is an abstraction from the whole situation, and criticism is an abstraction from literature. It necessarily selects those matters (be they textual or mythic, formalistic or philosophical) which possess in themselves certain abstract similarities. Isolated from the whole, these matters may better be analyzed and comprehended. Criticism then is intellectual, and it may be philosophical since it approaches art in something of the same manner that philosophy studies life. Even the most theoretical criticism, however, cannot turn literature into philosophy; for, like life, literature may not be deduced. Reductionist criticism may mistake its abstract theories about art for the art itself, but valid criticism functions not to replace art but to enhance man's understanding and experience of it; heightened experience of art should, in turn, enhance the experience of life itself. My intent is not to reduce or to replace, but rather to depart from the "aesthetic suspension" Spilka speaks of and to aim toward a sort of aesthetic immersion. To accomplish this end it is necessary first of all to abstract and then to reconnect. The abstraction which is this study should maintain its connectedness with the abstraction which is Faulkner's fiction and with the actuality beyond it, which is life.

---

4 I quote various philosophers rather extensively throughout this study, not to imply influence (except with Bergson), but rather to offer corroboration for Faulkner's understandings. Without direct influence, such corroboration seems an even more impressive testimony to the breadth and validity of Faulkner's insight.

Acknowledgments

THIS BOOK is dedicated to Weldon Thornton and Joseph K. Davis who have been my mentors and to Carl Foster who was my student. Together they have confirmed my conviction that ideas may live even in the dusty halls of academia. Both Weldon Thornton and Joe Davis helped make the modern world and that portion of it which is Faulkner's fiction comprehensible. Carl Foster reacted to literature and especially to Faulkner with such gusto that he helped make my own classes alive. That he survived Vietnam to die on a fishing trip in Tidewater Virginia is another of nature's insane absurdities.

I wish also to thank Joseph L. Blotner whose thorough knowledge of Faulkner's fiction and careful reading of this text have proved invaluable to me. Julius Raper, George Bedell, Quentin Gehle, and Barbara Hoagland have also offered many helpful comments and suggestions. Sue Moses and Emily Terry have given their time and care to work on the manuscript, and Janet Hobbs's assistance and support have been indefatigable and indispensable. Leslie E. Phillabaum of Louisiana State University Press has been especially considerate and perceptive. And Marie Carmichael's copy editing has been intelligent, efficient, and, as best I can tell, flawless.

The English Department and the College of Arts and Sciences at Virginia Polytechnic Institute and State University financed several excursions to Charlottesville for me to study the Faulkner collection at the Alderman Library. My thanks to them and to Jill Faulkner Summers for permission to quote from the manuscripts. Special thanks too go to Ruth and Miles Horton, whose studio was in itself a sanctuary from the storm.

I must also thank Jerolyn Deplazes, Lucile Griffin, Shirley Farrier, and Cecile and Ben Keller who saw more than their share of Reid Broughton while this book was in the works. I am deeply grateful to my parents John and Nell Reid for their long-term support and encouragement. And of course I must thank George and Reid Broughton who saw the first and the last of this; they endured.

P.R.B.
Gap Mountain
Newport, Virginia
May, 1974

List of Abbreviations

PRIMARY MATERIAL is cited parenthetically within the text of this study. The editions quoted and the abbreviations used are:

AA   *Absalom, Absalom!* New York: Modern Library, 1964.

AF   *A Fable.* New York: Modern Library, 1966.

AILD   *As I Lay Dying.* New York: Vintage Books, 1964.

A to SF   *Appendix to "The Sound and the Fury."* New York: Modern Library, 1946.

CS   *Collected Stories of William Faulkner.* New York: Random House, 1950.

ESPL   *Essays, Speeches, and Public Letters,* ed. James B. Meriwether. New York: Random House, 1965.

FD   *Flags in the Dust,* ed. Douglas Day. New York: Random House, 1973. The final complete typescript of *Flags in the Dust* has not survived (apparently Ben Wasson destroyed it when he trimmed *Flags* down to make *Sartoris*). Douglas Day compiled this 1973 edition from the composite typescript Faulkner preserved; thus it more closely approximates Faulkner's intentions than does *Sartoris*. I use this text to quote material deleted from *Sartoris*.

FIU   *Faulkner in the University: Class Conferences at the University of Virginia, 1957–1958,* ed. Frederick L. Gwynn and Joseph L. Blotner. New York: Vintage Books, 1965.

GDM   *Go Down, Moses.* New York: Modern Library, 1955.

H   *The Hamlet.* New York: Random House, 1940.

ID   *Intruder in the Dust.* New York: Random House, 1948.

KG   *Knight's Gambit.* New York: Random House, 1949.

LA   *Light in August.* New York: Harrison Smith and Robert Haas, 1932.

LG   *Lion in the Garden: Interviews with William Faulkner, 1926–1962,* ed. James B. Meriwether and Michael Millgate. New York: Random House, 1968.

Man.   *The Mansion.* New York: Vintage Books, 1959.

Mos.   *Mosquitoes.* New York: Liveright Publishing Co., 1955.

P   *Pylon.* New York: Harrison Smith and Robert Haas, Inc., 1935.

Req.   *Requiem for a Nun.* New York: Random House, 1968.

Rev.   *The Reivers.* New York: Vintage Books, 1966.

San.   *Sanctuary.* New York: Random House, 1962.

SP   *Soldiers' Pay.* Garden City, N.Y.: Sun Dial Press, Inc., 1937.

SF   *The Sound and the Fury.* New York: Jonathan Cape and Harrison Smith, 1929.

T   *The Town.* New York: Vintage Books, 1957.

U   *The Unvanquished.* New York: Random House, 1938.

WP   *The Wild Palms.* New York: Vintage Books, 1964.

Abstraction

and Aesthetics

I

THE MILIEU
Delineating Things

MAN'S DESIRE to differentiate between good and evil is apparently instinctive. Definitions of goodness may vary, yet each man tends to assume that only his own definition bears divine sanction. Rather than admit the anguish of uncertainty, he insists that circumstance confirms his concept of moral order. He has rarely found such confirmation to be self-evident; disasters have always plagued even the most virtuous of men, but man seems, nevertheless, to have such an innate craving for justice on his own terms that he has overlooked and rationalized and reconstrued events until they somehow have conformed to his expectations about the right order of the universe. Particularly in the ancient world were such rationalizations essential to existence: Job was being tested by God; Thebes was being punished for a disruption of the moral order. Even though the explanation for irrational circumstance was not readily apparent, there was always assumed to be, nevertheless, an explanation. Nowhere was it thought that man might break the moral code without facing retribution. Nowhere was it suggested that virtue would go unrewarded. If circumstance did not seem to favor the virtuous man on earth, it was assumed that recompense would come when he inherited

3

the kingdom of heaven. Always the presupposition was that man's concepts of moral order were underwritten by divine sanction and confirmed in existence either here or hereafter.

Since the Renaissance, however, it has become increasingly difficult to see in circumstance a confirmation of human moral order. The growth of man's knowledge, especially in the last century, has tended to invalidate all the precepts and concepts by which he traditionally has come to terms with existence. Science has given him a merely mechanical explanation for causality. An historical overview of time has established that catastrophe occurs quite arbitrarily to good and bad alike. Anthropology has revealed that there is no single absolute human value system and, therefore, apparently no such thing as "natural law." Psychology has encouraged us to think of heaven and hell as mere concepts growing out of man's yearning for justice but having no more validity than any other fantasy of wish fulfillment. The mass media have revealed that inanity and meanness and corruption are not just local but global phenomena. The empirical sciences have taught us to doubt the existence of anything which cannot be empirically demonstrated, so we deny the existence of heaven and hell. We are thus, as Edwin Arlington Robinson writes, "robbed of two fond old enormities," of God and of value itself. We see with Yeats that "The best lack all conviction, while the worst/Are full of passionate intensity" or with Eliot's Gerontion that "Unnatural Vices/Are fathered by our heroism. Virtues/Are forced upon us by our impudent crimes." And we also ask, "After such knowledge, what forgiveness?" and "With such knowledge, what action is possible?" Colin Wilson poses the question thus: "What will men *do* when they see things as they are?" [1]

In the twentieth century, seeing things as they are is virtually unavoidable for any human being who can bear to look, for the incredible upheavals and horrors which typify our age have

1 Colin Wilson, *The Outsider* (London: Victor Gollancz, Ltd., 1956), 19.

torn aside the veils and exposed the absurdity of man's confidence in order and in his own importance in the universe. As William Barrett writes, "We suffer not more than but differently from the Elizabethans. Our suffering is more confused." [2] Such confusion is particularly intense and seemingly insurmountable because traditional assumptions no longer manage to make suffering endurable; they no longer sustain in the face of chaos. The codes and concepts our ancestors relied upon to make existence tolerable have been exposed as ineffectual and largely irrelevant, but without them man stands defenseless and confused.

Ideally, the disruption and destruction of entrenched traditions would compel man to take off his blinders, to heighten his awareness, to enhance his vision, and finally to renew his life. Upheaval functioned so, according to Barrett (at least for those who opened their eyes to it) in the Russia of Dostoevski and Tolstoi:

A society that is going through a process of dislocation and upheaval, or of revolution, is bound to cause suffering to individuals, but this suffering itself can bring one closer to one's own existence. As long as they are securely in place, we need not consider what life means; its meaning seems sufficiently incarnate in the triumph of the daily habit. When the social fabric is rent, however, man is suddenly thrust outside, away from the habits and norms he once accepted automatically. There, on the outside, his questioning begins.[3]

The outsider's sight is unclouded, unimpaired; his questionings, therefore, may result in true insight, genuine vision. In some instances, then, the quality of vision may be directly proportional to the intensity of upheaval. Thus the disruptions of the modern age, like those of the Renaissance, may themselves be responsible for an art of great, perhaps apocalyptic, vision and stature.

2 William Barrett, *Time of Need: Forms of Imagination in the Twentieth Century* (New York: Harper and Row, 1972), 117.
3 William Barrett, *Irrational Man* (New York: Doubleday Anchor Books, 1962), 135.

Perhaps that is why so much insightful writing emerged after the First World War. And perhaps that is also why so much of that insight was distinctly southern. Because prewar America had such faith in its ideals, the South in its traditions, disillusionment after debacle was all the more acute. When ideals were revealed as frauds, traditions as shams, the social fabric was rent, and sensitive persons found themselves "on the outside." They began then, like Dostoevski and Tolstoi, to reject and also to question and search. To a certain extent, the reaction of the South is paradigmatic. Robert Penn Warren explains: "The South, then, offered the classic situation of a world stung and stirred, by cultural shock, to create an art, in order to objectify and grasp the nature of its own inner drama." [4] This art has offered us some of our most profound understandings of modern existence. When veils are pulled aside, our best artists see more clearly, to reverse Plato's allegory, for having been in the shadows.

If upheaval serves particularly to challenge and invalidate tradition, the question of what man will *do* when he sees things as they are may be most clearly revealed through his attitudes toward formerly sacrosanct traditions. That is, man may resist cultural shock by retaining the conventions of the past and using them as blinders against chaos. Conversely, man may attempt to accept shock and live unsustained in the glare of truth; in such a case he would attempt to unburden himself of traditions altogether. A third more balanced and mature reaction to cultural

4 Robert Penn Warren, "Faulkner: Past and Future," introduction to Robert Penn Warren (ed.), *Faulkner: A Collection of Critical Essays* (Englewood Cliffs, N.J.: Prentice-Hall, Inc., 1966), 4. There was of course a time lag for cultural shock in the South. Postbellum southerners refused to be disillusioned by the Civil War; they ignored actualities and dealt in grandiose self-justification. A third generation of southerners, however, gained perspective on that debacle: it saw the discrepancy between illusion and actuality. Catalyzed no doubt by the country's general disillusionment with World War I idealism, that generation rejected superannuated traditions. Belatedly it began to search for real meaning and for new expressions of that meaning.

disruption, however, is to reexamine traditional assumptions and to reject those abstract traditions which no longer have relevance. Such a mature reaction should involve, furthermore, retaining and revitalizing other abstractions so that they continue to play a meaningful role in existence. Such is the ideally balanced, but all too rare, reaction to upheaval. More typical are the extreme reactions of, on the one hand, clinging all the more adamantly to obviously outworn codes and concepts or, on the other, rejecting all codes and concepts as absurd and irrelevant.

William Faulkner began his writing career in the aftermath of World War I when mankind's reactions to trauma were by and large polarized between these two less satisfactory extremes. The masses were ill-equipped to cope with a fast-paced, iconoclastic, and often revolting new world. Harried and (figuratively if not literally) shell-shocked, most of mankind tried to deal with unsettling circumstance by pretending that it did not exist. Rather than admit that America might have been wrong or that the war did not make the world safe for democracy, such people became even more militant flag-wavers. Rather than revise defunct ideals, they insisted all the more intransigently upon their absolute validity. They reacted to a radically disoriented new world by ignoring disturbing facts and clinging to other details "just so they fit" (T, 330) into a comforting abstract hypothesis.

Such a reaction to trauma is (if we may believe Faulkner's fiction) most common. As Jean-Paul Sartre admits, "Most of the time we flee anguish in bad faith"; [5] for when veils are pulled aside, most persons only resent the glare. They seek frantically to restore the veils or to interpose new ones between themselves and existence. They erect, or resurrect, a framework of abstractions to serve as a barricade between themselves and shattering realities. Such people shirk enlightenment, resist awareness. As the icons by which they have lived are systematically shattered,

5 Jean-Paul Sartre, *Existentialism and Human Emotions* (New York: Philosophical Library, 1957), 59.

they seek only to establish new iconographies, more rigid, more inflexible, and more absolute than the last. As a release from chaos and uncertainty, such people retreat into dogmatism. As a defense mechanism against despair, they assert, all the more stringently, the absolute validity of their symbols and codes and concepts.

Faulkner's Eula Varner Snopes characterizes such a defense as essentially feminine: "women dont care whether they are facts or not just so they fit"; the opposite reaction, from Eula's viewpoint, is masculine: "men dont care whether they fit or not just so they are facts" (T, 330–31). Whether masculine or not, the second reaction may be more authentic, but hardly less extreme. It involves a disavowal of all the abstract concepts which would make facts fit together. Such a rejection of the tools of the intellect became, ironically, the typical intellectual reaction to World War I. Bitter over their exploitation by words without substance, shocked to see most of their contemporaries preferring ideas to facts, a small but very vocal number of sensitive and disillusioned moderns rejected (or claimed to reject) ideas. They determined to strip themselves of whatever defense or consolation an abstract idea might offer and to meet chaos face-to-face. They were the "lost generation," uprooted and dissociated by the war from all that had sustained their fathers.

However much the holocaust and atrocity of World War II have dwarfed by comparison the events of World War I, in terms of consciousness the First World War was a cataclysmic experience for all mankind. Not since the Renaissance had men's minds been so shaken and reoriented; probably never before had such a widespread shift in consciousness transpired in so brief a time span. Prewar and postwar existences in the United States seem as radically opposed as "before" and "after" photographs. "After the War, Miss [Gertrude] Stein said, we had the twentieth century." [6] In less than a decade this country's

6 Frederick Hoffman, *The Twenties: American Writing in the Postwar Decade* (Rev. ed.; New York: Free Press, 1965), 220.

mood passed from naïveté to cynicism, confidence in power to fear of impotence, idealism to nominalism, hope to despair. As William Barrett remarks, World War I was a "total *human* debacle." [7]

The First World War was such a debacle, partially at least, because it was fought for ideals. War has never been pretty or grand (though nonparticipants have often depicted it so), but the ugliness of World War I defied precedent. As the first mechanized war, it effected a tremendous revolution "in immorality": [8] filth, disease, senselessness, brutality, and atrocity were inescapable. For the first time propagandizing became a science; talk of a Holy War to End All Wars and Make the World Safe for Democracy continued to inundate civilians and soldiers alike. The man in the trench experiencing unalleviated horror could not but be sickened by the grandly flatulent homilies of war propaganda. As Robert Graves wrote in *Good-bye to All That,* "Patriotism, in the trenches, was too remote a sentiment." [9]

The discrepancy between expectation and reality, illusion and truth, was painfully revealed to the participants at least. Wilfred Owen addressed his reader:

> My friend, [if you had experienced what I have] you would
>   not tell with such high zest
> To children ardent for some desperate glory,
> The old Lie: *Dulce et decorum est*
> *Pro patria mori.*

Ezra Pound insisted in *Hugh Selwyn Mauberley:* "Died some, pro patria,/non 'dulce' non 'et decor.' " They enlisted "believing in old men's lies, then unbelieving/came home, home to a lie." For them it was neither sweet nor becoming to die for one's country; it was wasteful, grotesque, pointless:

7 Barrett, *Irrational Man,* 33.
8 Stanley Cooperman, *World War I and the American Novel* (Baltimore: Johns Hopkins Press, 1967), 13.
9 Robert Graves, *Good-bye to All That* (Rev. 2nd ed.; New York: Doubleday, 1957), 188.

There died a myriad,
And of the best, among them,
For an old bitch gone in the teeth,
For a botched civilization.

A whole generation of young men had sacrificed their lives, it now seemed, for nothing; and those who lived were sickened by the idea of sacrifice and, apparently, by almost all ideas. Civilization was now revealed as "botched," ideals as lies. E. E. Cummings, who volunteered to serve with the French army, was absurdly and unjustly imprisoned in a French detention camp. He describes this experience in *The Enormous Room* (1922), insisting that only when he was imprisoned did he come to realize "fully and irrevocably and for perhaps the first time the meaning of civilization": " '*CA PUE!*' " [10] And so the iconoclasm of the 1920s can be understood as a total rejection of civilization, of the Best that Has Been Thought and Said. As F. Scott Fitzgerald explained it, "We were tired of Great Causes." [11]

The disillusionment, frustration, and bitterness which followed the First World War have been amply documented.[12] History, literature, and criticism all remind us that the ultimate casualty of World War I was not human but abstract; it was, however, nonetheless real. In his essay "The Missing All" John

10 E. E. Cummings, *The Enormous Room* (New York: Modern Library, 1934), 167, 141. The first phrase is the narrator's, the second the Machine Fixer's. The latter's denunciation of civilization, the French government, and its representatives is violent and often obscene (the guards " '*qui ne se foutent pas mal . . . Sont. Des. CRAPULES!*' " p. 142). The respect Cummings expresses for the Machine Fixer and his point of view seems to justify equating perspectives and transposing terminology.

11 F. Scott Fitzgerald, *The Crack-Up*, ed. Edmund Wilson (New York: New Directions Books, 1945), 13.

12 The discussions of Hoffman, Barrett, Cowley, and others are, however, largely descriptive accounts. Ernest Earnest's *The Single Vision: The Alienation of American Intellectuals, 1910–1930* (New York: New York University Press, 1970) is a critical account; but Earnest indicts writers of the time chiefly for their criticism of America. He assumes such nea-saying to be an evasion of their duty to lift men's hearts. Apparently Earnest believes only in the power of positive thinking. I propose in this chapter to give a descriptive account of modern disillusionment and its aesthetic consequences and to evaluate as well as describe.

Peale Bishop wrote: "Not only did the young suffer in the war, but every abstraction that would have sustained and given dignity to their suffering. The war made the traditional morality inacceptable; it did not annihilate it; it revealed its immediate inadequacy. So that at its end the survivors were left to face, as they could, a world without values." [13] Values and ideals, the postwar generation bitterly concluded, had been frauds, in Cummings' terms, no more than "high falutin rigmarole." [14] One of Ford Madox Ford's characters explains, "You see, in such a world as this an idealist—or perhaps it's only a sentimentalist—must be stoned to death." [15]

"In such a world as this": the assumption is that the First World War has sundered the new from the old world. And in this new world neither idealists nor their outworn ideals have any place. In *The Enormous Room* Cummings treats idealists and ideals so scathingly that he does indeed verbally stone them to death. Here Cummings' style is a strange amalgam of realism and surrealism, prose and poetry, autobiography and fiction, fact and fancy. Despite its uniqueness, however, *The Enormous Room* is a seminal and even representative book of the 1920s; here is the era's disenchantment with abstractions rendered both thematically and stylistically. Cummings describes himself in the novel as a pilgrim searching not for ideals, but for life, the implication being that the two are mutually exclusive. Convinced that ideals destroy life, he meticulously prunes abstract phrases from his book; when they appear, they are the subject of stylistic ridicule. Cummings capitalizes ironically ("This Great War For Humanity, etc") [16] and adds the "etc." to establish the meaningless automatism with which such phrases are mouthed. The *plantons*, or prison guards, for instance, after completing guard

13 Edmund Wilson (ed.), *The Collected Essays of John Peale Bishop* (New York: Charles Scribner's Sons, 1948), 75.
14 Cummings, *Enormous Room,* 186.
15 Ford Madox Ford, *Some Do Not . . .* (New York: Alfred A. Knopf, 1950), 237.
16 Cummings, *Enormous Room,* 201.

duty were "shipped back to do their bit for world-safety, democracy, freedom, etc., in the trenches." [17] Cummings reduces stock phrases to initials ("g. and g. governments" are of course "great and good") and then manages stylistically as well as narratively to undercut any pretension of abstract value.

After the "veritable orgy of verbomania" [18] which characterized World War I, Cummings and his entire generation seem to have developed an almost paranoid fear of the abstract phrase. The Lawrentian persona in *Aaron's Rod* insists, " 'No, oh no, this was no war like other wars. All the machinery of it,' " [19] and afterwards concludes, " 'The idea and the ideal has for me gone dead—dead as carrion.' " [20] In "Man Against the Sky" Edwin Arlington Robinson, too, writes of "the time-born words/We spell, whereof so many are dead that once/In our capricious lexicons/Were so alive and final."

Words such as *glory, honor, sacrifice,* or *duty* were dead; they had to be expunged from literature or used only in derision. The stylistic consequences, as Frederick Hoffman explains, were far-reaching:

The worse victims among our language habits were the abstraction and the capitalized noun. The time-worn psychological values lying behind words were either canceled out or distorted, at the least revised. Broad and profane ironies marked the responses to slogans. The change in attitudes toward what the words stood for led to a minor revolution in style. The letter "i" often became lower case as the point of view of the narrator was lost in the general, reductive terror. Lower-case spelling—in the titles of magazines, in poetry, and in interior monologue—were as much a testimony of human doubt as they were literary novelties. Certain words were avoided, because they had too often been used by men who turned out to be either stupid or brutal, in speeches, directives, and the prose defenses of "ideals." [21]

17 *Ibid.,* 82.
18 Charles K. Ogden and I. A. Richards, *The Meaning of Meaning: A Study of the Influence of Language Upon Thought and of the Science of Symbolism* (New York: Harcourt, Brace, and World, 1946), 40.
19 D. H. Lawrence, *Aaron's Rod* (New York: Viking Press, 1961), 112.
20 *Ibid.,* 271.
21 Hoffman, *The Twenties,* 74–75.

Such hostility to what Malcolm Cowley describes as "The Big Words"[22] precipitated an aesthetic as well as a stylistic revolution. Artists readily embraced the conviction that beauty could exist, in T. E. Hulme's words, "in small dry things."[23] The noble sentiment, the abstract idea, the generalization were meticulously pruned from the modern literature, so that poetry and prose as well became a "sequence of images"[24] whose connections and explanations were rigorously suppressed. William Carlos Williams proclaimed that there are "No ideas/but in things." T. E. Hulme insisted that good art demands "sincerity," which he defined as a passion for "accuracy" in the "contemplation of finite things."[25] Pound insisted, "Bad art is inaccurate art."[26] Pound and T. S. Eliot structured their poetry by image patterns or clusters with abstraction and explanation expurgated. The objective correlative was set forth as not just a technical device but as a standard by which all poetry might be judged. F. R. Leavis attacked Shelley for "vagueness" and implied that most romantic poetry was inferior because the romantics used images which were not clear and fully visualized.[27] John Dos Passos' "camera eye" presentation was an experiment setting forth objectivity as the highest aesthetic end. As a level of meaning, style established that the concrete is true, the abstract false.

A canon of art emerged which was taken to be absolute and even retroactive (Shelley was vague, therefore not so good). However strange the imagist credo had sounded to a prewar

22 See Chapter 1 in Malcolm Cowley's *A Second Flowering: Works and Days of the Lost Generation* (New York: Viking Press, 1973), especially 13–18.
23 T. E. Hulme, *Speculations: Essays on Humanism and the Philosophy of Art*, ed. Herbert Read (New York: Harcourt, Brace, 1967), 131.
24 T. S. Eliot, introduction to Saint-John Perse's *Anabasis* (New York: Harcourt, Brace, 1949), 10.
25 Hulme, *Speculations*, 133–38.
26 T. S. Eliot (ed.), *Literary Essays of Ezra Pound*, introd. T. S. Eliot (New York: New Directions, 1968), 43.
27 See the chapter on Wordsworth, Shelley, and Keats in F. R. Leavis, *Revaluation: Tradition and Development in English Poetry* (New York: W. W. Norton, 1963), 154–275.

world, it became gospel to the postwar generation and has, for the most part, so remained.[28] The imagists of course began the movement before reaction against war rhetoric brought it to fruition. In 1913 F. S. Flint recorded the standards by which the imagists "judged all poetry, and found most of it wanting."[29] The supreme standard was, of course, the "Doctrine of the Image." All literature, they assumed, might be evaluated by its truth to "small dry things," by its freedom from abstraction.

Ultimately, then, the word itself seemed inimical to truth. Hulme attempted to destroy our confidence that "anything can be described in words."[30] Pound defined the good writer as the one who "uses the smallest possible number of words."[31] And Gertrude Stein instructed Ernest Hemingway: "If you keep on doing newspaper work you will never see things, you will only see words and that will not do, that is of course if you intend to be a writer."[32] And Hemingway worked meticulously to "strip language clean, to lay it bare down to the bone"[33] so that words would not obscure things but rather might succeed in delineating them. The assumption, as Stanley Cooperman explains, was "that the object, the thing, the experience-in-itself, stated boldly and without rhetorical flourish, would recreate truth."[34]

28 One example of deference to the canons of aesthetic nominalism is the recent study by Floyd C. Watkins entitled *The Flesh and the Word: Eliot, Hemingway, Faulkner* (Nashville: Vanderbilt University Press, 1971). Watkins begins by stating, "Most great writers of the early twentieth century wrote about object, fact, and person and rejected abstractions of all kinds." Rating writers according to their supposed conformity to the principle of concretion, Watkins equates Faulkner's point of view with Addie Bundren's; Addie's speech is "one of the most effective rejections of abstraction written in the early twentieth century." To Watkins, it reflects "the best aesthetic principles of Eliot, Faulkner, and Hemingway early in their careers."
29 F. S. Flint, "Imagism," *Poetry: A Magazine of Verse*, I (March, 1913), 199.
30 Herbert Read, introduction to Hulme, *Speculations*, xiv.
31 Eliot (ed.), *Literary Essays of Ezra Pound*, 50.
32 In Carl Van Vechten (ed.), *Selected Writings of Gertrude Stein* (New York: Random House, 1946), 176.
33 Ernest Hemingway, quoted by Carlos Baker, *Hemingway: The Writer as Artist* (Princeton, N.J.: Princeton University Press, 1956), 71.
34 Cooperman, *World War I*, 40–41.

The corollary assumption, of course, was that abstractions could create only falsehood. Apparently all abstractions were assumed to be as counterfeit as World War I slogans. Thus Ezra Pound instructed the poet: "Go in fear of abstractions." [35] The major premise of the times became the conviction that "meaninglessness is a correlative of abstraction." [36] As Hemingway bluntly put it in *Death in the Afternoon*, "unsoundness in an abstract conversation or, indeed, any over-metaphysical tendency in speech" is just simply "horseshit." [37]

Consequently, literature aimed not to *mean*, but rather to *be*. An extreme example of that aim occurs in James Agee's maverick *Let Us Now Praise Famous Men*. Agee wrote: "As a matter of fact, nothing I might write could make any difference whatever. It would only be a book at the best." Distrusting the ability of words to render subject, Agee exclaimed, "If I could do it, I'd do no writing at all here. It would be photographs; the rest would be fragments of cloth, bits of cotton, lumps of earth, records of speech, pieces of wood and iron, phials of odors, plates of food and of excrement. Booksellers would consider it quite a novelty; critics would murmur, yes, but is it art; and I could trust a majority of you to use it as you would a parlor game." [38] The logical outgrowth of such distrust of art is the literature Ihab Hassan characterizes as "the literature of silence" which "aspires to an impossible concreteness." What began philosophically as disenchantment and cynicism then resulted artistically in what Hassan terms "neoliteralism," [39] what I would describe as aesthetic nominalism.

The basic assumptions behind aesthetic nominalism are that

35 Eliot (ed.), *Literary Essays of Ezra Pound,* 5.
36 Ihab Hassan, *The Literature of Silence: Henry Miller and Samuel Beckett* (New York: Alfred A. Knopf, 1967), 27.
37 Ernest Hemingway, *Death in the Afternoon* (New York: Charles Scribner's Sons, 1960), 95.
38 James Agee, *Let Us Now Praise Famous Men* (Boston: Houghton, Mifflin, 1941), 13.
39 Hassan, *The Literature of Silence,* 10–11.

only the concrete is real and that, consequently, the artist serves merely to put human beings in touch with the concrete. Thus, art aims not at transcendence but rather at immediacy, not at imagining but rather at presenting. Such an aesthetic, formulated by the imagists in prewar times, confirmed by the war experience, and established as canon law in the postwar era, has served its function. Under its influence prose and poetry both became terse, blunt, tense. With presentational accuracy as an imperative, language startled us with sensory vividness and virile silences. We could measure the writer's achievement by his mastery of the hard bold metaphor. Consequently, our literature achieved a new vitality and specificity, a new method of dramatic presentation, and a new willingness to allow meaning to remain implicit. Aesthetic nominalism has revitalized our literature; yet it remains an essentially reductionist theory.

Nominalism is reductionist first of all because it ignores the complexity of reality, the evasiveness of truth. It is grounded in the assumption that truth is objectively knowable, that perception is entirely accurate. It subscribes, then, to what Nelson Goodman calls the "myth of the innocent eye." [40] Among nominalistic literary theories, furthermore, there are so many overt testimonials against *words* that it seems writers are not aware that they have chosen words, not paint or musical notes or objects themselves, as their medium. An author may speak of the building blocks of composition, or the contour of a sound, or the feel of a poem, but these words are images, happy ones at that, yet they remain words or abstract symbols of concrete experience. However hard he tries, the writer can never mold things from words. Nor can he pretend that, in being faithful to "the thing itself," he has minimized artistic intervention. (However boldly imagistic *The Cantos* and *The Waste Land* for instance may be, they hardly exhibit a minimum of art.) Even the most imagis-

40 Nelson Goodman, *Languages of Art: An Approach to a Theory of Symbols* (Indianapolis: Bobbs-Merrill, 1968), 7.

tic poetry can never be wholly concrete. ("April is the cruelest month" is an *idea*, not an image.) And Hemingway's fiction does considerably more than use simple declarative sentences to see things and transcribe minimals. Although Hemingway may say that all metaphysics is "horseshit," the speculation about meaning and causation in *A Farewell to Arms* is preeminently metaphysical. Hemingway's work, then, encompasses more than the bare minimum, but his nominalistic theory does not.

It may be instructive here to examine that passage from *A Farewell to Arms* which was "the great statement of protest against the butchery of the First World War." [41] Hemingway's Frederic Henry acknowledges:

I was always embarrassed by the words sacred, glorious, and sacrifice and the expression in vain. We had heard them, sometimes standing in the rain almost out of earshot, so that only the shouted words came through, and had read them, on proclamations that were slapped up by billposters over other proclamations, now for a long time, and I had seen nothing sacred, and the things that were glorious had no glory and the sacrifices were like the stockyards at Chicago if nothing was done with the meat except to bury it. There were many words that you could not stand to hear and finally only the names of places had dignity. Certain numbers were the same way and certain dates and these with the names of the places were all you could say and have them mean anything. Abstract words such as glory, honor, courage, or hallow were obscene beside the concrete names of villages, the numbers of roads, the names of rivers, the numbers of regiments and the dates.[42]

Lieutenant Henry's words clearly indicate how postwar disillusionment and disgust precipitated a retreat from the grandiose to the minimal, from the problematic to the certain. They confirm that suspicion of the abstract and respect for the concrete were corollary manifestations of postwar cynicism. Thus the passage became not only a protest but "a kind of manifesto of modern

41 Barrett, *Irrational Man*, 45.
42 Ernest Hemingway, *A Farewell to Arms* (New York: Charles Scribner's Sons, 1929), 196.

literature." [43] Yet the passage itself remains quite ambiguous. When Frederic Henry denounces the obscenity of certain abstract terms to proclaim the dignity of certain concrete names, he is still dealing in abstractions; "dignity" may be a less tainted abstraction than "glory," but it is nevertheless an abstraction. Furthermore, the names and numbers of villages and roads, rivers and regiments, are not the "thing itself"; they are abstractions. Yet, Hemingway's words have been taken to mean that all abstractions are necessarily obscene, necessarily extraneous to art. If the passage is a manifesto for modern art, its ambiguities suggest the inconsistencies in the modern aesthetic.

Just as Hemingway continues to use abstractions even while proclaiming their obscenity, so too do many modern literary theorists deal in a degree of doublespeak when they suggest that "art" be minimized for "direct treatment of the 'thing.' " [44] The commonsense implication of such an aesthetic is that "art" is merely artifice, the "thing itself" merely brute experience; but then, art could be only a secondhand facsimile. Whatever such theorists intend, they imply that art should seek only to reproduce the tangible world of surface.

In an early twentieth-century book on aesthetics entitled *Abstraction and Empathy*, Wilhelm Worringer put forth the proposition that "the simple line and its development in purely geometrical regularity was bound to offer the greatest possibility of happiness to the man disquieted by the obscurity and entanglement of phenomena." [45] Worringer is speaking of geometric form in the plastic arts, but his proposition holds true for literature as well; that is, the blunt minimal narratives of a Hemingway are another reaction against "obscurity and entanglement." Like cubism, his syntax represents a reduction of complexity to its

43 Barrett, *Irrational Man*, 45.
44 Flint, "Imagism," 199.
45 Wilhelm Worringer, *Abstraction and Empathy: A Contribution to the Psychology of Style*, trans. Michael Bullock (New York: International Universities Press, 1953), 20.

minimal elements. Such narratives are not then actually realistic; they are extreme selections from and distortions of the complete circumstance. They are, in other words, abstractions. Paradoxically, then, even the avant-garde's "brute fact" or "experience itself" is an abstraction; that is, it does not contain the complete situation. As Alfred North Whitehead writes, "Matter-of-fact is an abstraction." [46] With Whitehead, fact or event is "only an abstraction from a complete actual occasion. A complete occasion includes that which in cognitive experience takes the form of memory, anticipation, imagination, and thought." [47] In other words, the complete actual occasion includes elements which are human and cognitive. To Whitehead, then, the concrete is only a portion of reality. To equate the concrete and the real is to deny the fluid, the intellective, and the spiritual aspects of existence. Modern aesthetics seems, however, to make precisely that denial and to insist that art may aspire to do nothing more than put man into contact with the physical, the world's body.[48] Yet while that theory has revitalized our literature, it also has diminished it.

An aesthetic which acknowledges the constitutive function of abstractions in art and in life would better serve to appraise the achievements of both Hemingway and Faulkner. Such an aesthetic would reflect Whitehead's premise that the realm of art is "a realm not to be confused with the 'natural.'" [49] As Suzanne Langer states, "Everything in the arts is created, never

---

46 Alfred North Whitehead, *Modes of Thought* (New York: Free Press, 1968), 18.
47 Alfred North Whitehead, *Science and the Modern World* (New York: Macmillan Company, 1925), 238.
48 John Crowe Ransom's terms do carry nominalistic connotations when he asks, "Where is the body and solid substance of the world?" and suggests that poetry "wants only to know the untechnical homely fulness of the world." *The World's Body* (Baton Rouge: Louisiana State University Press, 1968), x, xi.
49 Donald W. Sherburne, *A Whiteheadian Aesthetic* (Hamden, Conn.: Archon Books, 1970), 110.

imported from actuality." [50] To Whitehead and to Langer (who was his pupil) the realm of art is not concrete but rather abstract. Langer insists that the arts "abstract from experience"; [51] they do not reproduce it. She writes:

> The aim of art is *insight*, understanding of the essential life of feeling. But all understanding requires abstraction. The abstractions which literal discourse makes are useless for this particular subject-matter, they obscure and falsify rather than communicate our ideas of vitality and sentience. Yet there is no understanding without symbolization, and no symbolization without abstraction. Anything *about* reality, that is to be expressed and conveyed, must be abstracted *from* reality. There is no sense in trying to *convey reality* pure and simple. Even experience itself cannot do that. What we understand, we conceive, and conception always involves formulation, presentation, and therefore abstraction. [52]

Aiming at insight, art should not be concerned to "convey reality" or faithfully transcribe. It does not conform to the photograph or the census. It is an abstraction. Being abstract, it is "comprehensible without reference to some one particular occasion of experience"; [53] in other words, the abstract is applicable to more than one instance; it is then universal. Fiction therefore may be considered an abstraction because its very concreteness is selected and ordered so as to convey significance beyond the particular. A good novel about Mississippi is comprehensible to those who have never been there. And the concreteness of a good novel or poem represents, as Wallace Stevens writes, "an intervention on the part of the image maker." [54] The artist intervenes in order to transpose contingency; thus his art transforms rather than duplicates. Selected and reordered and heightened, the particular in art is abstracted, the concrete universalized. Stevens explains that the poet must realize that "his

50 Suzanne K. Langer, *Problems of Art: Ten Philosophical Lectures* (New York: Charles Scribner's Sons, 1961), 84.

51 *Ibid.*, 94.

52 *Ibid.*, 92–93.

53 Whitehead, *Science*, 221.

54 Wallace Stevens, *The Necessary Angel: Essays on Reality and the Imagination* (New York: Vintage Books, n.d.), 128.

own measure as a poet, in spite of all the passions of all the lovers of the truth, is the measure of his power to abstract himself, and to withdraw with him into his abstraction the reality on which lovers of truth insist. He must be able to abstract himself and also to abstract reality, which he does by placing it in his imagination." [55]

Stevens himself is sometimes erroneously identified with those "lovers of truth"; certainly when he wrote "Not Ideas about the Thing, but the Thing Itself," he did indeed seem to be speaking for aesthetical nominalism. Yet even in that poem Stevens establishes that the *poem* is the thing itself because it deserves to be studied in its own right, not because it is *things* tangibly embodied. Even so concrete a poem as "Sea Surface Full of Clouds" is in no way equivalent to a sea surface, any more than a poem about making love is equivalent to making love. Speaking of one of Marianne Moore's poems, Stevens writes, "At first reading, this poem has an extraordinarily factual appearance. But it is, after all, an abstraction." [56] Poetry is not actuality, it is a "supreme fiction." Stevens continues to describe it as a "transcendent analogue composed of the particulars of reality, created by the poet's sense of the world, that is to say, his attitude, as he intervenes and interposes the appearances of that sense." [57] The poem is not the particulars, nor are the particulars the whole poem. It is still necessary, as he says in "The Glass of Water," to "contend with one's ideas." The poem or any "fictive thing" is, furthermore, perfect and immortal; nature, on the other hand, is imperfect and transient. The "object is merely a state," Stevens writes in "The Glass of Water"; and so accuracy and precision in describing objects are of minimal importance.

In "The Comedian as the Letter C," Stevens refutes most incisively the aesthetic nominalists who search for the "fecund

55 *Ibid.*, 23.
56 *Ibid.*, 95.
57 *Ibid.*, 130.

minimum." We are reminded of Hemingway in the character Crispin, who "in one laconic phrase laid bare/His cloudy drift."

[Crispin] savored rankness like a sensualist.
He marked the marshy ground around the dock,
The crawling railroad spur, the rotten fence,
Curriculum for the marvelous sophomore.
It purified. It made him see how much
Of what he saw he never saw at all.
He gripped more closely the essential prose
As being, in a world so falsified,
The one integrity for him, the one
Discovery still possible to make.

But such absorption in the physical and the prosaic has made Crispin and his kind "celebrants/Of rankest trivia, [which are] the strength of his aesthetic." Such writers are merely "clerks of our experience" serving "grotesque apprenticeship to chance event." They distort life by illuminating only "plain and common things" and so deserve to pass into oblivion. Stevens depicts the limitations of the "prickling realist" and in 'To the One of Fictive Music' urges that we reclaim "the imagination that we spurned and crave."

The perspective of Stevens, and Faulkner as well, is that a generation of Crispins has, in its talk of essential prose and actual things, stripped language and life and art bare. These Crispins have spurned the imagination and the intellect and have left us impoverished accordingly. They are like Robert Penn Warren's Willie Stark who began life as a man of idea but ended it as a man of fact. The challenge is to manage, as Jack Burden does at the close of Warren's novel, to keep facts and ideals in conjunction with one another, rather than to reject facts, as the idealists do, or to reject ideals, as the nominalists do. The challenge is both existential and aesthetic.

Whether or not he actually saw service in World War I, William Faulkner was a member in terms of chronology, experience, and, to some extent, attitude of the lost generation. He too was idealistic beforehand, disillusioned afterward, as that entire generation proclaimed itself to be. He too wrote out of a profound sense of cultural shock and an embittered dissatisfaction with the way of the world. Yet his fiction in no way duplicates the lost generation's wholesale rejection of abstractions on the grounds that abstractions had fostered the war. That rejection characterized the milieu in which he wrote, yet Faulkner himself makes no pretense of dismissing ideas; nor does he merely aim at delineating facts. In some ways, then, his fiction stands as refutation of the lost generation's stance: as evidence that such extremism is unnecessary, as testimony that facts need not (and may not) be divorced from ideas, as confirmation that the actual and the abstract may be conjoined in life and in art.

THE ALTERNATIVE
Sublimating the Actual

WHEN THE FICTION of William Faulkner is approached deductively, the result is singularly unsatisfactory. That critic who attempts to find in Faulkner corroboration for ready formulas about race or class or primitivism or naturalism or the South will be disappointed (unless, of course, he blinds himself to the frequent inapplicability of his formulas), for the fiction has a way of defying the system. Always resilient and apparently amorphous, it eludes the grasp of the deductive critic who would take an opened Pandora's box of legend, tall tales, short stories, novels, tragedy, comedy, grotesqueness, pathos, beauty, tenderness, and violence and package it all under a few ready categories.

Finding that the fiction eludes categorization, the critic may be tempted to despair of ever solving the riddles posed by William Faulkner's fiction. He may simply conclude, with Walter Slatoff, that "Faulkner might regard too much coherence as a kind of failure." [1] To assume that Faulkner was intentionally incoherent, though, is to deny the integrity of the works of art

1 Walter Slatoff, "The Edge of Order: The Pattern of Faulkner's Rhetoric," in Frederick J. Hoffman and Olga W. Vickery (eds.), *William Faulkner: Three Decades of Criticism* (New York: Harcourt, Brace, and World, 1963), 183.

and to slough off the responsibility of the critic. Faulkner's fiction is, indeed, too diverse, too multidimensional to be reduced to any simplistic formulas or convenient categories, but it possesses its own coherence, its own consistency. As Faulkner himself said, "The whole output or sum of an artist's work [has] to have a design"(LG, 255).

Faulkner never made any absolute clarification of his own design. And even though quite early in his career he wrote that "aesthetics is as much a science as chemistry," [2] he never formulated a precise or definitive aesthetic theory. Nevertheless, any man who created art through "a life's work in the agony and sweat of the human spirit" (ESPL, 119) must have evolved an aesthetic which, like his design, was at least implicit. Actually Faulkner did make his aesthetic fairly explicit in his numerous statements about the character, function, and value of art. And Faulkner explicitly considers aesthetic issues in his second novel *Mosquitoes*. In that novel a group of artists and aesthetes leaves New Orleans for a four-day cruise. The hostess Mrs. Maurier, a patron of the arts, expects that with so many artists aboard the trip will be scintillating. The excursion however is stalled, and the characters do little but talk about art.[3]

The conversation of Mrs. Maurier and the effete Talliaferro who "did Europe in forty-one days [and] gained thereby a worldly air and a smattering of esthetics" (Mos., 33) is trivial. Likewise, the pseudoartists Dorothy Jameson, Mark Frost, and Eva Wiseman discuss art superficially, inanely, and tediously. Gordon, the only accomplished, practicing artist, refuses to talk with them. Talk, however, is not per se inane. Dawson Fairchild, the novelist, and Julius Kauffman, the critic, talk perhaps rather tediously about art; but their conversations are nevertheless

2 In a review of Conrad Aiken's *Turns and Movies*, in Carvel Collins (comp.), *William Faulkner: Early Prose and Poetry* (Boston: Little, Brown, 1962), 74.
3 In 1953 Faulkner described such conversation as an attempt "to escape the responsibility of living." Joseph L. Blotner, *Faulkner: A Biography* (New York: Random House, 1974), II, 1477.

substantive. Though *Mosquitoes* is an apprenticeship novel, some of the opinions expressed, at least by these two characters, are consistent with Faulkner's lifelong attitudes and thus must not be overlooked.[4]

Mosquitoes contains an explicitly negative reaction to the aesthetic nominalism currently in vogue among lost generation artists. Such nominalism is voiced by Eva Wiseman when she says, "Only fools require ideas in verse" (Mos., 247). Mrs. Wiseman apparently considers herself an imagist. Her poetry jolts with such figures as "bleeding trees" and "droppings" from Philomel. Her brother Julius comments that this is "mostly words" and that although "you get quite a jolt from it. . . there's no nourishment in electricity" (Mos., 247).

Mrs. Wiseman has tried to dismiss ideas for images. Dawson Fairchild, the character patterned after Sherwood Anderson, has likewise tried to replace ideas with substance or what he considers the "thing itself." Fairchild's notion of the actual is photographic, one-dimensional (Mos., 246). Julius calls him "a bewildered stenographer" (Mos., 51) and speaks of "that bastard of a surgeon and a stenographer which you call your soul" (Mos., 131). Fairchild, we are led to believe, is like Stevens' Crispin: one of the "clerks of our experience." He too has proclaimed "the near, the clear" and has been a celebrant of "rankest trivia." Julius, however, explains that genius must do more than celebrate or detail trivia. What is wrong with Fairchild's art is that "clinging spiritually to one little spot of the earth's surface, so much of his labor is performed for him. Details of dress and habit and speech which entail no hardship in the assimilation and which,

4 In his dissertation, "On the Aesthetics of Faulkner's Fiction" (Vanderbilt University, 1968), F. F. Carnes writes of *Mosquitoes* "that the chief value of the work lies in its dealing with artistic principles," p. 12. Carnes, however, concentrates his discussion upon the two pieces of sculpture described in *Mosquitoes* and generally neglects the characters' discussions of artistic principles. No manuscript of *Mosquitoes* survives, but in the Alderman Library at the University of Virginia the bound typescript of *Mosquitoes* includes many autograph insertions, mostly to amplify and enliven conversation. None of the aesthetic conversations between Fairchild and Julius have been emended, which I would assume indicates some confidence about them on Faulkner's part.

piled one on another, become quite as imposing as any single startling stroke of originality, as trivialities in quantities will" (Mos., 184). As an aesthetic nominalist, what Fairchild lacks is "a belief, a conviction that his talent need not be restricted to delineating things" (Mos., 242–43). Julius goes on to explain in a language and with an attitude that is clearly Faulknerian: "Life everywhere is the same, you know. Manners of living it may be different . . . but man's old compulsions, duty and inclination: the axis and the circumference of his squirrel cage, they do not change. Details don't matter, details only entertain us" (Mos., 243).

Faulkner himself never contends that "details don't matter" or that "substance doesn't matter" (Mos., 250), but he does insist that substance is only the raw material of art. To omit it would 'ɔe impossible, unthinkable; but merely to delineate it is not to create art. In a 1931 review of Erich Maria Remarque's *The Road Back,* Faulkner skeptically wrote, "It still remains to be seen if art can be made of authentic experience transferred to paper word for word, of a peculiar reaction to an actual condition. . . . That does not make a book"(ESPL, 186-87). Fairchild's mistake is to think that it will, that faithful piling up of details, careful reproduction of trivialities in quantity, constitutes art. Apparently he equates words with "a kind of sterility" and things with virility. To him, the danger of art is that "you begin to substitute words for things and deeds" (Mos., 210). Like Gertrude Stein, Fairchild fears that dealing in words might interfere with his ability to "see things."

But seeing things is all that a Benjy Compson can do. In his preabstracting state Benjy, after all, achieves that same concentrated focus upon things which Fairchild and the nominalists aim toward. Benjy's consciousness can apprehend nothing but things (the nominalists imply that there is nothing else); he cannot begin to fathom the abstract manner in which these things are related. The game of golf, for instance, is an abstraction Benjy cannot grasp. He reduces it to tangible, separate, unconnected acts: "he hit and the other hit" (SF, 1). To Benjy even

the ball's movement is unrelated to the club's swing. Each movement and each item strike his consciousness as discrete entities.
For Benjy, experience is pulverized into details; they alone are
real.

The nominalists talk as if, for them as well, only details are
real; they are, of course, to a considerable extent deluding themselves, for theory is quite real to them, though it is not to Benjy.
The nominalists are certainly not Benjy Compsons, yet they
apparently wish they were. Their approach to life and to art
attempts a similar reductionism, different in degree but not in
kind. Such reductionism cannot succeed. Life will not be reduced;
art will not duplicate. To paraphrase Faulkner, transferring things
onto paper will not make a book. Yet art is diminished in
proportion to the strength of that determination.

Art which aims only at such a transference, at fidelity to
details alone, is hopelessly limited. The various aesthetes and
pseudoartists in *Mosquitoes* recognize the insufficiency of such
art, but they do not understand the cause. They do not understand that art which is intended to reproduce experience or
substitute for it will inevitably fail. Fairchild sees art only as
a hollow substitute for life. It might obey "arbitrary rules of
conduct and probability" (Mos., 181) even when life does not.
To him, art can never capture LIFE, and so he prefers (or claims
to prefer) "a live poet to the writings of any man" (Mos., 246).
Fairchild's point of view here is directly opposed to what
Faulkner expressed in 1955 when he said "the *Ode on a Grecian
Urn* is worth any number of old ladies" (LG, 239).

Unfortunately for his own art, however, Faulkner in *Mosquitoes* allows Fairchild for no apparent reason to reverse his opinion.
While Fairchild has talked about art as an insufficient "substitute" for life (Mos., 229) and while his own art has been described
as merely faithful treatment of material, late in the book Fairchild
begins to speak of the transforming power of the creative urge
and of the artist's amoral disregard for his subject matter (Mos.,

320). He had previously assumed that substance is all in art, yet later according to Julius, Fairchild implies " 'that substance doesn't matter, has no proper place in a poem. You have,' [Julius says to him] with curious speculation, 'the strangest habit of contradicting yourself, of fumbling around and then turning tail and beating your listener to the refutation' " (Mos., 250). Faulkner acknowledges then that Fairchild shifts his point of view; yet he provides no adequate pretext for the shift. Insufficiently motivated though it may be, the reversal is nevertheless pertinent since Fairchild clearly substitutes a proper for an improper understanding of art. Such a proper understanding is founded upon the assumption that words need not be feared, that "words brought into a happy conjunction produce something that lives" (Mos., 210), that reality is not solely concrete, and that art necessarily abstracts from the concrete.

That is what V. K. Ratliff comes to discover in *The Mansion* when he sees his first pieces of abstract sculpture. The sculptor Kohl asks if he is " 'Shocked? Mad?' " and Ratliff replies, " 'Do I have to be shocked and mad at something jest because I never seen it before?' " He is shocked only so long as he tries to relate the sculpture to the concrete or the literal. But finally Ratliff understands; he says:

I taken my time to look: at some I did recognise and some I almost could recognise and maybe if I had time enough I would, and some I knowed I wouldn't never quite recognise, until all of a sudden I knowed that wouldn't matter neither, not jest to him but to me too. Because anybody can see and hear and smell and feel and taste what he expected to hear and see and feel and smell and taste, and wont nothing much notice your presence nor miss your lack. So maybe when you can see and feel and smell and hear and taste what you never expected to and hadn't never even imagined until that moment, maybe that's why Old Moster picked you out to be the one of the ones to be alive. (Man., 173)

To respond to the literal, that which is expected, requires nothing of the viewer; to respond to something entirely new, unseen, abstract, or created, on the other hand, requires and confirms the aliveness of the viewer.

In this sense Faulkner would agree with Anais Nin who, in her study *The Novel of the Future,* writes that for the artist, "accepting what is . . . is an act of passivity, an act of resignation, of impotence, lack of invention and transformation, also an inability to discard *what is* and create *what might be.*" [5] Faulkner, in fact, insists that the artist discard *what is.* He says that it is the artist's prerogative to "distort facts in order to state a truth" (FIU, 282). The artist in fact must "take the sorry, shabby world which he finds and . . . can't change . . . physically [and use it] to create a world of his own." [6] He may not ignore the sorry, shabby world that is; for art must be grounded in substance, in things, in the hackneyed accidents, the postage stamps of earth which the artist knows best. But the artist may not simply transcribe; he must transform facts into truth. Thus, as Gavin Stevens observes, true poets are "not really interested in facts; only in truth: which is why the truth they speak is so true that even those who hate poets by simple natural instinct are exalted and terrified by it" (T, 88).

But that art which instead aims only at transcribing facts fails to exalt or to terrify. It is "ephemeral and doomed" precisely because it fails to join the temporal with the verities, "the old universal truths" (ESPL, 120). In such work, as Faulkner said at the University of Virginia, there is "something lacking" (FIU, 161). What Faulkner finds lacking in the work of the nominalists and specifically in that of Hemingway and Sartre is a sense of the infinite, the eternal, the universal, or God. He says, "I think that no writing will be too successful without some conception of God, you can call Him by whatever name you want" (FIU, 161).

5 Anais Nin, *The Novel of the Future* (New York: Collier Books, 1972), 174.
6 William Faulkner, "Faulkner in the University: A Classroom Conference," ed. Frederick L. Gwynn and Joseph L. Blotner, *College English,* XIX (October, 1957), 2. This answer is not included in the volume *Faulkner in the University.*

Such a statement may seem to be what Joseph Reed calls one of Faulkner's "universal bromides," [7] but I think it cannot be so easily dismissed. In the first place, Faulkner is by no means implying that the orthodox God-fearing writer is aesthetically better than the unorthodox; Faulkner's God does not even have a name, much less an institutionalized church. Secondly, Faulkner is speaking of the inadequacy of the finite, rather than setting forth some theory about the nature of the infinite. His perspective is simply that great art must embody something which is not mortal but rather immortal.

In *Mosquitoes* after Fairchild shifts his perspective, Faulkner has him acknowledge that true art is " 'invested with a something not of this life, this world, at all. It's a kind of fire, you know' " (Mos., 249). Fairchild is still fumbling among words for a definition, but later he defines the fire as " 'Genius' " and explains creativity as " 'that Passion Week of the heart, that instant of timeless beatitude which some never know . . . that passive state of the heart with which the mind, the brain, has nothing to do at all, in which the hackneyed accidents which make up this world—love and life and death and sex and sorrow—brought together by chance in perfect proportions, take on a kind of splendid and timeless beauty' " (Mos., 339). This "perfect proportion," this "splendid and timeless beauty," is achieved because in art the concrete is invested with something from beyond; the finite is conjoined with the infinite, the temporal with the eternal. When such a commingling occurs, a higher reality emanates from the synthesis. And that is why Faulkner can define God as "the most complete expression of mankind" (LG, 70); God seems incarnate in the highest expression of mankind, his art. And thus he is "a God who rests both in eternity and in the now" (LG, 70).

If in art the infinite becomes immanent in the finite, then such art seems to transcend itself and to claim an almost sacred

7 Joseph Reed, *Faulkner's Narrative* (New Haven: Yale University Press, 1973), 5.

level of meaning; thus it comes close to duplicating, for modern man, the function of myth for primitive man. Mircea Eliade explains that for the primitive "neither the objects of the external world nor human acts, properly speaking, have any autonomous intrinsic value. Objects or acts acquire a value, and in so doing become real, because they participate, after one fashion or another, in a reality that transcends them."[8] In the modern world such participation in a higher order is rarely achieved unless it be in art. Commingling with great art in what Whitehead calls "mutual immanence"[9] with the infinite, the finite there transcends itself and becomes once again "saturated with being."

Throughout his career, Faulkner spoke of the power of art to transform the hackneyed accidents of everyday into the timeless perfection of art. And he also insisted upon the power of art to exalt and encourage mankind. It is art's function to record man's "invincible durability and courage beneath disaster" and to postulate "the validity of his hope" (ESPL, 83). Art offers man "a matchless example of suffering and sacrifice and the promise of hope" (LG, 247). Like religion, it seems to be one of the "charts against which he measures himself and learns to know what he is" (LG, 247). To Faulkner, "the poet's voice need not merely be the record of man, it will be one of the props, the pillars to help him endure and prevail" (ESPL, 120).[10] When it does so, art saves man from "being desouled" (FIU, 245) and becomes the "salvation of mankind" (LG, 71).

Faulkner's aesthetic, then, is founded upon the assumption that art has ontological significance; its function is apocalyptic. From Faulkner's perspective the profound significance of art, furthermore, is directly proportional to its success in joining the finite with the infinite, in "sublimating the actual into the

8 Mircea Eliade, *Cosmos and History* (New York: Harper and Row, 1959), 3–4.

9 Alfred North Whitehead, *Adventures of Ideas* (New York: Free Press, 1967), 168.

10 Of these grand words and ideals Floyd Watkins writes, "Apparently Addie [Bundren] and Frederic [Henry] would have regarded Faulkner's own Nobel Prize speech as embarrassing and obscene." *The Flesh and the Word: Eliot, Hemingway, Faulkner* (Nashville: Vanderbilt University Press, 1971), 182.

apocryphal" [11] (LG, 255). Art, like the spirit of Robinson Jeffers' hawk, must be "unsheathed from reality"; like ancient myth it becomes then "saturated with being."

Faulkner's aesthetic stands in direct contradiction to that of the nominalists who want art only to delineate things. Furthermore, the assumptions, prescriptions, and achievements of the nominalists are challenged by the breadth and height of Faulkner's achievement in fiction. Faulkner's work differs from that of the nominalists most obviously in that he was willing to use abstract terms and ornate elaborate syntax; the nominalists were not. None of them would have described a bear as "an anachronism indomitable and invincible out of an old dead time, a phantom, epitome and apotheosis of the old wild life which the little puny humans swarmed and hacked at in a fury of abhorrence and fear like pygmies about the ankles of a drowsing elephant" (GDM, 193). None but Faulkner would tell how a woman seemed "one single inert monstrous sentient womb" (WP, 163) and let another describe herself as *"all polymath love's androgynous advocate"* (AA, 146). Only Faulkner would attempt such phraseology; only Faulkner could make it work.

Both Florence Leaver and Warren Beck acknowledge the importance of abstract terminology in Faulkner's fiction. Leaver writes that by using abstract terms, Faulkner "makes language transcend itself by hypersuggestion." [12] Beck acknowledges that

---

11 Faulkner uses the terms *apocrypha* or *apocryphal* to signify *myth* or *mythical.* Speaking of the artist's prerogative to "distort facts in order to state a truth," for instance, he says, "There's probably no tribe of Snopeses in Mississippi or anywhere else outside of my own apocrypha" (FIU, 282). And of *Sartoris,* it has "the germ of my apocrypha in it" (FIU, 285). To Malcolm Cowley he wrote, "By all means let us make a Golden Book of my apocryphal county" and suggested that the introduction to *The Portable Faulkner* might describe the book as a "chronological picture of Faulkner's apocryphal Mississippi county." Cowley revised to describe it as the "first chronological picture of Faulkner's mythical county in Mississippi," in Malcolm Cowley (comp.), *The Faulkner-Cowley File: Letters and Memories, 1944–1962* (London: Chatto and Windus, 1966), 25, 65, 69.

12 Florence Leaver, "Faulkner: The Word as Principle and Power," in Hoffman and Vickery (eds.), *William Faulkner: Three Decades of Criticism,* 201.

"Faulkner perhaps has no greater faith in the word than have his contemporaries who have partially repudiated it"; nevertheless, Faulkner expands the limits of language by using abstract words in "the old-fashioned way." [13] Willing to utilize such old-fashioned terms as *honor, sacrifice, pity, compassion, doom,* Faulkner through his vocabulary indicates the dimension of meaning that ideals add to life. [14]

Furthermore, his syntax implies that existence is not a pulverized sequence of discrete details. Faulkner uses ornate, involuted, and repetitive sentence structures to create a sonorous, almost hypnotic mood which is itself a level of meaning, for he knows that the simple sentence is no more true than the complex. He may write a 2,500-word sentence in order to "put the whole history of the human heart on the head of a pin" (FIU, 84); because life is a complex of *was, is,* and *will be,* "the long sentence is an attempt to get [a character's] past and possibly his future into the instant in which he does something" (FIU, 84).

Because Faulkner's vocabulary is often abstract and his syntax baroque, his work is readily contrasted with that of Hemingway, for example. His themes, however, are not always so clearly distinguishable from those of the nominalists. (He is as hostile to the defunct abstraction as Cummings and Hemingway ever were.) On one major thematic issue he does, however, differ radically; the elusiveness of truth is a major theme in his novels, not in theirs. To them truth is abundantly obvious to anyone who opens his eyes. Faulkner, however, is almost painfully aware of how inaccurate is vision, how subjective is experience, how distorted is perspective, how naïve is the myth of the innocent eye. Consequently, he does not allow even his most astute narrators to grasp all of the truth around them. Their fragmented

13 Warren Beck, "William Faulkner's Style," *ibid.,* 154–55.
14 Floyd Watkins expresses the converse opinion, insisting that Faulkner is "excruciatingly aware of the failure of all words except the concrete." Watkins, *The Flesh and the Word,* 233.

understandings must be synthesized finally in the mind of the reader, who alone creates "his own fourteenth image of that blackbird which I would like to think is the truth" (FIU, 274). In other words, Faulkner feels that no single perspective can corner truth. If truth is multivalent, to speak of art as an accurate reproduction of the "real thing" or truth itself is naïve.

Faulkner further challenges nominalistic theory in that even while his art is divorced or abstracted from the literal, it retains a vividly sensuous contact with the concrete. The vividness of Faulkner's imagery, in fact, surpasses almost anything the imagists themselves achieved. A typical example of Faulkner's ability to render the visual and tactile is his description of Ab Snopes's coat which "had once been black but which had now that friction-glazed greenish cast of the bodies of old house flies" (CS, 11); another is Miss Emily Grierson's eyes which "looked like two small pieces of coal pressed into a lump of dough" (CS, 121); and there are the convicts "packed like matches in an upright box" (WP, 61) in a truck pushing ahead of itself "a thick slow viscid ridge of chocolate water" (WP, 64); and the overcooked machine-made food that tastes more "like one of the paper napkins" (Man., 382) than food; and the gallant fire truck with men and boys clinging about it "with the astonishing disregard of physical laws that flies possess" (LA, 272).

In fact, even a cursory study of the manuscripts indicates that Faulkner painstakingly revised with maximum vividness of image in mind. The manuscript of *As I Lay Dying*, for instance, reads that as the barn is burning, Mack "slaps at the widening crimson-edged holes in [Jewel's] undershirt"; [15] the passage is literally accurate, but the revised typescript is incomparably more vivid. Now he "slaps at the widening crimson-edged holes that bloom like flowers in his undershirt." [16] The superiority of the

15 William Faulkner, "As I Lay Dying" (MS in Alderman Library, University of Virginia, Charlottesville), 91.
16 William Faulkner, "As I Lay Dying" (Typescript in Alderman Library, University of Virginia, Charlottesville), 224.

second image lies not so much in its concretion, however, but rather in its abstraction. The metaphor of the fire's blooming on his shirt is vivid precisely because it is more than literally true. Metaphor, in fact, according to Langer, "is the natural instrument of our greatest mental achievement—abstract thinking." She continues: "At first blush it may appear as a paradox that metaphor, which enriches poetry and prophecy with concrete imagery should be an instrument of abstraction. Yet that is its true nature; it *makes us conceive* things in abstraction." [17] And so even the vividness of images which Faulkner preeminently masters seems to be a function of abstraction rather than an example of fidelity to the thing itself. His writing is thus concrete without being literal.

Faulkner follows his own aesthetic, in fact, by managing to fuse the concrete with the abstract, the finite with the infinite. With Faulkner, as Jean-Jacques Mayoux observes, "reality is perhaps only the concrete vesture of ideas [;] similarly in the style, these concrete details are united to abstractions, in the most singular combinations, and lend them a strange life. . . . In all that is abstract, everything is charged with the physical, the immediate; in all concrete particulars, everything is charged with the highest abstractions." [18] Mayoux discerns the central thematic and stylistic achievement in Faulkner's fiction, yet he does not elaborate upon it. And he continues somewhat irrelevantly to conclude that Faulkner is "an idealist, for whom as for Berkeley *esse est percipi*, for whom all takes place in the consciousness and between consciousnesses." [19]

For the idealist, matter-of-fact does not exist except in consciousness. For Faulkner, however, it exists as a given in perception which may be faithfully recorded by the clerks of experience

17 Suzanne K. Langer, *Problems of Art: Ten Philosophical Lectures* (New York: Charles Scribner's Sons, 1961), 104.
18 Jean-Jacques Mayoux, "The Creation of the Real in Faulkner," in Hoffman and Vickery (eds.), *William Faulkner: Three Decades of Criticism,* 171–72.
19 *Ibid.,* 172.

or transformed by the artists. It is transformed, however, only when it comes into congruence with the ideal or the abstract, as it does in Faulkner's fiction. As William V. Nestrick writes, "Probably no writer since the Renaissance has shown such an ability to bind together the human, the natural and the divine orders." [20] Faulkner does not choose to disregard concrete experience (as so many disoriented moderns and most of the character types in his fiction do); nor does he choose to dismiss the abstract (as his generation of artists claimed to do). His fiction suggests that life should and art must be a blend of the two.

Certainly Faulkner's fiction embodies such a synthesis. In it, as Florence Leaver writes, "by the rhetoric of abstractions Faulkner repeatedly impregnates the simplest acts with cosmic significance." [21] In other words, from Leaver's point of view, as well as mine, it is precisely because of his willingness to use abstractions that Faulkner's fiction transcends his material. Knowing that reality may be expanded and enhanced by its linguistic and metaphysical dimensions, Faulkner is not afraid of words or of ideas. Although he is painfully aware of the ways in which abstractions are misused, Faulkner does not refuse to use them, nor does he pretend to do without them. For it is the abstract dimension of his art which sublimates the actual into a creation saturated with being. Convinced that he can "improve on the Lord" (FIU, 123), Faulkner creates a new actuality or supreme fiction. As such his work becomes, in Ernst Cassirer's words, "not an imitation but a discovery of reality." [22]

---

20 William V. Nestrick, "The Function of Form in *The Bear*, Section IV," *Bear, Man, and God: Eight approaches to Faulkner's "The Bear"* (Rev. ed.; New York: Random House, 1971), 303. Nestrick's comments refer only to the fourth section of "The Bear." I suggest that Faulkner exhibits that synthesizing ability throughout his fiction.

21 Leaver, "Faulkner: The Word as Principle and Power," 202.

22 Ernst Cassirer, *An Essay on Man: An Introduction to a Philosophy of Human Culture* (New Haven: Yale University Press, 1944), 143.

Abstraction

and Inauthenticity

EVADING
Becoming Impervious
to Actuality

TO THE UPHEAVALS which were generally modern and more precisely post–World War I, the most vocal intellectual reaction was rejection of all tradition and suspicion of all abstraction. The more typical mass reaction, however, was trust in any abstraction which survived the debacle more or less intact. Faulkner differed in the rather important ways elaborated in the previous chapter from the vocal minority who were the lost generation and his contemporaries. They assumed that all abstractions are devoid of life and therefore defunct. Faulkner understood the difference between an inert and a vital abstraction. He knew that abstractions cannot be pruned, nor should they be, from either life or art. Faulkner understood, as the nominalists did not, the role of abstractions in human existence, yet he shared their contempt for an abstraction-fettered populace.

His entire canon, in fact, stands as a caveat against the fixed abstraction. He peoples his pages with characters of different races, classes, ages, and personalities who are nevertheless alike in their dependence upon defunct abstractions. When existence is difficult and disconcerting, such persons make a wholesale retreat from the actual into the abstract, for the fixed abstraction seems to offer them "the one sanctuary" (Man., 181) from life's onward flow.

In a paragraph prefatory to *The Mansion* Faulkner asserts that "'living' is motion." That point of view is similar to that of any number of philosophers from Heraclitus on. Nevertheless, these images of flux carry a peculiarly contemporary authenticity. In accelerated modern times, according to Robert Jay Lifton, "change and flux characterize not only our external environment but our inner experience" [1] as well. In his study *Boundaries: Psychological Man in Revolution*, Lifton describes the modern age as one of incredible upheaval and change resulting in a breakdown of traditional boundaries. He writes principally about the amount of change modern man must assimilate, yet Lifton also cautions that man may refuse to encounter change:

> One response to the crisis of boundaries is a desperate attempt to hold fast to all existing categories, to keep all definitions pure. This is, unfortunately, the impulse of a great deal of political, military, and cultural thought throughout the world, including that of classical psychoanalysis. More than being merely conservative, this response is a *reaction* to a perceived threat of chaos; it all too readily lends itself to nostalgic visions of restoring a golden age of exact boundaries, an age in which men allegedly knew exactly where they stood. The approach is self-defeating and, moreover, impossible to maintain. [2]

It is just such a reaction against the threat of change upon which William Faulkner concentrates in his fiction. For, if he presents life as flux, he also presents the typical human reaction as an attempt to bottle up, dam, stymie, fix, or otherwise impede the flow.

In "Old Man" the flooding river serves as an appropriate emblem for an existence which is fluctuating, uncontainable, and unjust. The entire narrative of "Old Man" then becomes allegory. "Old Man" has a fablelike quality established by its title; by its beginning, "Once . . . there were two convicts" (WP,

---

1 Robert Jay Lifton, *Boundaries: Psychological Man in Revolution* (New York: Vintage Books, 1970), 37.
2 *Ibid.*, xi.

23); by their associations with animals; by the biblical and historical references; and of course by the elemental nature of the conflict itself. Given power, volition, and even malignancy, the river serves as symbol for the "living and fluid world of his time" (WP, 25) into which man is doomed "unwitting and without choice" (WP, 177). And the narrative framework of the tale itself is an apt allegory for man's confrontation with and capitulation before that motion.

The river presents to the tall convict trial upon trial: "the sort of thing that shouldn't happen to a dog"(FIU, 173). It shouldn't happen, but it does, and to man as well as beast. For the convict comes to represent all men in their struggle against irrational happenstance and the "arbitrariness of human affairs" (WP, 146). He encounters incredible hardships with Job-like fortitude and endurance. But finally "mischance," or "a power, a force," or "the cosmic joker" (WP, 264) heaps upon him such a malevolent and unending sequence of disasters that the convict can bear no more. He has had quite enough of encountering circumstance. Human freedom is too much to bear; so like the plump convict who says, "Free. He can have it" (WP, 80), the tall convict at last says, "This is too much" (WP, 280); he seeks sanctuary at the price of servitude. Likewise, most of Faulkner's characters do not act so much as they react. They find circumstance an outrage simply because it moves.

Perhaps even the most casual reader of Faulkner's fiction would hazard a guess that *outrage* is Faulkner's favorite word.[3] Any number of his fictional creations are "husbanded . . . with the abstract carcass of outrage" (AA, 180) because of their "helpless rage at abstract circumstance" (H, 215). The explanation for their outrage is that these characters have been forced to encounter that "motion, which is life" (LG, 253). They have tried to approach life in terms of a few rigid demands and fixed

3 John T. Flanagan, on the other hand, contends that the "epithet *implacable*" is Faulkner's favorite. "Faulkner's Favorite Word," *Georgia Review,* XVII, No. 4 (Winter, 1962), 431.

expectations. They have demanded that life be contained within definite boundaries, that it be ordered, predictable, and rational, that humanity be simple, classifiable. Repeatedly, they have been forced to encounter multifarious humanity and irrational circumstance; they have, in short, been forced to meet life; and they have found the shock almost unbearable. Like the tall convict, they too seek sanctuary. Read allegorically, "Old Man" reminds us that throughout history man has met and survived incredible hardships. It suggests, however, that the encounter with "blind and risible Motion" (WP, 335) has overwhelmed humankind. Especially in the modern world when upheaval is his normative but "absolutely gratuitous predicament" (WP, 155) does man seek refuge from actuality, escape from freedom, sanctuary from the flood.

Man can find only a specious and brief sanctuary from the flux of human existence, but his quest for that immunity is nevertheless, Faulkner's fiction affirms, as frantic and indefatigable as it is futile. He may seek the "illusion of iron impregnability" (WP, 301) or a *"beautiful attenuation of unreality in which the shades and shapes of facts . . . move with the substanceless decorum of lawn party charades, perfect in gesture and without significance or any ability to hurt"* (AA, 211); but either way he is resisting flux, denying the motion which is life, in a fated attempt to find an *"apathy which [is] almost peace"* (AA, 155). By Faulkner's logic, however, achieving such a static apathy is tantamount to being dead. He makes that clear in his brief preface to *The Mansion:* "Since 'living' is motion, and 'motion' is change and alteration . . . therefore the only alternative to motion is un-motion, stasis, death." That is why old Mr. Nightingale in *The Mansion* dies; he will not allow change and alteration. We learn that the old man, "having set his intractable and contemptuous face against the juggernaut of history and science both that April day in 1865 and never flinched since," was killed "by simple inflexibility" (Man., 187). To seek the static is essentially to seek death; but Faulkner's characters still retreat from flux, hoping to find a sanctuary that is "fixed, forever safe from change and alteration" (Man., 203).[4]

Some of them, like Mr. Nightingale, try to do so by simply denying the present and the future and picking some moment (1865 for Mr. Nightingale) beyond which they do not acknowledge change. They choose a time simplified, as Robert Frost in "Directive" phrases it, "by the loss/Of detail." Like Quentin Compson and Gail Hightower, old Mr. Nightingale refuses to admit progression in time. He has isolated out of flux one segment of time and has attempted to reside therein. With Mr. Nightingale, Quentin, and Hightower, that segment is the past, but it would be an equivalent falsification of time to attempt to live only in the present, as Temple Drake does, or only for the future, as Thomas Sutpen does. William Faulkner insists that we may not evade the now and that time-present necessarily carries within it the weight of the past, the possibilities and responsibilities of the future. Man cannot disavow the past, nor should he wish to. In the interviews in Japan, Faulkner said that time has "got to go forward and we have got to take along with us all the rubbish of our mistakes and our errors" (LG, 131). That is what Quentin realizes in *Absalom, Absalom!*: *"Maybe nothing ever happens once and is finished. Maybe happen is never once but like ripples maybe on water after the pebble sinks"* (AA, 261). Because events continue to reverberate throughout all time, no occurrence is ever lost. Sartre writes that for Faulkner "the past is *unfortunately* never lost" [italics mine].[5] With Faulkner, the past is indeed an inescapable burden, but not an unfortunate one.

---

4 Writing to Ben Wasson in 1933 about one of his stories, Faulkner suggested a footnote explaining man's fear of change: " 'But [man] naturally and humanly prefers the sorrow with which he has lived so long that it not only does not hurt anymore, but is perhaps even a pleasure, to the uncertainty of change.' " Quoted by Joseph L. Blotner, *Faulkner: A Biography* (New York: Random House, 1974), I, 809.
5 Jean-Paul Sartre, "Time in Faulkner: *The Sound and the Fury,*" in Frederick J. Hoffman and Olga W. Vickery (eds.), *William Faulkner: Three Decades of Criticism* (New York: Harcourt, Brace, and World, 1963), 229.

On the contrary, in Faulkner it is dissociation from history, as with Jason Compson and the aviators and the modern industrial South, which is unfortunate. To lose the past is to become "ephemeral," substanceless; the past is a burden, to be sure, but "anything worthwhile is a burden" (LG, 121).

Explaining the philosophy of Henri Bergson, T. E. Hulme writes, "The whole of your past life is in the present," ⁶ or as Faulkner's Gavin Stevens phrases it, "The past is never dead. It's not even past" (Req., 92). That is why Thomas Sutpen cannot revoke his beginnings in the West Virginia hills and the West Indies and why Mrs. Gowan Stevens cannot deny her past as Temple Drake. As Gavin Stevens reminds Temple, at anytime the past may "foreclose on you without warning" (Req., 162). Thus the dramatic sections of *Requiem for a Nun* demand that she acknowledge and accept her past as Temple Drake; unless she does so, Temple can come to no satisfactory present existence nor can she be in any way prepared for "tomorrow, and tomorrow, and tomorrow" (Req., 275). She therefore must reject the example apparently recommended by Hemingway in *For Whom the Bell Tolls.* Temple's mind returns to the book by "Hemingway, wasn't it? . . . about how it had never actually happened to a gir—woman, if she just refused to accept it" (Req., 154). Refusing to accept one's past seems to offer the option of escaping from it. Faulkner's fiction, on the other hand, establishes that man escapes history only by coming to terms with it, by living with it and accepting all its implications. Thus Mink Snopes is mistaken to believe that "a man can bear anything by simply and calmly refusing to accept it, be reconciled to it, give up to it" (Man., 21). To refuse to accept the past is to grant it power and to doom oneself to repeating it. Only by accepting the past, living with it, does one gain control over experience.

Faulkner's fiction affirms that both past and future are mutu-

6 T. E. Hulme, *Speculations: Essays on Humanism and the Philosophy of Art,* ed. Herbert Read (New York: Harcourt, Brace, 1967), 201.

ally immanent in the present as memory and tendency. Any attempt to set boundaries around a category of time and abstract it from the "becomingness of nature"[7] is to deny reality. We can live neither in the past, as Hightower attempts, nor in the future, as Sutpen attempts. We must live in the now, accepting that in the present are both the weight of the past and the responsibility for the future. Neither past nor future can be denied, Jack Houston in *The Hamlet* finds out belatedly: "He fled, not from his past, but to escape his future. It took him twelve years to learn you cannot escape either of them" (H, 242).

Characters throughout the Faulkner canon, however, want to escape time by fragmenting it into discrete units and attempting to live in only one such unit. Such characters disregard the fact that "once the advancement stops then it dies" (LG, 131) and that it is possible to be destroyed "by simple inflexibility" (Man., 187). They make an autistic attempt to secure their existences within boundaries that are "fixed, forever safe from change and alteration" (Man., 203).

Such boundaries may be temporal or they may be spatial; either way they represent an attempt to escape flux and to deny reality. Byron Bunch, for instance, knows that life was simpler "yesterday"; he too wishes, for a while at least, that he could "just turn back to yesterday and not have any more to worry me than I had then" (LA, 76). Byron also knows that life is simpler when one isolates oneself physically and psychically from other human beings. Thus Byron works on Saturdays, not for the overtime pay, but because he "believed that out here at the mill alone on Saturday afternoon he would be where the chance to do hurt or harm could not have found him" (LA, 50). Byron's concern is to protect others. A more typical Faulknerian character, however, seeks to place himself "beyond the

7 Alfred North Whitehead, "The First Physical Synthesis," *Interpretations of Science: Representative Selections* (Indianapolis: Bobbs-Merrill, 1961), 18.

reach of passion and blood's betrayal" (H, 141) for his own self-protection. Extreme examples are Gail Hightower who, although he has made it "appear that he was being driven" into isolation, had actually desired (LA, 463) to be so ostracized from the human community; and there is Goodhue Coldfield who "retired into the impregnable citadel of his passive rectitude" (AA, 63) by boarding himself up in his attic where he died four years later; or the tall convict to whom a prison suit is not only "the known" but also "the desired" (WP, 337) and who is grateful for an added ten-year prison sentence, because in Parchman he can be "safe, secure, riveted warranted and doubly guaranteed by the ten years they had added to his sentence for attempted escape" (WP, 164).

At Parchman he can avoid the motion which is life and can secure himself from "all pregnant and female life forever" (WP, 153). The female represents to him the unpredictable, the irrational burden. He does not know "that anything worthwhile is a burden" (LG, 121), and he sees only that involvement with a woman would demand a giving of himself. Thus he can have a quick affair with someone else's wife (WP, 334–35) where he knows, as Olga Vickery writes, "the risks he is taking and the punishment he may receive. The affair, the outraged husband, and the convict's trouble follow in familiar and predictable succession." [8] But he cannot involve himself in a relationship which is unpredictable, unstructured, or demanding—which is, in short, alive.

Faulkner repeatedly presents characters who, with "that same air of perpetual bachelorhood" (H, 48), are ostensibly retreating from women but actually are withdrawing from all human involvement. Byron Bunch, Gavin Stevens, Horace Benbow, Jody Varner, and, probably, V. K. Ratliff,[9] as well as the tall convict,

8 Olga W. Vickery, *The Novels of William Faulkner: A Critical Interpretation* (Rev. ed.; Baton Rouge: Louisiana State University Press, 1964), 163.
9 See my article "Masculinity and Menfolk in *The Hamlet," Mississippi Quarterly,* III (Summer, 1969), especially pp. 187–89 for a discussion of Ratliff's bachelorhood.

see their bachelorhood in such terms. As Faulkner said of Gavin, "He was probably afraid to be married. He might get too involved with the human race if he married one of them" (FIU, 141). The assumption is not, of course, that fulfillment can exist only in marriage or that bachelorhood is necessarily 'a retreat. But, like Kierkegaard, Faulkner presents marriage as an ethical responsibility. And he often uses "all pregnant and female life" to represent life's rich fecundity. Bachelorhood, therefore, may be an attempt to hold the self outside ethical and emotional complexity. But bachelorhood is just one paradigmatic instance of the retreat from human commitment. Married and unmarried men and women throughout the fiction mistakenly conceive of a life disentangled from human ties as an ideal existence.

Throughout his fiction Faulkner displays a predilection for a set of oft-recurring words which imply retreat, disengagement, attempted invulnerability, or stasis in the midst of motion; among them are *sanctuary, immunity, insulation,* and *impervious.* Their frequent appearance in the fiction affirms that Faulkner sees the impulse for sanctuary as an overriding psychic impulse in times such as our own when disruption threatens to engulf all humankind. Thus he writes mostly about people who refuse to move with the current. These characters, as we have seen, want to set boundaries around particular units of time and to live in that time, inviolate. Or they wish to set boundaries around their own psychic existences so that they remain unscathed by others' trouble and pain.

Of course they fail. No one (not even Flem Snopes) can be totally objective. No one can withdraw from time present. No one can totally dissociate from the human community (even Mr. Coldfield must have Rosa pass food up to him in the attic). Nevertheless, the desire to find refuge from the flood remains. The convict and Mr. Coldfield may attempt a physical retreat to find a literal refuge, but most of Faulkner's characters discover that the most effective barrier against a recalcitrant external world is not physical but rather mental withdrawal.

In a world fraught with anguish and turmoil, these persons tend to envy, or identify with, or even emulate whatever is immobile and thus beyond anguish. A good example is Horace Benbow, who makes a rather strained identification between hand-blown glass objects and his sister's supposed purity. Horace retreats from the world's chaos by making the fragile objects which seem "macabre and inviolate; purged and purified" (FD, 153) of life. Gavin Stevens retreats by translating the Old Testament back into classic Greek. And in *Pylon* a similar retreat from flux appears in Jiggs's absorption in his new but ill-fitting boots which he determines to keep forever "unblemished and inviolate" (P, 7). Such objects fascinate because, purged of life, they appear impervious.

Introducing *Pylon,* Reynolds Price considers the aura of glamour which surrounds even these rather tawdry aviators. Price supposes that they are idolized because "the Heroes are always incapable of love." [10] This answer seems to me, however, to beg the question, which still remains, "Why does man love what is incapable of love?" At the University of Virginia, Faulkner said of the tawdry heroes in *Pylon* that "they were outside the range of God, not only of respectability, of love, but of God too. That they had escaped the compulsion of accepting a past and a future, that they were—they had no past. They were as ephemeral as the butterfly that's born this morning with no stomach and will be gone tomorrow" (FIU, 36). They seem, in other words, out of life. Like Jiggs's boots or Horace's glass flowers or their own airplanes, these characters, the spectators suppose, "aint human" (P, 46). They are idolized because they seem unfeeling, impervious. Rather than being overwhelmed by experience, they appear to be unscathed by it. Of course, the reader realizes, as does the reporter finally, how human the aviators are—how very profound are their passion and their anguish. But the point remains that, inundated himself in a petty

10 Reynolds Price, introduction to *Pylon* (New York: New American Library, 1968), xii.

welter of incomprehensible and uncontrollable circumstance, man tends to admire whoever or whatever appears to rise above it.

The fiction indicates, however, that no human being rises above experience by retreating from it. Heroes only appear to be impervious; no human can be a still-unravished bride. In *Flags in the Dust* we read that Horace Benbow has "produced one almost perfect vase of clear amber, larger, more richly and chastely serene and which he kept always on his night table and called by his sister's name in the intervals of apostrophising both of them impartially in his moments of rhapsody over the realization of the meaning of peace and the unblemished attainment of it, as Thou still unravished bride of quietude" (FD, 162). In both *Flags in the Dust* and *Sanctuary*, Horace's sister Narcissa appears dressed in white, apparently impervious to human soilure. But such imperviousness is essentially a measure of inhumanity. For we also learn that Narcissa bears the "serene and stupid impregnability of heroic statuary" (San., 102). And, similarly, in *Soldiers' Pay* Cecily's mother appears "like a rock . . . imperishable, impervious to passion and fear. And heartless" (SP, 233). And in *The Hamlet* we are told that the Texan's gaze is "at once abstract and alert, with an impenetrable surface quality like flint, as though the surface were impervious or perhaps there was nothing behind it" (H, 325). The implication is obvious; these associations do not imply rocklike stability so much as lifelessness. Statuary and machinery and stone may be impregnable to human anguish, but they are also impervious to human bliss. To idealize and emulate the out-of-life existence is to attempt exclusion from human ravishment and to accomplish instead exclusion from human bliss.

Nevertheless, to avoid being ravished by or inundated in flux man mentally restructures it into fixed shapes. The fixity of these shapes seems to imply imperviousness, yet it establishes lifelessness. Such shapes are the abstractions Faulkner's characters so persistently misuse. Disconcerted by the onslaught of change and outraged over their own helplessness, such people suspect that objects and codes and precepts remain "unblemished" (ID, 200). Therefore, they assume that if only they can possess the magic symbol, or invoke the proper code, or rely upon the ideal concept, then they too will be impervious to actuality. It is through abstractions, then, that these characters make autistic attempts to guard themselves from truth.

The abstract may be defined as thought apart from substance, as whatever is not concrete. Yet man finds it difficult to imagine the nonsubstantive or totally abstract. Paradoxically he tries to congeal even his abstractions into concrete entities. He remodels them into objects, or formulas, or labels which his intellect can readily grasp. These fixed representations are constrictions of the vast into the little, the complex into the simple. A further denotation of the word *abstracted* is *preoccupied;* in other words it means to be mentally withdrawn. Our present use of the term *abstraction* also carries the connotation of withdrawal. Faulkner's characters extract or withdraw their symbols, codes, and concepts from the flux of actuality. Though they seem to be concretions, such representations are, in fact, then abstractions. To rely upon them is to make a mental withdrawal from actuality.

The ability to abstract or isolate details from the shifting welter of experience is a uniquely human achievement. It has utilitarian function; the ability to reduce the totality of an experience to a chart, a map, a code, or a concept facilitates acting upon it. And it has aesthetic and moral significance; the ability to symbolize lends life form, coherence, and purpose; it is through our symbols of the ideal that we manage to lift ourselves above the inertia of complacency and to transcend a merely phenomenological existence. Abstractions, then, can afford invaluable enrichment of existence, and they are absolutely necessary to order and to sustain life; to contend otherwise is to delude oneself. Faulkner saw, however, that all too often they become fixed shapes which are so absolute and devitalized that they distort rather than enhance man's existence. As they lose reference to the flux of experience, as they are allowed to become rigid and absolute, their influence is indeed pernicious.

Although the ability to abstract is necessarily human and valuable, it is fraught with dangerous liabilities. As Whitehead explains: "Thus a fortunate use of abstractions is of the essence of upward evolution. But there is no necessity of such good use. Abstractions may function in experience so as to separate them from their relevance to the totality. In that case, the abstractive experience is a flicker of interest which is destroying its own massive basis for survival." Whitehead further explains that we have a "preservative instinct aiming at the renewal of connection" [11] with the totality of existence. When, however, that instinct is obscured and the abstraction is considered in its own right as a fixed entity, apart from and independent of experiential reality, then its effect may indeed be deleterious.

The fatal error in empiricism and in most modern Western thought is what Whitehead terms the "Fallacy of Misplaced Concreteness" or simply "mistaking the abstract for the concrete." [12] Man not only lifts the abstraction from experience, but he tends to assign reality status to the abstraction and deny the existence of ultimate reality which, according to Whitehead, is "not static matter but the flux of physical existence." [13] Examining the same phenomenon, Bergson explains, "Consciousness, goaded by an insatiable desire to separate, substitutes the symbol for the reality or perceives the reality only through the symbol. As the self thus refracted, and thereby broken to pieces, is much better adapted to the requirements of social life in general and language in particular, consciousness prefers it, and gradually loses sight of the fundamental self." [14] To see

11 Alfred North Whitehead, *Modes of Thought* (New York: Free Press, 1968), 123, 124.
12 Alfred North Whitehead, *Science and the Modern World* (New York: Macmillan Company, 1925), 72.
13 Whitehead, "Synthesis," 18.
14 Henri Bergson, *Time and Free Will: An Essay on the Immediate Data of Consciousness,* trans. F. L. Pogson (London: George Allen and Unwin, 1950), 112.

reality in terms of abstract configurations is legitimate: as long as man does not commit the fallacy of misplaced concreteness, forgetting that there is a living, moving reality beyond these configurations; as long as he does not refuse to revise his abstractions by continued reference to fluid reality.

Faulkner's fiction shows us, however, just how determined man is to disregard the complexities of the ever-fluctuating real world and, instead, to assign reality status to a few fixed and frozen abstractions. As Henri Bergson explains in *An Introduction to Metaphysics,* man tries to "reconstruct reality—which is tendency and consequently mobility—with precepts and concepts whose function it is to make it stationary." [15] Faulkner, who in a 1952 interview acknowledged being influenced "by Bergson obviously" (LG, 72), presents life as tendency, mobility, flux. An overwhelming number of his characters, however, refuse that awareness and try to use fixed symbols and codes and concepts to evade the difficult and ever-fluid realities of existence in time. They seek to find refuge from "the becomingness of nature" [16] by fixing human relationships or by raising a symbol or a code or a single interpretation of reality to an absolute status.

When Thomas Sutpen struggles "to hold clear and free above a maelstrom of unpredictable and unreasoning human beings, not his head for breath and not so much his fifty years of effort and striving to establish a posterity, but his code of logic and morality, his formula and recipe of fact and deduction whose balanced sum and product declined, refused to swim or even float" (AA, 275), he is committing his version of Whitehead's fallacy of misplaced concreteness; for Sutpen refuses to renew his code's reference to the maelstrom of experience. Denying that experience, he endows the fixed code with more validity than the changing reality it is supposed to interpret. A definite majority of Faulkner's characters likewise try to contain or chan-

15 Henri Bergson, *An Introduction to Metaphysics,* trans. T. E. Hulme (Indianapolis: Bobbs-Merrill, 1955), 51.
16 Whitehead, "Synthesis," 18.

nel actuality, which is experiential, under the rubric of a few convenient abstractions. They rely upon three types of abstract configurations: symbols, codes, and concepts. Though each is used to deny the "motion, which is life," each may best be examined as a separate attempt to contain and thereby evade actuality.

These characters symbolize or codify or conceptualize to create a barrier against the onslaught. That barrier is, of course, not impregnable; flux cannot be contained. Erecting shields against it is (as Faulkner writes in another context) only the "rank stink of baseless and imbecile delusion" (GDM, 278). Yet these characters continue in their delusion and, when the living world chances to intrude beyond the barrier, they are not outraged over the ineffectuality of their presuppositions, the fraudulence of their guarantees. They do not seem to notice that these barriers are invalid; instead they try to resurrect and rebuild abstract shields which are even more out-of-life and thus opposed to life.

Their attempt evolves into a sort of downward spiral in which life is devitalized by abstractions, and abstractions are devitalized by lifelessness. The problem is that such persons are using the abstract and the actual to deny, rather than to complement, each other; neither is revised in relation to the other. And, according to Whitehead, "Those societies which cannot combine reverence to their symbols with freedom of revision, must ultimately decay either from anarchy, or from the slow atrophy of a life stifled by useless shadows." [17] Faulkner himself believes that abstractions need not be useless shadows. He knows that ideas may be fecund and that traditions may enrich life. He writes, however, mostly about people whose ideas are sterile, whose traditions are impoverished. These abstractions remain empty precisely because they are used to evade actuality, not to embrace it.

---

17 Alfred North Whitehead, *Symbolism: Its Meaning and Effect* (New York: Capricorn Books, 1959), 88.

OBJECTIFYING
The Abstraction
Nailed in a Box

IN *The Hamlet,* Jack Houston goes all the way to Texas to escape Lucy Pate's "unflagging will not for love or passion but for the married state" (H, 238). After seven years with another woman, however, Houston returns to marry Lucy. He sees his marriage as a capitulation to her "female ruthlessness" (H, 240), as a sacrifice of masculinity. So he buys a stallion to represent that "polygamous and bitless masculinity which he had relinquished" in marriage; to the horse he makes an "actual transference" (H, 246) of his masculinity. The example is typical of a determination by the characters, seen throughout Faulkner's fiction, to find tangible embodiments for their abstractions.

The fiction testifies that man finds it very convenient to give his abstractions a local habitation and a name, to embody the concept in the object. But all too often man's notion of "embodiment" is not an ever-fluctuating relationship between the object and the quality signified; on the contrary, it is simply a static embalming of the quality in the thing. Because the object is valued only for its signification, which is then abstracted from it, the object itself no longer retains its place in the flux of experience. It becomes invariable, in Bergson's word's, "a mere symbol," or "in any case a motionless view of the moving reality." [1] And, all too often, the motionless object comes to replace human quality. With Wash Jones, for example, the "spurious bronze medals that never meant anything to begin with" (AA, 328) do not just represent bravery; they embody and establish it.

Man prefers to deal with motionless objects rather than ambiguous flux. Embodied in a motionless object, the abstraction is clear, concrete, and usable. Life, therefore, is simpler, but it is also less human. As novel after novel reiterates, man objectifies his abstractions in order to circumvent his responsibilities. One clear instance of man's tendency to use the object as a surrogate for human commitment occurs in *Go Down, Moses;* for Uncle Hubert Beauchamp obviously finds it convenient to leave Isaac McCaslin a tangible thing, "possessing weight to the hand and bulk to the eye and even audible: a silver cup filled with gold pieces" (GDM, 301), which can be exhibited and rattled and passed from hand to hand for twenty-one years. He prefers to bequeath a cup rather than to accept any responsibility for conveying to Ike a meaningful heritage. But this "Legacy, a Thing" (GDM, 301) would be no substitute, even if it remained silver and gold, for a tradition of honor and compassion and bravery.

Faulkner's characters, however, persist in trying to replace human commitment with an object. In "Wild Palms" the doctor's wife is suspicious of Harry and Charlotte's relationship, outraged over their presence on her property. Nevertheless she cooks a pot of gumbo for them as a surrogate for concern or as "symbol" of the "uncompromising Christian deed" (WP, 10). Carothers McCaslin tries to replace his obligation to Tomey's Turl with a legacy of one thousand dollars because, as Isaac realizes, *"that was cheaper than saying My son a nigger. . . . Even if My son wasn't but just two words* (GDM, 269–70). Using a gift to fulfill human

---

1 Henri Bergson, *An Introduction to Metaphysics,* trans. T. E. Hulme (Indianapolis: Bobbs-Merrill, 1955), 42.

obligations is indeed cheaper than giving the self, just as it is cheaper for Flem Snopes to pacify Mrs. Armstid with a nickel's worth of candy, " 'A little sweetening for the chaps' " (H, 362), than to repay the five dollars he has cheated from her. The gift may indeed provide an easy illusion of a debt amortized. The thing, as a gift, may then serve as a convenient cover for an ungenerous heart.

The gift need not, of course, be an evasion of obligation. Here Faulkner would strongly disagree with Jean-Paul Sartre who writes that "the craze to destroy which is at the bottom of generosity is nothing else than a craze to possess. . . . To give is to enslave." [2] Throughout Faulkner's novels, in fact, the gift may appear as a genuine expression of the heart's concern. A few examples include the egg money Mrs. Armstid gives to Lena Grove, or the wooden effigy Eck gives to Ike Snopes, or the dollar Isaac gives to Boon, or the birthday cake Dilsey buys with her own money and bakes for Benjy. But the fiction also details man's readiness to use an object as a substitute for the heart's involvement. So used, the gift mocks true generosity.

If he expects the object to absolve him from human responsibility, to perform his obligations for him, man has endowed the object with properties which are, in fact, magical. As Sartre explains, and here Faulkner would agree, such foisting of magical properties upon experience is "an inert activity, a consiousness rendered passive." [3] It eliminates tension with the external world and justifies inertia. Sartre explains that magic objects are "captivating, enchaining; they seize upon consciousness," and he insists that when man allows his consciousness to be captivated by magic objects, he in effect denies his own freedom [4] and ends by "eliminating consciousness itself." [5] Such a denial of

2 Jean-Paul Sartre, *Being and Nothingness: An Essay on Phenomenological Ontology,* trans. Hazel Barnes (New York: Washington Square Press, 1969), 758.
3 Jean-Paul Sartre, *The Emotions: Outline of a Theory* (New York: Philosophical Library, 1948), 84.
4 *Ibid.,* 79
5 *Ibid.,* 62–63.

freedom or elimination of consciousness is abhorrent to Sartre and to Faulkner; many of the people Faulkner writes about, however, find it most enticing. They crave sanctuary and absolution and would readily sacrifice their humanity for a magic symbol. Fonsiba's husband, for instance, sees his pension as symbol of absolution. On his Arkansas farm he worries about neither livestock nor crops, neither himself nor his wife. Hard times will be ameliorated because he can say, " 'I have a pension.' . . . He said it as a man might say *I have grace*" (GDM, 279). To endow, as he does, the object with magic properties (with a sort of secularized grace) is to imagine that possession of it offers a means to the abundant life. People may give the symbol away as surrogate for human commitment or retain it as a surrogate for human accomplishment. Either way, when they invest the object with magical potency, they justify inertia; either way, they expect from the symbol absolution from the ethical and emotional demands of human existence.

Labove, the schoolmaster at Frenchman's Bend, is clearly one such character who is captivated by magical objects. Faulkner writes that Labove "still had his hill-man's purely emotional and foundationless faith in education, the white magic of Latin degrees, which was an actual counterpart of the old monk's faith in his wooden cross" (H, 133). With Labove, the degree itself becomes a fetish endowed with magic properties. In these terms, the remaining paraphernalia of Labove's existence are seen only in abstract terms according to their relation to that degree. He spends time poring over the "books which he did not love so much as he believed that he must read, compass and absorb and wring dry . . . measuring the turned pages against the fleeing seconds of irrevocable time like the implacable inching of a leaf worm" (H, 125–26). Labove's asceticism and his virginity, as well as his book reading, are simply conditions necessary for the attainment of that degree. Eula Varner is neither a girl nor a woman but a threat to his inexorable determination. That is why "he did not want her as a wife, he just wanted her one time as a man with a gangrened hand or foot thirsts after the axe-stroke which will leave him comparatively whole again" (H, 134). But for Labove, being whole again means only being free of human involvement, being free once more to dedicate himself to "the power of words as a principle worth dying for if necessary" (H, 119). Essentially, Labove wants to abstract himself from the welter of human uncertainties. If he can set himself on the narrow pristine path toward a degree, then he will assuredly obtain a diploma which will solve the problems of his existence. Labove's dedication not only renders the football games, his schoolteaching, and his books mere abstractions valued according to their relation to his goal, but also denies the existence of Eula and ultimately of Labove himself as living human realities.

Other characters, too, make a fetish of an object and assume that possession of it will unfold the abundant life. What they want, of course, is to get something for nothing: life abundant, without any expenditure of anguish, suffering, or sacrifice. That is why buried money offers such an irresistible temptation. Whatever grief and struggle the money originally represented is long past. Unearthed, it is wealth made manifest; without agony or trial, it offers "one blinding glimpse of the absolute" (GDM, 39). In "The Fire and the Hearth," Molly Beauchamp is afraid that Lucas will find the buried money because she knows that, abstracted from human effort, such money will corrupt rather than enrich. Molly's point of view is corroborated by the unnamed woman in "Delta Autumn" who tells Uncle Ike, " 'You spoiled [Roth]. . . . When you gave to his grandfather that land which didn't belong to him, not even half of it by will or even law' " (GDM, 360). Abstracted from toil and sacrifice, the gratuitous inheritance has ruined Roth Edmonds just as found money, Molly is sure, would ruin Lucas.

Molly sees, as V. K. Ratliff does in *The Hamlet*, " 'what even the money a man aint got yet will do to him' " (H, 393). But neither money nor the pursuit of it is necessarily noxious. It may be self-perpetuating, as even Will Varner realizes (H, 24), or demoralizing as Molly and Roth's lover and Ratliff realize, but it is not necessarily so. In *The Wild Palms*, in fact, at the climax of "Old Man," the convict experiences, if the word does not seem too pretentious for him, an epiphany directly relating to the value of money. Working then with the Cajun in mutual trust and independence, the convict realizes, " *'I reckon I had done forgot how good making money was. Being let to make it'* " (WP, 262), and again, " *'I had forgot how good it is to work'* " (WP, 264), and again, he "had not even known until now how good work, making money, could be" (WP, 266). Money here is emphasized not for its own sake but as a concrete manifestation of work done freely with pride and skill. It manifests an ideal relationship between man and nature, one in which work means use but not exploitation.

Maurice Friedman explains such an ideal concept of work: "Work, too, is a part of spontaneity—not compulsion or domination of nature, but an act of creation that unites one with nature without dissolving one in it." [6] Free in the swamps of Louisiana, the convict finds such work. His reiterated remarks about the goodness of money along with his recognition that in prison he had spent "seven wasted years during which . . . he had been permitted to toil but not to work" (WP, 263–64) constitute a profound moment of self-awareness for the convict. If the man had remained true to this awareness, he would doubtless have deserved the kind of accolades accorded him by the critics who consider the convict an exemplar of primitive heroism. Unfortunately, however, the convict does not retain that awareness; he withdraws from it.

In the swamp the convict had a spontaneous relationship, in work, with nature. His money was the visible emblem of that work; it was not expected to replace the work. Lucas, on

6 Maurice Friedman, *To Deny Our Nothingness: Contemporary Images of Man* (New York: Delacorte Press, 1967), 229.

the other hand, seeks dollars with no sweat on them, and the convict retreats to Parchman where there will be sweat but no dollars. Either way, money or work is abstracted from human involvement and hence is without human meaning. Jean-Paul Sartre considers money itself a magic object, an abstract shortcut of the normal relation between man and nature: "Money suppresses the *technical* connection of subject and object and renders the desire immediately operative, like the magic wishes of fairy tales." [7] Faulkner, on the other hand, seems to feel that money may be more than a *mere* abstraction if it retains its connection with the work which produced it. To such a man as Ratliff, for instance, money continues to represent whatever hurt and grief somebody went through to earn it (Man., 176–77). And to the convict the money he earns in the swamps is simply the tangible embodiment of his working skill. With Lucas Beauchamp and Henry Armstid, on the other hand, money would obviate skill. The frenetic desperation of their search and the human sacrifices they make without compunction indicate that buried treasure means more to them than a release from poverty. Treasure has become for them a magic symbol, an easy shortcut to the good life.

That the desire to own things can be obsessive is reiterated throughout *The Hamlet;* there Henry and the other menfolk sell body and soul for some uncatchable spotted horses, and "Miz Snopes" (Ab's wife) trades off her only cow for a milk separator. That the desire to get something for nothing is debilitating is further affirmed by our last glimpses in *The Hamlet* of Henry Armstid. Frantically digging, he screams to his cospeculators, " 'I warn you. Get outen my hole' " (H, 393). Duped by Flem with the salted gold mine, Henry nevertheless will not give up; he continues to dig, furiously "spading himself into the waxing twilight with the regularity of a mechanical toy and with some-

7 Sartre, *Being and Nothingness,* 752–53.

thing monstrous in his unflagging effort" (H, 419). Still digging at the end of the book, his face is "now completely that of a madman" (H, 421).

Henry's madness is the logical outcome of greed which exists heedless of human concerns, which seeks reward without human accomplishment. "The Bear" ends similarly with Boon Hogganbeck under a tree alive with squirrels. Boon is "hammering the disjointed barrel against the gun-breech with the frantic abandon of a madman." He screams to Isaac, " 'Get out of here! Dont touch them! Dont touch a one of them! They're mine!' " (GDM, 331). In the classroom sessions at the University of Virginia, Faulkner commented upon this ending: "To me it underlined the heroic tragedy of the bear and the dog by the last survivor being reduced to the sort of petty comedy of someone trying to patch up a gun in order to shoot a squirrel. That made the tragedy of the dog and the bear a little more poignant to me" (FIU, 60). Here is a *reductio ad absurdum* of human desire to gain status through possession. Boon wants to possess the squirrels without skill as a woodsman; Henry wants to possess the gold without working for it. Both expect from the magic object absolution from human difficulties; both are crazed by that expectation.

The fiction indicates, however, that, dehumanizing as the desire to possess may be, no answers may be found in a simple refusal to possess anything. That is, of course, the solution Isaac McCaslin attempts. Seeing Boon's frantic greed and equating his grandfather's corruption with absolute power over land and slaves, he relinquishes his inheritance. Isaac not only refuses to own McCaslin property, but he refuses to own anything. *Go Down, Moses* begins by making two points about Uncle Ike: the first is that he is "father to no one" (GDM, 3). Admittedly, sonlessness was not Isaac's intention, and it is part of his pathos that in "saving and freeing his son, [he] lost him" (GDM, 351). But the sterility of Isaac's vow to virtue is established by his inability to pass on the code of pride and humility to posterity. Though he may be "uncle to half a county [he is] still father to none" (GDM, 300), not even to his kinsman Roth Edmonds. His life does indeed seem to have been "drawing inward" (GDM, 335) ever since his sixteenth year.

The beginning pages of *Go Down, Moses* further emphasize the fact that Isaac owns almost nothing. Faulkner calls him "a widower these twenty years, who in all his life had owned but one object more than he could wear and carry in his pockets and his hands at one time, and this was the narrow iron cot and the stained lean mattress which he used camping in the woods for deer and bear or for fishing or simply because he loved the woods; who owned no property and never desired to since the earth was no man's but all men's" (GDM, 3).

The repeated emphasis upon Isaac's sonlessness and propertylessness establishes these as the two salient facts about the old man. But they both seem to be emblems of his vow's limited scope. Uncle Ike seems powerless to perpetuate humility and pride beyond himself and to expand virtue beyond relinquishment. There is, furthermore, a fundamental paradox in Isaac's refusal to own land; for, like a woman such as Eula Varner, the land is impervious to man's mortgages and deeds and titles. In *The Hamlet* we are told that Eula's husband will actually be "no more a physical factor in her life than the owner's name on the fly-leaf of a book. . . . [He will] not possess her but merely own her by the single strength which power gave, the dead power of money, wealth, gewgaws, baubles, as he might own, not a picture, statue: a field say . . . the fine land rich and fecund and foul and eternal and impervious to him who claimed title to it" (H, 134–35).

Aware of the land's imperviousness, Isaac tells Cass Edmonds, " 'I cant repudiate it. It was never mine to repudiate . . . because on the instant when Ikkemotubbe discovered, realised, that he could sell it for money, on that instant it ceased ever to have been his forever, father to father to father, and the man who bought it bought nothing'" (GDM, 256–57). In "The Old People" Isaac has realized that although someday it "would be his own land which he and Sam [now] hunted over, their hold upon it actually was as trivial and without reality as the now-faded and archaic script in the chancery book in Jefferson which allocated it to them and that it was he, the boy, who was the guest here and Sam Father's [sic] voice the mouth-piece of the host" (GDM, 171). Isaac does then believe that titles of ownership are irrelevant abstractions. Actual ownership is, on the other hand, as Cleanth Brooks explains, a spiritual quality founded upon respect: "One can 'possess' the wilderness only by respecting and loving the wilderness, not by filing legal title and turning its trees into so many board feet of lumber, or even more abstractly, into so many shares on the stock exchange." [8] As the spiritual son of Sam Fathers, Isaac does then have some claim upon the land. But that claim cannot be refused by revoking the title of ownership. And certainly if Isaac accepts any of the monthly allotment Cass sends him or allows himself to be, as Lucas suspects, "supported by what Roth Edmonds chose to give him" (GDM, 36), then his refusal to own the land itself is an empty, self-deceptive gesture.

It is Ratliff in *The Hamlet* who thinks of men as having "established the foundations of their existences on the currency of coin" (H, 228), but that novel and the rest of Faulkner's fiction as well depict man's intention to establish his existence on a currency of symbols: objects endowed with magic properties and sought as surrogates for human qualities. Isaac's wife, for example, wants to define her existence through a plantation. Faulkner at the University of Virginia said of her, "Well, she assumed when they got married that she was going to be cha-telaine of a plantation and they would have children. And she

---

8 Cleanth Brooks, *William Faulkner: The Yoknapatawpha Country* (New Haven: Yale University Press, 1963), 270.

was going to be as—according to the rules of the book a good wife to him. She'd still be frigid and cold and a shrew probably but she'd still be a good wife" (FIU, 275–76). To this woman, marriage is not love but possession. She expects her life to be defined by the plantation just as Lucas expects his to be defined by the three thousand dollars which he banks and refuses to spend. Since Lucas will not use the money he already has, we have no indication that he will do anything, except bank it, with the buried money if he finds it. From Lucas' point of view, money is an absolute, a magic symbol for defining the worth of a person's life. He hopes to establish, with easily acquired money, the definition for his life he is not always willing to provide himself. To be sure, it appears that the whites establish their worth just that simply; we understand why Lucas assumes money is such a panacea, but we know that found money offers only an easy way to respectability, as artificial as I. O. Snopes's lensless spectacles, his paper dickey, and his cuffs that are simply "attached to the coat sleeves themselves" (H, 229). Snopes hopes to establish his erudition with such fake representations; he hopes that, in other words, the objects will serve as stand-ins for the quality, just as Lucas hopes that money will serve as a surrogate for human worth and Mrs. Isaac McCaslin hopes that a plantation will establish gentility.

Flem Snopes is another character who apparently does believe that quality may be established by the ownership of a few objects. He assumes that owning the de Spain mansion and having it remodeled to appear older and more antebellum than it really is will prefabricate his heritage. He buys a Cadillac and a "black felt hat somebody told him was the kind of hat bankers wore" (Man., 65), expecting these trappings of a heritage to establish his respectability for him. With many people, of course, heritage is assessed only in terms of trappings, for it is easier to judge a man's value by the knot in his tie and the size of his house than to examine the complex issue of personal integrity or actual aristocracy. But to judge only in terms of things, to consider the symbol rather than the actuality, is to commit the fallacy of misplaced concreteness.

Thomas Sutpen offers the most clearly defined example in the fiction of that fallacy, for an understanding of the irrelevance of things completely eludes Sutpen. As a boy, he was outraged to discover that men actually presumed to establish their superiority through the dead fact of ownership alone, by buying a rifle, for instance, not necessarily by being able to use it. Apparently a man can say, *"Because I own this rifle, my arms and legs and blood and bones are superior to yours"* (AA, 229). Until Sutpen made this discovery "it had never once occurred to him that any man should take any such blind accident as [ownership] as authority or warrant to look down at others, any others" (AA, 222). But once Sutpen discovers that the "ones who owned the objects" (AA, 221) do feel superior, he assumes that the superiority may be established by the objects alone: "You got to have land and niggers and a fine house to combat them with" (AA, 238). The house must of course be filled with the proper furniture, "not the least of which furniture was that wedding license" (AA, 51). Land, slaves, house, license, all these things are invested with a magical capacity to establish the respectability of Thomas Sutpen. To Sutpen, acquiring them will replace the tenuous and difficult business of establishing a tradition based upon human values. As Cleanth Brooks explains:

Sutpen's manners indicate his abstract approach to the whole matter of living. Sutpen would seize upon "the traditional" as a pure abstraction—which, of course, is to deny its very meaning. For him the tradition is not a way of life "handed down" or "transmitted" from the community, past and present, to the individual nurtured by it. It is an assortment of things to be possessed, not a manner of living that embodies certain values and determines men's conduct. The fetish objects are to be gained by sheer ruthless efficiency. (Sutpen even refers to "my schedule.") Thorstein Veblen would have understood Sutpen's relation to traditional culture. Sutpen is on all fours with the robber baron of the Gilded Age building a fake Renaissance palace on the banks of the Hudson.⁹

Here Brooks is dealing with a central question posed in Faulkner's fiction: how can such an amorphous quality as "tradition" be handed down or transmitted except through things or fetishes? The dilemma is that Faulkner believes in the absolute necessity of passing on tradition, yet sees the paradoxical difficulty of keeping it alive. For he knows that once tradition is ossified or frozen into an inert abstraction it loses its vitality and hence its relevance to the human heart. Man finds it convenient to suppose that tradition can be embodied and passed down through blood or in an object or by a code, but Faulkner reiterates that value resides elsewhere. It lies in relationships which emerge from the heart's involvement with people in time. It is embodied in the idea that the old times should "become a part of the boy's present, not only as if they had happened yesterday but as if they were still happening" (GDM, 171), and that the old people should "continue to live past the boy's seventy years and then eighty years" (GDM, 165). Tradition, then, must continue to live. Value and quality may not be appropriated simply through using an objective symbol of quality. Human commitment may be ordered, but not replaced, by symbols.

Faulkner's characters, however, want to use not just objects but people as inert abstractions, as symbols or replacements for some deficiency. To Ellen Coldfield Sutpen, Charles Bon is not a man but rather a symbol. She expects the same sort of transmogrification of her station from Bon that Flem Snopes expects from his mansion. She speaks "of Bon as if he were three inanimate objects in one, or perhaps one inanimate object for which she and her family would find three concordant uses: a garment which Judith might wear as she would a riding habit or a ball gown, a piece of furniture which would complement

9 *Ibid.*, 298.

and complete the furnishing of her house and position, and a mentor and example to correct Henry's provincial manners and speech and clothing" (AA, 75). This young man, whom Miss Rosa Coldfield calls *"the abstraction which we had nailed into a box"* (AA, 153), does not exist for Ellen or Rosa as a human being. He is simply the ultimate shape of their fantasies, a mere embodiment of certain abstract qualities. Ellen may consider him totally possessable only because, like Labove's degree or Miz Snopes's separator, he has been abstracted from the flux of experience. Charles Bon is, to Ellen, not a human being but an "object of art, the mold and mirror of form and fashion which Mrs. Sutpen . . . accepted him as and insisted . . . that he be (and would have purchased him as and paid for him with Judith even . . .)" (AA, 320). As the mere embodiment of an abstraction, Charles Bon may be bought and owned. Ellen wants to buy Bon because she has invested him, as an object, with magic properties. Like Flem Snopes with his mansion or the Arkansas Negro with his pension, Ellen wants to relinquish to an object her responsibility for creating a meaningful existence. House, pension, person—all are treated as mere fetishes whose possession offers an easy solution to human problems.

Ellen's attitude toward Bon is not unlike Flem's toward Eula. Flem has not only purchased the proper hat, car, and house, expecting them to establish his respectability for him, but he has also purchased a wife for the same reason. As Gavin Stevens realizes, Flem just wanted " 'a vice president's wife and child along with the rest of the vice president's furniture in the vice president's house' " (T, 224). Flem, in fact, maintains no human contact unless it may ultimately be useful to him (T, 279).

The use of another person as a commodity is humorously treated in *The Town* with the story of Mrs. Hait, "who as Ratliff put it had sold her husband to the railroad company for eight thousand percent profit" (T, 232); but underlying even that tale is Faulkner's horrified recognition that, as Lucius Priest in *The*

Reivers realizes, "there are people like Butch who don't remember anybody except in the terms of their immediate need of them" (Rev., 207). When Charles Bon or Eula or any human being is valued only as property, the intention is to simplify human existence; the result, however, is simply to deplete and dehumanize it.

In *Absalom, Absalom!* Ellen is not the only character who renders a human being an abstraction by valuing him according to his utility alone. She herself is, in fact, the subject and victim of just such a dehumanizing estimate. For, to her husband, Ellen is only the inert embodiment, the mere shape of respectability. Sutpen had come "to town to find a wife exactly as he would have gone to the Memphis market to buy livestock or slaves" (AA, 42). Ellen is chosen rationally, ruthlessly, because she represents impeccable respectability. Sutpen values Ellen, the architect, his slaves (the two women among them chosen probably "with the same care and shrewdness with which he chose the other livestock" [AA, 61]) only for what he can get out of them. Like octoroons who are, according to Mr. Compson, "more valuable as commodities than white girls" (AA, 117), these people are, to Sutpen, only so much merchandise. For, with Sutpen, as with the group commander in *A Fable*, man is not a "gallant and puny creature" but a mere "functioning machine" (AF, 51). Thus he has interest in Rosa Coldfield only if she can produce a son for him; he *"spoke the bald outrageous words* [propositioning Rosa] *exactly as if he were consulting with Jones or with some other man about a bitch dog or a cow or mare"* (AA, 168).

Throughout the fiction, disastrous consequences result from seeing human beings as abstract symbols, using them as means to an end. Treated as symbol of her mother's shame or of her uncle's lost job (SF, 382), Caddy Compson's daughter Quentin hardly has a chance to develop into a complete individual. She runs away from home and is not heard of again. Eula Varner Snopes commits suicide so that Flem will no longer be able to own and manipulate her like a piece of merchandise on a seller's market. In *Light in August,* Gail Hightower has considered the girl he married as little more than an abstract shape embodying the things he wants from her. As he himself comes to realize, " 'You took her as a means toward your own selfishness. As an instrument to be called to Jefferson' " (LA, 463). Her flight, adultery, and suicide are reactions motivated by a simple and pathetic attempt to declare her human identity. Joe Christmas' violence toward himself and others may, similarly, be understood as a reaction against the various abstract identities that haunt him and against the relationship with his foster father who accepts the boy only after examining him with "the same stare with which he might have examined a horse or a secondhand plow" (LA, 133).

In *Absalom, Absalom!* furthermore, it is because they have been treated as just so many usable objects that characters react so vehemently. In that novel, acts of violence are reactions to rejection; they are assertions of personal identity and individuality; they are protests which proclaim *I am not an object.* After his discovery that to the planters his people were mere cattle (AA, 235), Thomas Sutpen formulated the design which was simply a violent attempt to wrest from life an identity for himself. Rejected by him, Eulalia Bon has used her son as an agent of vengeance against Sutpen. (The vengeance theory is Quentin and Shreve's interpretation, but it seems to be validated by context and Faulkner's remark that Shreve's hypotheses are "probably true enough," AA, 335.) And certainly the rejected Rosa Coldfield does want to be "an instrument of retribution" against Sutpen (AA, 61). Rejected by his father, Bon too seeks vengeance; he is perhaps using the marriage plans as a lever to force recognition from Sutpen. But if Henry kills him, Bon will in turn deny his Sutpen kin. That is probably why he exchanges Judith's picture for that of the octoroon mistress and child. If he lives, the pictures may be reversed again. But if he is killed and the locket opened, Bon wants to be identified with the octoroon mistress, not with the Sutpens who rejected him. Charles Etienne de Saint Velery Bon too, in his fights first with black men then with white men, is attempting through violence to find his identity. His marriage to the black, apelike woman is a final vengeful gesture to make concrete his abstract identity as a black.

Ironically, these various assertions of identity, these proclamations that *I am not an object,* are predicated most often upon the use of others as objects. Rebelling against his family's being evaluated as cattle, Sutpen uses two wives and everyone else he can lay claim upon as just so much livestock. And Eulalia Bon probably uses Charles and Charles uses Judith to retaliate. Obviously, one's humanity is difficult to retain when one has been valued and used only as the tangible embodiment of an abstraction. Eula Varner Snopes manages to retain her humanity; Sutpen and Ellen and Joe Christmas and any number of other characters do not. Lifted out of flux and considered a mere mold and form, an ultimate shape or static embodiment of some abstraction, these characters tend to assimilate the out-of-life classification foisted upon them, for bad faith is easier than good faith. It is easier to fit a mold than to take upon oneself the manifest burden of self-definition.

To repeat, Faulkner's fiction details man's attempt to objectify his abstractions in objects or persons. To do so simplifies his dealings with the circumambient universe, for it allows him the illusion that the symbol may be used as a surrogate for human commitment. Such an illusion, however, is maintained only at the cost of depleting his humanity and the vitality of his symbol, since the object, lifted out of flux, soon loses its relevance. In *Go Down, Moses* the meaningful symbols in Rider and Mannie's marriage are imitated by Nat and George. Yet, as Lucas realizes, his daughter Nat is too young to know that "just a stove and a new back porch and a well were not enough" (GDM, 73).

Nat and George tried to use these things as surrogates for meaning, but they abstracted the symbols from the quality and thus rendered them meaningless. With Rider and Mannie, on the other hand, not even money is abstract, for they spend most of Rider's weekly "bright cascade of silver dollars" and save some too (GDM, 138). Rider and Mannie can be sensible about money; they can use it because they do not need it as a symbol of or substitute for value. A part of living, money for them is not abstracted from either work or pleasure; unlike Lucas' money or Flem's mansion, their dollars are used.

The mansion may have been a living symbol for the de Spains of their heritage; Flem purchases it, however, along with his wife, to cover his lack of heritage. With the de Spains it may have retained its connection with man's grief and pride and hope. Ratliff realizes that the mansion is the " 'physical symbol of all them generations of respectability and aristocracy' " (Man., 153), but by treating it as symbol alone, Flem reduces it to an abstraction, an empty husk. As Olga Vickery explains, Flem "must fall back on the urge to keep, to protect and conserve. Such conservation depends on not spending, not using, and not risking. Aside from his two extravagances necessary to consolidate his position in Jefferson—Eula's tombstone and De Spain's mansion—Flem apparently lives on less than he did as a clerk at Varner's store. Furthermore, his house is unlived in, his car rarely driven, his tobacco unchewed. His very hat is unsweated though, according to Montgomery Ward, he has worn it night and day for three years." [10] The relationship between mansion and heritage must be a vital one, continually revivified. Unused, unrelated, abstracted, the symbol becomes a dead thing; unused, it is misused.

In order to be used as a mere symbol, the object or person must be completely abstracted from the flux of actuality. Labove's

10 Olga W. Vickery, *The Novels of William Faulkner: A Critical Interpretation* (Rev. ed.; Baton Rouge: Louisiana State University Press, 1964), 202–203.

desire to possess Eula Varner once is based upon the assumption that she is little more than a thing subverting him from his design. Abstracted from flux, she may be seized once as a totality. Labove will have *had* that experience; Eula can offer him nothing more. The sex act is as absolute to Labove as it is to the crazed deputy in *Pylon* who sees Laverne only as the "ultimate shape of his jaded desires" (P, 196): " 'I'll pay you!' the man screamed. 'I'll pay her! I'll pay either of you! Name it! Let me . . . . her once and you can cut me if you want!' " (P, 200). To such men, the woman is only a "shape," an abstract vessel into which he may project whatever qualities he wants to possess. He can consider a woman as an "ultimate shape" only because he considers her abstracted from life. With these men, as with Lucy Pate who wants Houston only as an accessory to the "married state" (H, 238) or Lucas Beauchamp who refuses to use the three thousand dollars he has in the bank, possession is a finished, absolute condition, predicated upon the assumption that a person or object may be abstracted from flux. Miz Snopes provides perhaps the most extreme example of a character who abstracts a possession from existence, for, though she has no fresh milk, she is nevertheless determined to "get a heap of pleasure and satisfaction outen" her milk separator (H, 53).

Objects may be meaningful as symbols only so long as their connections with the human heart and soul are continually renewed. The courthouse in *Requiem for a Nun* is such a symbol because it expresses human aspirations. Similarly, in *Go Down, Moses* the fire on the hearth may exist as an "ancient symbol of human coherence and solidarity" (GDM, 380) because neither Rider and Mannie nor Lucas and Molly try to use it as a stand-in for coherence. And the objects on Mannie's grave are "insignificant to sight but actually of a profound meaning" (GDM, 135) because they express the heart's anguish; they are not expected to serve as substitutes for that anguish.

Nor are these symbols placed out of life as Flem's mansion is. The symbol continues to express value in man's life only when it is a part of his life. The symbol should be, in fact, put to use, like the gun given Isaac after his first winter in the big woods. That gun is a symbol of his manhood or at least his apprenticeship to manhood, but he does not enshrine it: "he would own and shoot it for almost seventy years, through two new pairs of barrels and locks and one new stock, until all that remained of the original gun was the silver-inlaid trigger-guard with his and McCaslin's engraved names and the date in 1878" (GDM, 205). Used, the gun maintains its connections with the humility and pride it is intended to signify.

In "The Old People" Isaac has shot his first buck, and Sam has marked him with the blood of the slain beast. Then a specter buck appears whom Sam addresses as "Oleh, Chief . . . Grandfather" (GDM, 184). Later Isaac tells his cousin about it. " 'You dont believe it,' the boy said. 'I know you dont—' 'Why not?' McCaslin said" (GDM, 186). Cass goes on to explain:

You cant be alive forever, and you always wear out life long before you have exhausted the possibilities of living. And all that must be somewhere; all that could not have been invented and created just to be thrown away. And the earth is shallow; there is not a great deal of it before you come to the rock. And the earth dont want to just keep things, hoard them; it wants to use them again. Look at the seed, the acorns, at what happens even to carrion when you try to bury it: it refuses too, seethes and struggles too until it reaches light and air again, hunting the sun still. (GDM, 186)

Isaac understands what Cass means. Like the earth which does not just keep and hoard things, Ike does not enshrine or shelve or just keep his gun; he uses it. And he is not concerned because the tokens which he places on Sam's grave likewise will not be permanent and inviolable. Without regret, he leaves on the grave "the twist of tobacco, the new bandanna handkerchief, the small paper sack of the peppermint candy which Sam had used to love; that gone too, almost before he had turned his back, not vanished but merely translated into . . . myriad life" (GDM, 328). Isaac does not mind the transposition of his gifts because he knows that meaning lies in human feeling, not in the mere tokens of affection. He also should have known that meaning lies in a right relationship to the land, not in the mere token of ownership. To reject his token title was to grant to that title tangible reality status. Isaac makes that mistake, however, with the token of ownership; he does not make it with the tokens of affection.

His attitude toward such tokens is directly opposed to that of Flem Snopes, Thomas Sutpen, Rosa Coldfield, and Judith Sutpen, each of whom shows an excessive concern with the tombstone, the token itself. Judith has arranged for the tombstone of Charles Etienne Bon before he arrives at Sutpen's Hundred; thinking of that, Mr. Compson remarks, "They lead beautiful lives—women. Lives not only divorced from, but irrevocably excommunicated from, all reality. That's why although their deaths, the instant of dissolution, are of no importance to them . . . yet to them their funerals and graves, the little puny affirmations of spurious immortality set above their slumber, are of incalculable importance" (AA, 191–92). It is not, of course, just women who attach such importance to an external symbol. Flem Snopes and Thomas Sutpen go to incredible expense and trouble to procure suitable tombstones. They expect these things to establish respectability or virtue or immortality because their approach to life is abstract rather than vital. They rely upon the permanence of rock as stand-in for evanescent human qualities. Isaac, on the other hand, does not mind if his graveside tokens of love are translated back into flux because there is still love.

Man's desire to objectify his abstractions, to give them a local habitation and a name, is explained inadvertently by Miss Rosa Coldfield when she compares the still-living Henry with the just-murdered Charles Bon: *"for the fact that he was still alive* [made him] . . . *just that much more shadowy than the abstraction which we had nailed into a box"* (AA, 153). Whatever is alive is shadowy, flickering, undefinable; whatever is nailed in a box or tangibly embodied is concrete, unambiguous, certain. Henri Bergson tells us that "to try to fit a concept on an object is simply to ask what we can do with the object and what it can do for us"; [11] he further explains that immobility seems clearer than mobility because the mind has "an irresistible tendency to consider that idea clearest which is most often useful to it." [12] Man objectifies his abstractions, then, to make them useful and to render his dealings with the universe clearer and simpler. If, however, he replaces the abstraction with the object or considers a human being to be a mere embodiment of an abstraction, then he has travestied the symbolizing process and constricted his own existence accordingly.

11 Bergson, *An Introduction to Metaphysics*, 39.
12 *Ibid.*, 44.

CODIFYING
The Abstraction Held Symmetrical
Above the Flesh

IN *The Sound and the Fury* Mr. Compson talks of Quentin's desire for "an apotheosis in which a temporary state of mind will become symmetrical above the flesh" (SF, 220). Abstracted from the uncertain and impermanent human world, Quentin's apotheosis would be fixed, absolute, imperishable. Being above the flesh, its symmetry would be neither organic nor cyclical, but rather angular and linear. Quentin might desire such a state because whatever is bounded by the symmetry of angles and lines is indeed neat, fixed, circumscribed; its substance is readily apprehended, its limits controlled. But, because life is organic flux, whatever is fixed into a final angular shape is out-of-life. Man's reducing the untamed wilderness to "oblongs and squares of . . . earth" (GDM, 257) seems to symbolize his humanizing of the nonrational world, but actually when the "untreed land [has been] warped and wrung to mathematical squares of rank cotton" (GDM, 354), man has only defaced nature and denied himself the opportunity to "hold the earth mutual and intact in the communal anonymity of brotherhood" (GDM, 257).

The attempt to impose structure on the world may be manifested in the absolute and dehumanized terms of geometry, for linear formulas necessarily simplify the natural world, but they may also distort it. Man nevertheless finds it consoling to project out onto the natural world his mathematical and geometrical constructs. And just as he attempts to transform jungle and wilderness into squares and oblongs, so too does he attempt to project mathematical formulas in the shape of codes and precepts onto the human world. The attempt, in either case, is to lend some semblance of order and control, but it involves a retreat from a vital and full relationship with both nature and man whenever the formulas exist "above the flesh." Codes are, of course, essential to order chaos and transcend anarchy, but they lose their validity when man so abstracts them from flux that their reference to the totality of existence is severed.

That totality is what Karl Jaspers terms the "unconquerable non-rational" [1] which eludes proof and demonstration, which cannot be deduced from precept, and which defies categorizing. It is then unconquerable because it is inaccessible to reason. In a rationalistic era, however, when he has lost his faith in almost everything except the empirical sciences, man is reluctant to admit the existence of this nonrational element; thus he tends to rely upon code and precept and formula not only to explain and order his world but to deny it. He works deductively by imposing a system of rational codes upon the unconquerable nonrational. These codes may be directed either outward upon the world or inward upon the self, or they may be used simply as a static barrier between the world and the self. In other words, man may impose codes upon external nature, denying that there is anything in existence which cannot be deduced from it, or he may allow codes to be imposed upon himself from without, maintaining that there is nothing in his behavior not determined by precept. Either way, validity is granted to symmetrical rules rather than to organic life. Man may use the rule as a barrier

1 Karl Jaspers, *Reason and Existenz,* trans. William Earle (New York: Noonday Press, 1955), 19.

between himself and existence, on the other hand, without insisting upon its validity. The idea in that case is so to absorb the self in the mechanics of codes and rules that the remainder of existence is excluded from consciousness; to do so is to grant the rule validity, not in itself, but only in its power to shut out existence.

Whether then the code is outer directed, insulatory, or inner directed, if it exists in denial of the totality, the code diminishes rather than augments life. Richard Chase explains the predominantly negative function codes play in Faulkner's fiction; he writes:

Mr. Robert Penn Warren suggests that Faulkner's objection to the modern world is that it lacks the ability to set up "codes, concepts of virtue, obligations" by which man can "define himself as human" and "accept the risks of his humanity." In *Light in August*, Faulkner seems to be concerned with showing that the codes modern man *does* set up do not allow him to define himself as human—that codes have become compulsive patterns which man clings to in fear and trembling while the pattern emasculates him.[2]

Even though they contradict each other, there is truth in what both Chase and Warren write, for compulsive codifying does distort, as Chase maintains, and meaningful codifying could enrich, as Warren maintains. Most of Faulkner's characters, however, codify only to evade the unconquerable nonrational; they deal, as Chase suggests, in codes, not actualities, and distort or reduce existence accordingly.

Although a rule may in fact be, as Quentin Compson phrases it, the "reducto absurdum of all human experience" (SF, 111), it is at least easily understood and mastered. Life is not. Lucas Beauchamp assumes that he may enter the white man's world by following the white man's rules for fighting duels. Lucas makes a move and then stops to ask, "That's right, aint it?"

2 Richard Chase, "The Stone and the Crucifixion: Faulkner's 'Light in August,' " *Kenyon Review*, X (Autumn, 1948), 542–43.

(GDM, 56). Imagining the alternating moves in the duel, Lucas thinks: *"He will do something and then I will do something and it will be all over. It will be all right"* (GDM, 51). Lucas searches for security, a sense of well-being, through following procedure. His obsession with order, apparatus, system can be understood as a desire to exclude the unconquerable nonrational and to restrict existence to that which can be mastered. Similarly, Talliaferro in *Mosquitoes* assumes that there is a formula, "the trick, the only trick" (Mos., 348), which will enable him to seduce women; everything will be "all right" if only he can find the magic formula. He expects procedure alone to offer an entree, to establish automatically for him a right relation to the world. He has, in other words, endowed the code with magical properties.

The assumption is that a formula will grant an entree or that the mere repetition of a gesture will be sufficient to allay difficulties. Gowan Stevens expects as much from being a Virginia gentlemen, Temple Drake from saying "my father's a ju-judge" (San., 54). These two characters are forced, in *Sanctuary*, to encounter a situation in which their social status is irrelevant; the bootleggers in Frenchman's Bend are neither impressed nor placated. Temple and Gowan have to face, for a time at least, the inefficacy of their codes. Most of Faulkner's characters avoid that recognition. Because it is easier to master a code than to confront the nonrational, they persist in believing in the solvency of certain formulas. Narcissa Benbow Sartoris, for example, in "There Was a Queen," spends two nights in a Memphis hotel with a Yankee federal agent. When she comes home, she and her son Bory spend all evening sitting in the creek with their clothes on. Miss Jenny snaps at her, " 'In Jordan. Yes, Jordan at the back of a country pasture in Missippi' " (CS, 741). Miss Jenny sees the absurdity, as well as the amorality, in Narcissa's actions, but Narcissa does not. Her brief affair had nothing to do with affection; it was just a way to buy back some obscene letters addressed to her. She assumes, however, that the mechanical performance of the externals of a rite of absolution will wash her clean of sin.

Narcissa expects absolution from the mere repetition of a codified gesture. Other characters expect salvation to be a state purchasable by "simple adherence to a simple code" (LA, 446). Rather than acknowledge the indeterminate, elusive nature of existence, such characters construe their experience on this earth in the unambiguous mathematical terms of debits and credits. Dawson Fairchild in *Mosquitoes* explains such a codified recipe for salvation: If duty " 'were just unpleasant enough, you got a mark in heaven' " (Mos., 228). Goodhue Coldfield has founded his existence on such a formula. Coldfield "intended to use the church into which he had invested a certain amount of sacrifice and doubtless self-denial and certainly actual labor and money for the sake of what might be called a demand balance of spiritual solvency, exactly as he would have used a cotton gin in which he considered himself to have incurred either interest or responsibility" (AA, 50). Coldfield's life of "fortitude and abnegation" results in a certain amount of hoarded money and goods, but the old man takes pleasure "not in the money but in its representation of a balance in whatever spiritual counting-house he believed would some day pay his sight drafts on self-denial and fortitude" (AA, 84).

Though the terminology of bookkeeping schematizes and belittles human moral responsibilities, it is an essential part of the frame of mind and vocabulary of those characters who want to approach the larger questions of existence with methodology alone. Gail Hightower accepts his martyrdom "with voluptuous and triumphant glee: [saying] *Ah. That's done now. That's past now. That's bought and paid for now*" (LA, 464). Later, when asked to emerge from his isolation, "his sanctuary" (LA, 293), in order to save Joe Christmas' life, Hightower thinks, " 'I wont! I wont! I have bought immunity. I have paid. I have paid' " (LA, 292).

Temple and Gowan Stevens in *Requiem for a Nun* too conceive of human accountability as if it were a credit and balance sheet on which the debits of sin might be balanced and erased by a proportionate amount of suffering. Temple asks, "Why cant you buy back your own sins with your own agony?" (Req., 277). Gowan talks bitterly of *paying* with his "bachelor freedom" and "man's self-respect in the chastity of his wife" for something his wife didn't even regret (Req., 74). And Temple speaks of their marriage as being worth to Gowan "less than he paid for it" (Req., 137). The absurdity and horror of reducing human ethical and emotional ties to a mathematical tally sheet is most vividly rendered in the Act I exchange between Gowan and lawyer Gavin Stevens:

GOWAN   I got a cut rate. I had two children. I had to pay only one
         of them to find out it wasn't really costing me anything—Half
         price: a child, and a dope-fiend nigger whore on a public
         gallows: that's all I had to pay for immunity.

STEVENS There's no such thing.

GOWAN   From the past. From my folly. My drunkenness. My coward-
         ice, if you like—

STEVENS There's no such thing as past either. (Req., 71)

The reader cannot but sympathize with Clytie in *Absalom, Absalom!* when she insists, " 'Whatever [Henry] done, me and Judith and him have paid it out' " (AA, 370). Yet the fiction in no way guarantees that Clytie and the Sutpens, any more than Hightower or Temple and Gowan Stevens, can buy immunity from the past. Even the most disinterested moral deeds do not enable one " 'to balance the books, write *Paid* on the old sheet so that whoever keeps them can take it out of the ledger and burn it, get rid of it' " (AA, 325). As General Compson tells Thomas Sutpen, immunity cannot be bought, not through martyrdom or sacrifice, or even with justice (AA, 265).

Such moral account keeping is a convenient emollient and,

like the McCaslin ledger which records commissary trade in feed and flour and grain and slaves, it does simplify existence. Indeed the McCaslin ledger, as it belittles human life and responsibility into only a matter of bookkeeping, may serve as metaphor for the obtuse moral account keeping these characters attempt. They refuse to acknowledge that absolution or salvation or immunity can never be bought by a calculated input of sacrifice or respectability or, indeed, by any calculations. And, like unused books, their calculated moral formulas become only "ordered certitudes long divorced from reality" (SF, 155).

Nevertheless, these characters assume that their codes bear absolute authority. And if the code is book derived, its certitude is objectively established, its validity beyond question. In *A Fable*, for instance, the aide distrusts his own judgment and experience with bravery and cowardice and reads books to find definitions of bravery (AF, 45). In *Go Down, Moses* Miss Sophonsiba Beauchamp has derived her definition of chivalry apparently from Sir Walter Scott. Though she lives in backwoods Mississippi in the nineteenth century, she wishes to live by romanticized medieval prescriptions: by rules which decree that Uncle Buck McCaslin put on a necktie before he chases Tomey's Turl toward "Warwick" or that she send him the red ribbon that she'd worn on her neck with a wish for "success" (GDM, 16) or that Buck marry Miss Sophonsiba after accidentally entering her bedroom at night. Miss Sophonsiba hopes to transform her commonplace existence into one with some semblance of glamour and refinement, but she would do so by rubric alone. The absurd inadequacy and superficiality of her attempt affirm that existence cannot be so easily mastered.

The tall convict in "Old Man" has such a discovery thrust upon him when he is arrested at the age of nineteen for attempted train robbery. "He had laid his plans in advance, he had followed his printed (and false) authority [dime novels] to the letter" (WP, 24), yet his plans are ludicrously inappropriate; they might have worked in books, but in the actual world they are absurd. In *Light in August* we learn that a younger Gail Hightower too followed procedures for courtship learned "not from her or from himself, but from a book" (LA, 454). And thus he discovered early "how false the most profound book turns out to be when applied to life" (LA, 455). Profound books are, of course, abstract, not false. Hightower's problem apparently was that he approached romances like the convict approached dime novels. Expecting "the stamp of verisimilitude and authenticity" rendered in "unspoken good faith," the convict feels that it is "criminally false" (WP, 23) that the techniques described in books fail to be prescriptions for living. Such faith in rational procedure, of course, constitutes these characters' innocence, for to have faith in the exclusively rational is to be innocent of the actual. As Cleanth Brooks explains, "The only people in Faulkner who are 'innocent' are adult males; and their innocence amounts finally to a trust in rationality—an overweening confidence that plans work out, that life is simpler than it is." [3]

Thomas Sutpen offers the most astonishing example of such a character who simply refuses to admit that there are elements in life which cannot be rationally calculated. Thus when his life begins to crumble around him, Sutpen does not reexamine his design; he only wonders how he miscalculated. He says to General Compson: " 'Whether it was a good or a bad design is beside the point; the question is, Where did I make the mistake in it, what did I do or misdo in it . . . I had a design. To accomplish it I should require money, a house, a plantation, slaves, a family—incidentally of course, a wife' " (AA, 263).

The wife is hardly a human being at all; she is only one of those ingredients in Sutpen's recipe. Quentin Compson tells Shreve McCannon how Sutpen "just told Grandfather how he had put his first wife aside like eleventh- and twelfth-century

3 Cleanth Brooks, *William Faulkner: The Yoknapatawpha Country* (New Haven: Yale University Press, 1963), 308.

kings did: 'I found that she was not and could never be, through no fault of her own, adjunctive or incremental to the design which I had in mind, so I provided for her and put her aside' " (AA, 240). Sutpen's only concern, after spending several years with one wife and then having to put her aside, seems to have been getting, as he told General Compson, " 'behind with my schedule' " (AA, 264).

Though his schedule or design was self-derived according to his outsider's appraisal of social mores, Sutpen is no more capable of scrutinizing and revaluating it than the convict is capable of judging his book-derived code. Sutpen has invested his "code of logic and morality, his formula and recipe of fact and deduction" (AA, 275) with absolute authority. And he has reduced existence to its quantitative and rational elements alone. His, then, is an "innocence which believed that the ingredients of morality were like the ingredients of pie or cake and once you had measured them and balanced them and mixed them and put them into the oven it was all finished and nothing but pie or cake could come out" (AA, 263).

Such a trust in rationality is a tempting simplification of existence. The more reluctant a character is to face the nonrational, the more vehemently he insists upon the power of rational codes to render existence predictable, malleable, accommodating. Such an insistence, however, is founded upon the assumption that existence is an aggregate of static entities whose properties may be added or subtracted in neat mathematical recipes or computations. The inefficacy of a code which merely assembles and computes is best exemplified, again, in Thomas Sutpen, for his morality, though it *"had all the parts . . . refused to run, to move"* (AA, 279). Sutpen has the mere ingredients of a dynasty. Similarly, Horace Benbow tells Ruby Lamar, " 'I lack courage: that was left out of me. The machinery is all here, but it wont run' " (San., 16).

Obviously, if existence were no more than an aggregate of

fixed ingredients which could be measured and properly combined to achieve the expected results, a recipe or code would be absolutely efficacious to conquer it. The inefficacy of codes affirms, however, that the universe includes mystery as well as matter. The futility of codifying is particularly apparent when the codes are directed outward upon other human beings, because human behavior defies empirical schematizing. Man wants to believe, however, that other human beings will react within the roles assigned them according to established rules. But to ask that man be predictable is to ask that he be mechanical. Lucas Beauchamp, imagining the white man's world as one structured by the symmetry of codes, expects such mechanized predictability from Roth Edmonds. He intends to "speak his word [to Roth] and it would be like dropping the nickel into the slot machine and pulling the lever" (GDM, 36). Roth, of course, does not react as predictably as a slot machine. Nor do the women in *Mosquitoes* about whom Talliaferro exclaims, "Why is it that they never act as you had calculated?" (Mos., 348). As Karl Jaspers writes, "Man cannot be deduced." [4] It is, in fact, only through a loss of humanity that human behavior becomes in any way deducible, calculable, or machinelike. I. O. Snopes may be "like one of the machines in railway waitingrooms" (H, 228), Henry Armstid may dig for gold with the regularity of a metronome (H, 413), and Flem Snopes may have a purely "mechanical morality," [5] but the extent of their mechanization is measure of their inhumanity. That is why " 'folks dont like it' " (H, 65) when Flem Snopes never makes a mistake; his impersonal, unfailing accuracy implies that he is not quite human. Flem will not cheat, because, like Jason Compson, he finds that being true to the letter of a money contract extricates him from personal entanglements.

4 Karl Jaspers, *Man in the Modern Age*, trans. Eden and Cedar Paul (New York: Doubleday and Co., 1957), 76.

5 Paul Levine, "Love and Money in the Snopes Trilogy," *College English* (December, 1961), 198.

The structure of law itself encourages this point of view. It maintains with Flem (who takes the menfolks' money for worthless horses) or with the sentry in *A Fable* (who loans money for the privilege of becoming the beneficiary of apparently hundreds of soldiers) that if the law has not been violated, there is no crime. The many courtroom scenes in Faulkner's fiction imply that whether the defendant is innocent, as are Lee Goodwin and Popeye Vitelli in *Sanctuary* and Monk Odlethrop in *Knight's Gambit,* or guilty, as are Harry Wilbourne in "Wild Palms," Nancy Mannigoe in *Requiem for a Nun,* and Mink Snopes in *The Mansion,* the court's judgment is simply beside the point. Like Mink Snopes, we find it difficult "to listen . . . when the Judge bang[s] his little wooden hammer on the high desk" (Man., 3), because we feel that his judgment will never be quite relevant or pertinent.

Only pertinent are the questions of background, motivation, intent, consciousness, and conscience that lie forever outside the law's jurisdiction. Lawyer Gavin Stevens tries, from time to time, to bring such matters before the court. In *Knight's Gambit* he remarks of Monk's death, " 'They didn't hang the man who murdered Gambrell. They just crucified the pistol' " (KG, 50). The half-wit Monk was only a tool, a pistol, used by the man Terrel to kill the warden. Gavin convinces the governor of Terrel's actual guilt, but it is a guilt not punishable by law, so Terrel goes free. Held symmetrical, outside the flesh, the law is pathetically inapplicable to Terrel's situation, for it can deal only with technical, not actual, guilt.

In "Smoke," another story in *Knight's Gambit,* Faulkner writes of an old judge who believed "that justice is fifty per cent legal knowledge and fifty per cent unhaste and confidence in himself and in God" (KG, 11). But apparently the judge's percentages are inexact, for any number of injustices are committed in Faulkner's world with the proclamation, " 'It's the law' " (KG, 102). Indeed, the fiction indicates that legal knowledge plays little or no part in justice. Legality offers us, in fact, only "a rule provided . . . and a penalty provided for the rule" (AF, 59). As Olga Vickery writes:

The result is a static morality in which the moral is identified with the lawful. Because he pays scrupulous attention to the legal aspects of his actions, Jason Compson considers himself not only legally blameless but morally right. The same attitude is revealed in *Sanctuary* and *Requiem for a Nun* by Temple Drake's inability to see the moral significance of her actions. This diminution of the moral involves also a shrivelling of the concept of sin to a mere violation of a formal law for which an exact and often arbitrary punishment is meted out. It is Nancy Mannigoe's trial that most dramatically juxtaposes the moral and legal aspects of sin. Her concern is with God and her own soul, not with the judges, lawyers, bailiffs, and jury. With her quiet words, "Guilty, Lord," she acknowledges her sin as distinct from her legal culpability. Through her action, responsibility and dignity are once more restored to man.[6]

In asserting her guilt before God, Nancy acknowledges the irrelevance of the court and its legal judgment. Most Faulknerian characters, however, reverse Nancy's insight. They insist upon a dichotomy between temporal and ultimate standards, but they value only the temporal and local. They confuse law with justice, propriety with morality, or the literal terms of an agreement with its intent. They grant full reality status to procedure alone. They evade the complications of human existence by believing that, when the letter of the law is followed, all obligation is amortized. That is why Anse Bundren is so determined to obey the letter of his promise to bury Addie in Jefferson. The journey becomes "a monstrous burlesque of all bereavement" (AILD, 74), but Anse nevertheless sees it as duty decently fulfilled, for he deludes himself into believing that he owes her no obligation other than fulfillment of that single promise. Gail Hightower too, momentarily at least, theorizes that the church fathers " 'did

6 Olga W. Vickery, *The Novels of William Faulkner: A Critical Interpretation* (Rev. ed.; Baton Rouge: Louisiana State University Press, 1964), 292.

their part; they played by the rules. . . . I was the one who failed, who infringed. Perhaps that is the greatest social sin of all; ay, perhaps moral sin' " (LA, 461). Such thinking implies that emotional ties and ethical obligations do not exist; only the code of propriety has validity.

Jason Compson sees his human obligations only in terms of following a series of inflexible codes. Jason acknowledges no emotional or moral or aesthetic claims upon him. Even his affair with Lorraine is handled like a business contract. Delegating only his weekends to Lorraine, Jason makes sure that she does not touch him vitally. "A sane man always," (A to SF, 17) Jason assumes that, unencumbered by the illusions which plague the other Compsons, his literal vision is alone true. But, as Olga Vickery writes, "It is his very insistence on facing facts that causes his distorted view of Caddy, his family, and the whole human race." [7] To keep up appearances is all that Jason feels life requires of him; certainly it is all he requires of his niece. Quentin offends because she violates, not morality, but discretion, for to Jason, external appearances alone constitute reality. That is why he can feel that, when the letter of the law is followed, an obligation is fulfilled. Caddy has paid him fifty dollars to let her see her baby. Jason lets her do just that—see it through a moving carriage window—and congratulates himself on causing Caddy more heartbreak while at the same time fulfilling his agreement with her and being, therefore, blameless.

Like Mrs. Compson, Jason grants reality status to the code of propriety alone. As Mr. Compson remarks of his wife, she is concerned over impropriety, but "whether it be sin or not has not occurred to her" (SF, 126). Mrs. Compson simply dismisses all moral issues which lie outside her rigid code of propriety. It is conveniently reductionist to do so; she manages neatly and finally to differentiate between right and wrong and to maintain some semblance of morality without the slightest bit

7 *Ibid.*, 43.

of soul-searching. Like the old doctor in "Wild Palms," she has "contrived to retire into pure [and irrelevant] morality" (WP, 280).

Persons like Mrs. Compson, the old doctor and his wife, and the Reverend Mr. Hightower seek to dwell "by serene rules in a world where reality [does] not exist" (LA, 448). They fail precisely because their serene rules and rituals exist outside of actuality. As Dawson Fairchild remarks in *Mosquitoes*, they " 'destroy life by making it a ritual' " (Mos., 117). Such persons destroy life because, rather than using rules and rituals and formulas to order existence, they use them to shut out existence. In *Light in August*, for example, the townspeople find Hightower's ravings and his wife's suicide incomprehensible. But rather than deal with that problematic situation, they disregard most facts, while seizing upon and embroidering others, so that they can fit circumstance into a preconceived pattern. On well-trodden ground, they simply make the conditioned, and therefore least scrutinized, response. Accordingly, Hightower is "punished" for an unpardonable sin with which they know how to deal: for having an affair with a Negro. Their response is itself a cliché.

Man resorts to clichés in hopes that "bluff and simple adherence to a simple code" (LA, 446) will deny life's complexities. But, as Richard Chase explains, "The tragic irony of the linear consciousness, Faulkner seems to say, is that it is an illusion." [8] Precisely because codes shut out reality, because they are self-contained and symmetrical, they fail. Alfred North Whitehead insists that there can be "no self-contained abstraction"; every abstract code must involve "reference to the totality of existence." [9] Faulkner's characters, however, sever that reference to the totality and assume that, being self-contained, their codes and rituals will prevail over uncertainty and indeterminancy.

8 Chase, "The Stone and the Crucifixion," 541.
9 Alfred North Whitehead, "Immortality," *Interpretations of Science: Representative Selections* (Indianapolis: Bobbs-Merrill, 1961), 251.

Codes and rituals may, on the other hand, be invoked not to master but simply to avoid the nonrational. As Herbert Dingle explains in an introduction to Bergson's *Duration and Simultaneity:* "It is our practical routine that has militated against a renewal, or deepening, of our perception." [10] Bergson, of course, deplores the way in which routine militates against a renewal of perception. Most of Faulkner's characters, on the other hand, find in routine a welcome respite from consciousness. Thus we may find them living with defeat or even choosing it in order *"to be allowed to cling to the habit"* (WP, 324). In such cases, habit and routine, the mechanics of code following, become so absorbing that everything else is excluded from consciousness. That is why Quentin Compson, before committing suicide, nevertheless paints his cut finger with iodine and brushes his teeth. Continuing with habitual routine enables him to avoid fully recognizing the awesome nature of the deed he plans; it is a defense against awareness, a device for closing off thought. As Dawson Fairchild insists in *Mosquitoes,* man renders himself "out of life . . . [when] living becomes a conscious process" (Mos., 231).

By concentrating on conscious process alone, Quentin seeks the sort of absolution from and evasion of complexity his brother Benjy is cursed with. For Benjy, routine is an unalterable absolute. At the close of the novel when Luster turns left rather than right at the monument, "for an instant Ben sat in an utter hiatus. Then he bellowed. Bellow on bellow, his voice mounted, with scarce interval for breath. There was more than astonishment in it, it was horror; shock; agony eyeless, tongueless; just sound, and Luster's eyes back-rolling for a white instant. 'Gret God,' he said, 'Hush! Hush! Gret God'" (SF, 400). With Queenie's direction reversed, the novel ends as "the broken flower drooped over Ben's fist and his eyes were empty and

10 Herbert Dingle, introduction to Henri Bergson, *Duration and Simultaneity,* trans. Leon Jacobson (Indianapolis: Bobbs-Merrill, 1965), v.

blue and serene again as cornice and façade flowed smoothly once more from left to right; post and tree, window and doorway, and signboard, each in its ordered place" (SF, 401).

Benjy craves order because his minimal-level consciousness is incapable of apprehending fluctuating temporal and human actualities. Benjy possesses some degree of immunity to existence because, unable to abstract, he remains unaware of the fluid, conscious only of the fixed. Paradoxically, other characters use the sort of high-level abstractions Benjy is incapable of to accomplish a constriction of existence as rigid and unthinking as Benjy's. They seek to avoid the human need for what Karl Jaspers terms "infinite reflection" [11] and to find solace in what amounts to subhuman rigidity.

Such rigidity is essential to Benjy's sense of well-being, but it is a retreat and an evasion for Quentin, as it is for Joe Christmas. Through mechanical absorption in detail alone, Joe avoids, as Quentin did before the suicide, too close a scrutiny of his projected course of action. Joe destroys the whisky still with a thoroughness that implies pleasure in technique alone. He reads a magazine "straight through as though it were a novel," stopping only to count the remaining pages; Faulkner says that Joe "read now like a man walking along a street might count the cracks in the pavement" (LA, 104). Such single-minded absorption in detail is mechanical and dehumanizing. As Faulkner writes of Roger Shumann in *Pylon*, he is not only "single-purposed" but "fatally and grimly without any trace of introversion or any ability to objectivate or ratiocinate . . . like the engine" (P, 171). The engine never deviates from a fixed track or pattern; its behavior is straightforward and determined.

Throughout *Light in August* there appear images of lines, paths, tracks, and corridors, images of what Richard Chase terms "linear discreteness." Chase explains, "The linear discrete image

11 Jaspers, *Reason and Existenz*, 32.

stands for 'modernism': abstraction, rationalism, applied science, capitalism, progressivism, emasculation, the atomized consciousness and its pathological extensions. The curve image stands for holistic consciousness, a containing culture and tradition, the cyclical life and death of all the creatures of earth. Throughout the novel, Lena retains her holistic consciousness and she is strong, enduring, hopeful. All the other characters in one way or another are victims of the linear delusion." [12] This delusion is most repeatedly exemplified in the corridor image. Man hopes to place himself in a corridor or on a track which will so dictate and determine his behavior that he himself will be absolved of responsibility. For example, when the dietitian sees Eupheus Hines and realizes how she can get rid of Joe, she finds that "her life now seemed straight and simple as a corridor" (LA, 426). For Joe, the day when he will kill Joanna opens "peacefully on before him, like a corridor, an arras" (LA, 104).

The corridor, rigid and symmetrical, seems uncomplex and simple because it is above the flesh; Joe even "follows a straight line, disregarding the easier walking of the ridges" (LA, 318) because he feels absolved of the need to make decisions when a track or corridor or straight line determines his direction. And that is why he finds it a "respite" (LA, 113) to deal with such a ruthless man as McEachern, who even when he is cruel is at least predictable. Faulkner writes that McEachern, "the hard, just, ruthless man, merely depended on [Joe] to act in a certain way and to receive the as certain reward or punishment, just as he could depend on the man to react in a certain way to his own certain doings and misdoings" (LA, 157). Joe and McEachern are in fact "in their rigid abnegation of all compromise more alike than actual blood could have made them" (LA, 139). They are alike because they both approach life through a code which leaves no room for the personal factor. McEachern's "voice was not unkind. It was not human, personal, at all. It was just

12 Chase, "The Stone and the Crucifixion," 540.

cold, implacable, like written or printed words" (LA, 139). McEachern is not quite human because his code, like Joe's straight line through the woods, remains rigid and uncompromising, regardless of human realities.

When he is fourteen and is late coming home one Saturday, Joe knows that "when he reached home he would receive the same whipping though he had committed no sin as he would receive if McEachern had seen him commit it" (LA, 146). But Joe prefers it that way. McEachern is a man "whose immediate and predictable reaction to the knowledge would so obliterate it as a factor in their relations that it would never appear again" (LA, 157). Joe wants to "get his whipping and strike the balance and write it off" (LA, 115). The whipping is perfunctory and passionless; it seems to offer a convenient way to obliterate consciousness and to write off the past. But, as Lucius remarks in *The Reivers* when his father is about to whip him: "It was wrong, and Father and I both knew it. I mean, if after all the lying and deceiving and disobeying and conniving I had done, all he could do about it was to whip me, then Father was not good enough for me. And if all that I had done was balanced by no more than that shaving strop, then both of us were debased" (Rev., 301).

Indeed, man is debased whenever he assumes that the mere enactment of a code can absolve him of human responsibility. Joe Christmas, of course, wants to debase himself because he is afraid of the fully human existence. He is comforted because "he and the man could always count upon one another. . . . Perhaps he saw no incongruity at all in the fact that he was about to be punished, who had refrained from what McEachern would consider the cardinal sin which he could commit, exactly the same as if he had committed it" (LA, 149). And so Joe submits to the punishment in which McEachern's strap "rose and fell, deliberate, numbered, with deliberate, flat reports. The boy's body might have been wood or stone; a post or a tower" (LA, 150).

These images of rigidity—the tower, the stone, the post—are decidedly masculine. But in *Light in August* rigidity is masculine not only because it is phallic, but also because it is impersonal, outside the flesh. In *Light in August* whatever is rigid, hard, predictable is associated with the white man, while images of caves, pits, "the original quarry, abyss itself" (LA, 108) are associated with the female and the Negro, with whatever is soft, emotional, and unpredictable. Joe resents the kindness of Mrs. McEachern, who "would try to get herself between him and the punishment which, deserved or not, just or unjust, was impersonal, both the man and the boy accepting it as a natural and inescapable fact until she, getting in the way, must give it an odor, an attenuation, and aftertaste" (LA, 157). Joe's resentment is projected outward upon whatever is feminine; he comes to hate the "soft kindness" of all women "which he believed himself doomed to be forever victim of and which he hated worse than he did the hard and ruthless justice of men" (LA, 158).

To Joe the feminine is soft, supine, disordered, unpredictable, and demanding, while the masculine is hard, erect, ordered, and predictable, demanding no more than simple adherence to a simple code. That is why he is pleased to find in Joanna Burden "not woman resistance," for she resists "fair, by the rules" (LA, 222). In fact, between them the sex act "was as if he struggled physically with another man for an object of no actual value to either, and for which they struggled on principle alone" (LA, 222). Whatever follows absolute, rigid rules is masculine and, to Joe, a respite, because it is lifted out of an emotional, cluttered, and soiled female world.[13] Joe's violent reaction to Bobbie's

13 To Richard Chase, Joe's yearning for whatever is hard, linear, erect, implies necessary homosexuality. Chase is not quite clear on this point, however, as he says both: "Joe's many adventures with women are attempts to escape the abstract quality of a latently homosexual life" (*Ibid.*, 544) and "He goes through life with this same attachment to his pattern, hating the women in underclothes [that he sees in the cheap magazine], longing for a purely masculine annihilation" (*Ibid.*, 545). That Chase posits a formula on Joe's

menstrual period is a clear-cut example of his inability to accept human soilure. Joe "seemed to see a diminishing row of suavely shaped urns in moonlight, blanched. And not one was perfect. Each one was cracked and from each crack there issued something liquid, death-colored, and foul. . . . He vomited" (LA, 177–78). Here, as elsewhere in Faulkner, the urn is associated with out-of-life stasis or perfection. Joe hopes to find that sort of perfection in a rigidly codified masculine world; the feminine world, to Joe, is obviously imperfect, and it is dangerously unpredictable and demanding.

Joe kills Joanna because she ceases to play by manlike rules. She seeks to involve him in a world which is complex and emotional and uncertain. They meet in the bedroom now, "as though they were married" (LA, 249); she wants to have a child; she tries to remake Joe into "something between a hermit and a missionary to Negroes" (LA, 257); she even makes allowance for Joe to break the rules and steal from the Negroes he would be bringing "up out of darkness" (LA, 261); she prays over him. All this Joe sees as an attempt to unman him by taking him off the rigid path and involving him in an uncertain and ambiguous human world.

In his study *The Flight from Woman,* the psychiatrist Karl Stern characterizes such behavior as symptomatic of our times. He describes the compulsive activism of a number of his patients.

Many of these ulcer patients were found to be hard-working and spartan in their habits; they shied away from any pleasure of "receiving," from accepting tenderness, from all forms of passivity, even healthy ones. Yet deep down there persisted an extra-ordinary need to be mothered, to be fed. "Deep down" is the right term, because the conflict manifests itself literally deep down in the body, on an organic level. The patient protests in his life against "being fed," while

---

entirely latent homosexuality seems, to me, decidedly uncertain and unnecessary. That Joe seeks whatever is rigid, linear, and predictable establishes his desire not for a homosexual relation but for an abstract existence which is metaphorically masculine. Chase seems here to have confused, in I. A. Richards' terms, "vehicle" and "tenor."

his stomach revolts against "not being fed." However, feeding here means much more than the intake of nourishment; it means receptiveness in a large sense, receptiveness to love, and openness in a childlike attitude of trust.[14]

Dr. Stern might well have had Joe Christmas himself for a patient, for with Joe there is precisely this same refusal to accept tenderness. The young Joe rebels against Mrs. McEachern because " 'she was trying to make me cry' " (LA, 158). Crying would be an acknowledgment of his own inadequacies, and, rather than admit his need for others, Joe cuts off the buttons Joanna has sewed on for him (LA, 100) and hurls the plates of "woman's muck" (LA, 225) proffered by Joanna and Mrs. McEachern onto the floor.

Joe Christmas spends all his life trying to run on a narrow manlike path that is symmetrical and outside the flesh. His attempt is, of course, doomed. He wanted to be "an eagle: hard, sufficient, potent, remorseless, strong. But . . . he did not then know that, like the eagle, his own flesh as well as all space was still a cage" (LA, 150–51). Human flesh forever resists rigidity. For a time a code or a system such as the war machine "stiffens the malleable mass and even holds it cohered and purposeful for a time," but "the vast seething moiling spiritless mass" of fleshly man is too amorphous to be held symmetrical and cohered for any length of time (AF, 30). Man overflows and destroys the neat symmetrical boundaries which attempt to contain him. Even Joe, after running all his life to escape whatever is soft, emotional, and unregimented, realizes that acceptance in the relaxed Negro world " 'was all I wanted. . . . That was all, for thirty years. That didn't seem to be a whole lot to ask in thirty years' " (LA, 313). Joe has left the "cold hard air of white people" and has "returned to the lightless hot wet primogenitive Female" (LA, 107). This is the "black abyss" (LA, 313) which he had earlier defined as the "woman-

14 Karl Stern, *The Flight from Woman* (New York: Noonday Press, 1965), 2.

shenegro" (LA, 147) and which "had been waiting, trying, for thirty years to drown him" (LA, 313). Only when he leaves the "manshaped life" (LA, 107), meaning a life tied to nothing but a rigid code, can Joe become what John L. Longley, Jr., terms a "Hero in the Modern World." Joe can become a hero only with his acceptance of "the risk of the human condition." [15] And he can accept these risks only when he steps off the rigid path and ceases to demand that life be fixed and rational and mechanical and predictable.

When the codes are directed outward, as with Thomas Sutpen, the intention, again, is to render existence predictable and circumstance workable, to conquer the nonrational. When codes are used to insulate the self against the nonrational, as with Quentin Compson and Joe Christmas, they are barriers, static and without direction. But when the intention is to see the self as conquered by an external, rational order, the codes are directed inward. To soothe his psyche from the burden of responsibility for his own acts, man may insist that his behavior is dictated by social mandate. Therefore, he lapses from conscious decision making into following codes automatically and often unconsciously.

V. K. Ratliff theorizes that it is the northerner who " 'when he does something . . . does it with a organised syndicate and a book of printed rules" (H, 91) and that it is " 'federal folks' " who are "not interested in whether anything worked or not, all they were interested in was that you did it exactly like their rules said to do it" (T, 155–56). But Faulkner's fiction establishes the ubiquity of such behavior that Erich Fromm terms "automaton conformity." According to Fromm, whenever behavior is conditioned, "the individual ceases to be himself; he adopts entirely the kind of personality offered to him by cultural patterns; and he therefore becomes exactly as all others are and

15 John L. Longley, Jr., "Joe Christmas: The Hero in the Modern World," in Frederick J. Hoffman and Olga W. Vickery (eds.), *William Faulkner: Three Decades of Criticism* (New York: Harcourt, Brace, and World, 1963), 272.

as they expect him to be." [16] He sacrifices his own individuality in order to adopt behavior which is, in Faulkner's terms, "formally pre-absolved" (WP, 293). Fromm further explains: 'Human existence begins when the lack of fixation of action by instinct exceeds a certain point. . . . In other words, *human existence and freedom are from the beginning inseparable.*" [17] The problem, however, is that freedom is such a terrifying burden that man is all too often willing to relinquish it. Liberated from the fixity of instincts, he retreats from the burden of freedom into the fixity of precepts.

In *Intruder in the Dust* the mob exemplifies such "automaton conformity." To Chick Mallison the mob appears not as "faces, but a face, not a mass nor even a mosaic of them but a Face" (ID, 182). Chick remembers the faces in the mob as being "myriad yet curiously identical in their lack of individual identity, their complete relinquishment of individual identity into one We" (ID, 137). The mob is ready to follow a code according to which Negroes are automatically lynched for killing white men, but when Lucas Beauchamp's innocence is verified, the mob turns and runs as one rather than acknowledge that it almost lynched an innocent man. Their actual physical flight is intended as an escape from self-recognition. Whenever individual identity is relinquished to "one We," the intention is an escape from the awesome responsibility of being one's unique self. It is intended, in Fromm's terms, as an "escape from freedom," but the truth is that, as Faulkner writes, "you escape nothing, you flee nothing" (ID, 195). Man, nevertheless, attempts to flee personal responsibility by lapsing into the kind of reflex action that is actually 'hindered by thought" [18] and by feeling as well.

Persons resort to such reflex actions particularly when existence threatens to overwhelm them. At moments of impending

---

16 Erich Fromm, *Escape from Freedom* (New York: Rinehart and Co., 1941), 185–86.
17 *Ibid.*, 32.
18 Alfred North Whitehead, *Symbolism* (New York: Capricorn Books, 1959), 81.

disaster or death, Faulkner writes, men gather "with that curious vulture-like formality which Southern men assume in such situations" (U, 267). Such formality is a conditioned response. Its codified externality is a defense against ultimate trials. It is a measure of their emotional and intellectual insensitivity that the menfolk, Anse among them, at Addie Bundren's funeral can be conscious of their role, can in fact strike a pose. Like the deputy in "Pantaloon in Black," the men in *As I Lay Dying* are most concerned with funereal proprieties. Tull describes their pose: "We do not go in. We stop at the steps, clumped, holding our hats between our lax hands in front or behind, standing with one foot advanced and our heads lowered, looking aside, down at our hats in our hands and at the earth or now and then at the sky and at one another's grave, composed face" (AILD, 86).

The mourners' composed role playing is set against the anguish of people like Addie's sons and Rider in "Pantaloon in Black" who truly grieve and who therefore cannot simply maintain a pose or play a role. To Anse and his kind the ritual is a mandate for behavior; they expect the conventions to serve, like the magic object, as surrogates for human feeling. They refuse to acknowledge that, in Olga Vickery's words, "any ritual, as Addie herself suggests, can become a travesty, even though it has been ordained and sanctioned in its fixed order from the beginning of time. Since there is no virtue attached to the meticulous repetition of its words and gestures, it is the individual who must give meaning and life to ritual by recognizing its symbolic function." [19] Anse and the men see no symbolic function to their behavior; they play the role of bereaved mourners only because such role playing is expected of them. The pose may come automatically, unbidden, as it did to Quentin Compson when he confronted Dalton Ames. Quentin remembers how

19 Vickery, *The Novels of William Faulkner*, 52–53. Actually it is Darl who sees Anse's mourning as a "monstrous burlesque of all bereavement" (AILD, 74).

abstracted his own voice was: "then I heard myself saying I'll give you until sundown to leave town" (SF, 198). Or the pose may be consciously adopted; either way it offers an escape from feeling and thinking and authentic living.

Jean-Paul Sartre considers such posing or role playing as an example of *mauvaise foi* ("bad faith" or, in Walter Kaufman's translation, "self-deception"). Sartre sees role playing as an evasion of the individual responsibility for being the authentic self. He writes, "But the first act of bad faith is to flee what it cannot flee, to flee what it is." [20] In *Flags in the Dust* Belle Mitchell and Horace Benbow are trying to flee self-recognition through "unflagging theatrics" (FD, 167). Belle adopts a "self-imposed and tragic role, [with Horace] himself performing like the old actor . . . who can play to any cue" (FD, 180). Similarly, Ellen Coldfield Sutpen speaks "her bright set meaningless phrases out of the part which she had written for herself" (AA, 69), and Thomas Sutpen "act[s] his role too" (AA, 72). Joanna Burden also behaves "as if she had invented the whole thing [her affair with Christmas] deliberately, for the purpose of playing it out like a play" (LA, 244–45). These characters use role playing to escape themselves; they feel that, by playing a role, they may lapse out of their own personal identities.

Role playing may provide man with a positive means to enrich his existence, but, as Maurice Friedman explains in his study *To Deny Our Nothingness*, role playing may, on the other hand, offer man "a means of escaping from the *shame* of the self by seeing oneself as an object, in categories, or as rationally comprehensible and explicable." [21] The military, in particular, as Faulkner's fiction indicates, encourages man to see himself, in Friedman's terms, as "not responsible as the unique person that

20 Jean-Paul Sartre, *Being and Nothingness: An Essay on Phenomenological Ontology*, trans. Hazel Barnes (New York: Washington Square Press, 1969), 115.
21 Maurice Friedman, *To Deny Our Nothingness: Contemporary Images of Man* (New York: Delacorte Press, 1967), 249.

one is but only in terms of a social role."[22] In *A Fable* the commander himself denies responsibility and insists upon seeing himself as an object: " 'It wasn't we who invented war,' the group commander said. 'It was war which created us' " (AF, 54). The group commander and most military personnel insist that " 'there are rules' " (AF, 53); they therefore transfer responsibility to the system itself. Olga Vickery explains that man's dependence upon system serves "as a way of circumventing the recalcitrance of experience by fixing a code or formula which clearly, definitively, and finally orders that experience and hence all reactions to it. The result is a kind of linguistic determinism inflicted on himself by man because of his desire for order."[23]

When he construes his codes and formulas to be fixed, absolute, and determining, man hopes to excuse himself from responsibility, to buy immunity from the consequences of his own actions. The military establishment, with its rigid "old obsolete methods" (AF, 125), seems to offer man absolute immunity, because in the military, system alone is supreme. It is the officers' insistence that " 'there are rules' " (AF, 53); it is their ability to decree "for half the earth a design vast in its intention" (AF, 232); it is their concern with system alone which renders military officers particularly "immune to nationality, to exhaustion, even to victory" (AF, 22). Faulkner defines officers as "they who by avocation and affinity had been called and as by bishops selected and trained and dedicated into the immutable hierarchy of War to be major-domos to such as this, to preside with all the impunity and authority of civilised usage over the formal orderly shooting of one set of men by another" (AF, 136).

These men are characterized as immune, impervious, insulated, impregnable, and indestructible because they have relinquished their ties with the flesh. They have, in fact, placed an "insuperable barrier of . . . vocation and livelihood" (AF,

22 *Ibid.*
23 Vickery, *The Novels of William Faulkner*, 272–73.

9) between themselves and the entire human race. Faulkner writes that the officer is "by the badges on his tunic also forever barred and interdict from the right and freedom to the simple passions and hopes and fears" of mankind (AF, 66). It is the fury and hatred of his men that irrevocably isolates the officer (AF, 26) and alienates him from the human race.[24] Such an officer is the group commander Bidet, who becomes "more immune to harm as his stars increased in number and his gift for war found field and scope, but no more pitiless" (AF, 33). Cut off from man's simple passions and hopes and fears, Bidet cares not about justice, or even about himself, but only about "vindication of his military record" (AF, 32). Like the system, he too is "impervious and even inattentive to the anguish, the torn flesh" (AF, 124-25). The impunity of rank atrophies the human sympathies and sensitivities. As George Bedell writes in his book on Faulkner and Kierkegaard, "To allow one's self to be pushed and directed by outside forces means that one becomes less and less a self and more and more an object."[25]

Nevertheless, Bidet and characters like him throughout the fiction grant special reality status to a system (whether military or not) precisely because, by diminishing the human factor, it renders them no more responsible than an object is. In *The Hamlet* Labove insists, as military officers do, that there are "rules for violence" (H, 123). In *Light in August* McEachern maintains "firmly fixed convictions about the mechanics" (LA, 189) of both good and evil. Cora Tull knows that there are rules for salvation. Joe Christmas assumes that apparently " 'there is a rule to catch me by, and to capture me that way [by his own surrender] would not be like the rule says' " (LA, 319). And Percy Grimm respects Joe's procedural control: "He said, 'Good man' " (LA, 437).

---

24 Taken exclusively from *A Fable*, these quotations represent Faulkner's later viewpoint toward the military, an attitude for the most part absent from the earlier work, in which the military was treated indifferently or, as in *The Unvanquished*, in rather romantic terms.

25 George C. Bedell, *Kierkegaard and Faulkner: Modalities of Existence* (Baton Rouge: Louisiana State University Press, 1972), 143.

The attempt to schematize existence with rules and codes is often an effort to evade responsibility and escape consciousness. Man does not know that "you escape nothing" (ID, 195). He wants only to avoid coming face-to-face with life by doing what Darl Bundren calls the "safe things," which are "just the things that folks have been doing so long they have worn the edges off" (AILD, 125). These folks do not care that " 'when anything gets to be a habit, it also manages to get a right good distance away from truth and fact' " (LA, 69). They would gladly crucify Joe Christmas (as they would Lucas Beauchamp), whether or not the punishment is deserved, " 'since to pity him would be to admit selfdoubt' " (LA, 348). Self-doubt would necessitate Jasper's "infinite reflection" or Whitehead's "reference to the totality": in other words, a continual reexamining of one's human responsibilities and of the interrelationship between existence and the codes used to order it. Many of Faulkner's characters prefer, however, to keep their codes fixed at "a right good distance from truth and fact" in order to evade just such a necessary reexamination. Held symmetrical outside the flesh, such codes seem to offer another sanctuary from the ongoing flood which is life.

Their attempt fails, of course, because, abstracted "a right good distance" from a fluctuating, ever-incomprehensible human existence, their codes become devitalized and irrelevant. Faulkner writes of Wash Jones's morality that it "was a good deal like Sutpen's" (AA, 287) and of Quentin and Shreve's "ratiocination [that it] after all was a good deal like Sutpen's morality and Miss Coldfield's demonizing" (AA, 280). The similarity lies in the fact that such morality or ratiocination or demonizing is each, like Sutpen's design, abstracted from the flux of existence. Each, therefore, is an empty abstract formula contrived in denial of actuality. Always refractory, however, actuality will not be so readily dismissed. It refuses to be coerced by such formulas or to conform to such rational schemes as Sutpen's recipe for establishing a dynasty or Hightower's formula for buying immunity. The code is, therefore, an ineffective barrier between man and the "living and fluid world of his time" (WP, 25); that world necessarily intrudes, washing away the barriers and outraging that man who has expected to buy immunity with his neat little maxims, precepts, and formulas.

To recapitulate then: man codifies his existence in order to conquer the nonrational. He arranges the world according to arbitrary designs which would exclude the irrational. He insists that *the way* is knowable and seeks to devise a formula or code which will enable him to master the chaos of experience, to make it an object for his will. Or he concentrates his attention upon procedure so that the code stands as a barrier between himself and a disconcerting world. Or he tries to "slough that which conscience refuses to assimilate" (LA, 323), to deny his accountability for his own deeds, by seeing himself as a volitionless agent in the service of an inexorable code. Indeed, man tries "to use all sorts of shabby and shoddy means and methods to assuage himself" (LG, 102) but none are genuinely efficacious.

As Ned McCaslin remarks in *The Reivers*, " 'There's somewhere the Law stops and just people starts' " (Rev., 243). In that novel Lucius Priest, now comprehending the code and the behavior dictated by it, says to Everbe, " 'It wasn't your fault then.' " But she replies, " 'Yes it was. You can choose. You can decide. You can say No' " (Rev., 160). There are characters in Faulkner's fiction who do say no to the dictates of a code, who do choose themselves in Kierkegaard's sense. The runner in *A Fable* who relinquishes his military rank does. Everbe does. Chick Mallison does. Isaac does when, at the age of ten, he abrogates "all the ancient rules and balances of hunter and hunted" (GDM, 207) in order to experience the epiphany of an encounter with Old Ben. And young Bayard Sartoris does when "in the face of blood and raising and background" (U, 249) he confronts Benjamin Redmond without the dueling pistols Drusilla has offered him according to the code of "succinct and formal vio-

lence" (U, 252). The scarcity of such examples evidences, however, Faulkner's awareness of how much easier it is to believe
in the efficacy of formulas and the suitability of the codified
response than it is to confront face-to-face, without the defense
of code or precept, a living and fluid irrational world.

CONCEPTUALIZING
The Abstraction Grasped as a Fine Dead Sound

MODERN EPISTEMOLOGY tells us that the mind can deal only in "models" of experiential reality; it can never "have" reality itself and should be under no delusion about fully comprehending and containing actuality. Most of Faulkner's characters, however, make the mistake of insisting that the models or categories they deal with are the reality. They tend to forget that they are dealing with models which may be functional tools for comprehending and ordering reality but which cannot replace that actuality; thus they manage to be only in touch with the shape of their own concepts and models rather than with the living and fluid world of their time. They expect fixed objects or rigid codes to offer a stay against chaos, a sanctuary from the flood. Similarly, yet even more abstractly, they may expect concepts themselves to offer a sanctuary of sorts. They mold these convenient beliefs into an elaborate conceptual framework which so obscures the workings of the universe that it seems a shield against actuality or an agent for rendering it known and malleable. They use abstract concepts in two ways: either as barriers against actuality to block it out or as inscriptions upon it to coerce it into apparent congruence.

Horace Benbow calls such a restructuring of existence "lying" and adds that it is a " 'struggle for survival. . . . Little puny man's way of dragging circumstance about to fit his preconception of himself as a figure in the world' " (FD, 189). But man lies or drags circumstances about or reconceptualizes for psychic not physical survival. He does so to keep "the shock of reality [from] entering [his] life" (AA, 79). He does so, in other words, to preserve his impunity. With an "insuperable barrier" (AF, 9) between himself and reality, man has "surrounded himself, enclosed himself, insulated himself from the penalties of his own folly" (Man., 236).

Preferring insulation to exposure, most of Faulkner's characters display an " 'infinite capacity no: passion for unfact' " (AF, 348) because actuality is problematic, the unfactual concept is not. Such a concept is passively adopted "for no other reason than that [they] happened to be believing it at the moment" (KG, 25). As Bergson explains in *Time and Free Will*: "The beliefs to which we most strongly adhere are those of which we should find it most difficult to give an account, and the reasons by which we justify them are seldom those which have led us to adopt them. In a certain sense we have adopted them without any reason, for what makes them valuable in our eyes is that they match the colour of all our other ideas, and that from the very first we have seen in them something of ourselves." [1] Because these beliefs are familiar, they are unthreatening and therefore may pass unexamined; they are, in other words, static and stale. As Bergson explains, man tries to "reconstruct reality—which is tendency and consequently mobility—with precepts and concepts whose function it is to make it stationary." [2]

Man's fear of time present was discussed in Chapter III in order to illustrate the impulse for sanctuary. Misconceptions of

1 Henri Bergson, *Time and Free Will: An Essay on the Immediate Data of Consciousness*, trans. F. L. Pogson (London: George Allen and Unwin, 1950), 135.
2 Henri Bergson, *An Introduction to Metaphysics*, trans. T. E. Hulme (Indianapolis: Bobbs-Merrill, 1955), 51.

time may further serve here as illustration of man's fondness for fixing and freezing any concept. Faulkner once remarked in an interview that "time is a fluid condition which has no existence except in the momentary avatars of individual people. There is no such thing as *was*—only *is*" (LG, 255). To see time in discrete units of past, present, and future (or *was*, *is*, and *will be*) is therefore to distort and deny actuality. One of the stories in *Go Down, Moses* is entitled "Was," but the novel affirms that *was* is to some extent an abstraction; there is "no such thing as *was*." No story in *Go Down, Moses* is discrete or isolated. Each is a part of the whole, not because it deals with the McCaslin clan (one story, in fact, deals not with the McCaslins but with one of their tenants), but because theme, motif, and symbol recur throughout. The novel shows generations repeating themselves and the sins of the fathers being perpetuated, not because an authoritarian God curses a family with a particular sin, but because man cannot accept the past as an irrevocable part of the present and learn from it. Ignoring the past, he does not subdue it but instead grants it license to reassert itself. Thus Isaac McCaslin hopes to dissociate himself and his son from old McCaslin's sins, but he accomplishes instead his own childlessness and manages to so spoil (GDM, 360) his kinsman Roth Edmonds that Roth hasn't the humanity to love or the decency to accept responsibility toward man or beast. Roth, in fact, repeats the sins of old Lucius Quintus Carothers McCaslin. And he too assumes that sins can be paid off with money.

Isaac does try to find out about the past and attempts to deal with it in, he assumes, something of the manner of John Brown who "was crude enough to act" (GDM, 284). But Isaac's "action" is chiefly one of dissociation from the evils of the past. And there is some sense in which, by ignoring the past, he grants to it a peculiar potency, for, regardless of man's efforts to deny it, the past persists, and it must be acknowledged. All of *Go Down, Moses* asserts that point. We find there that generations repeat themselves (GDM, 110), that Sam Fathers will live on in Isaac (GDM, 165), and that, indeed, all time may be "crammed and crowded into one instant of time" (GDM, 140). Isaac's boyhood experience serves to insure that "those old times would cease to be old times and would become a part of the boy's present" (GDM, 171). Isaac's mistake, however, is to attempt, on the one hand, to freeze the old wilderness times so that they may not become a living part of the present; on the other hand, it is to try to dismiss the plantation past altogether. Repudiating it, Isaac believes he may escape it.

But the past is an undeniably and irrevocably real part of the living present. It may be neither frozen nor dismissed. In Faulkner, in fact, those people who appear to have escaped their past never seem quite human. The aviators in *Pylon* seem "ephemeral" because they have "no past" (FIU, 36). Similarly in *Go Down, Moses,* Butch, the grandson of Molly and Lucas Beauchamp, who dissociated himself from his Mississippi past and fled to the glitter of Chicago, speaks now "in a voice which was anything under the sun but a southern voice or even a negro voice"; thus he seems out of time, "imperishable and enduring" (GDM, 369). Charles Bon too appears to be "impervious to time" (AA, 74). The brass-haired woman in *Light in August* with the "false glitter of the careful hair" (LA, 164) has about her also that same quality of being "impervious to time: a belligerent and diamondsurfaced respectability" (LA, 163). These characters seem out of time and therefore imperishable because they have no visible past. They have become only walking abstractions, brittle and imperishable and unalive.

With his overwhelming sense of the past, Gail Hightower is, however, just as ephemeral as Butch, the brass-haired woman, and those aviators who seem to have no past at all. Hightower simply has no present. He retreats from the world of living people, about whom he cares nothing (LA, 56), and from his responsibilities as husband and minister, instead, he embraces what is ostensibly the past but is really an illusory world of his own construction. Hightower's inflated image of his grandfather's cavalry charge bears little resemblance to the actual ignominious raid on the chicken house. The important point is that for Hightower "time had stopped there" with his grandfather's death and "nothing had happened in time since, not even him" (LA, 59). As the community realizes, "if Hightower had just been a more dependable kind of man, the kind of man a minister should be instead of being born about thirty years after the only day he seemed to have ever lived in—that day when his grandfather was shot from the galloping horse—she [his wife] would have been all right too" (LA, 56–57). But Hightower evades being a "dependable kind of man" because his fantasies extricate him from the demands of the present moment. Hightower is mistaken in assuming that he may disavow the present to live in the past. He is further mistaken in assuming that the past is finished and therefore unthreatening. In the war tales he finds "no horror here because they were just ghosts, never seen in the flesh, heroic, simple, warm; while the father which he knew and feared was a phantom which would never die" (LA, 452). Hightower is unlike V. K. Ratliff, who can accept "change, because it's motion" and who is "never one to say, I wish I had been born a hundred years ago" (FIU, 253), for Hightower denies time present. Like Isaac McCaslin who thinks that the ledgers out of the past are fixed and static and therefore harmless (GDM, 268), Hightower assumes the past to be finalized and therefore safe.

Quentin Compson too, like Gail Hightower, would choose to live in the past. He faces backward in time: "his very body was an empty hall echoing with sonorous defeated names; he was not a being, an entity, he was commonwealth. He was a barracks filled with stubborn back-looking ghosts" (AA, 12). As Cleanth Brooks explains, "Quentin's obsession with the past is in fact a repudiation of the future. It amounts to the sense of having no future." Brooks further insists that "man's very freedom is bound up with his sense of having some kind of future." [3] Or, as Warren's Jack Burden comes to understand, man has to have the future to have the past. Similarly, Ernst Cassirer writes that the future is "more than mere expectation; it becomes an imperative of human life." [4] Quentin Compson, however, chooses to reject that imperative. He commits what Frederick Hoffman calls "the ultimate act of abstraction, death by suicide." [5] Becoming himself a "stubborn back-looking ghost," Quentin denies his involvement in both present and future. He consciously sets out to destroy the interconnectedness of time, to forestall progression.

To Quentin, progression bears no relation to the Bergsonian concept of fluidity; with Quentin it is strictly mechanical. Unlike Spoade who refuses to be programed or scheduled (SF, 96–97), unlike Dilsey who can tell time by a one-handed clock three hours off (SF, 342), and even unlike Hightower who "lives dissociated from mechanical time [and who] for that reason . . . has never lost it" (LA, 346), Quentin is obsessed with mechanical time. He conceives of progression as being embodied in clocks themselves. Thus, to get out of time, Quentin twists the hands off his watch. His gesture is, of course, futile, but Quentin reflects, "I suppose it takes at least one hour to lose time in, who has been longer than history getting into the mechanical progression of it" (SF, 102).

Without its hands, Quentin's watch is only a "blank dial with little wheels clicking and clicking behind it, not knowing any better. Jesus walking on Galilee and Washington not telling lies" (SF, 99). Quentin associates the myths about Jesus and

3 Cleanth Brooks, *William Faulkner: The Yoknapatawpha Country* (New Haven: Yale University Press, 1963), 329.

4 Ernst Cassirer, *An Essay on Man: An Introduction to a Philosophy of Human Culture* (New Haven: Yale University Press, 1944), 55.

5 Frederick Hoffman, *The Twenties: American Writing in the Postwar Decade* (Rev. ed.; New York: Free Press, 1965), 248.

Washington with the watch's clicking, because to him now they are each equally meaningless falsifications. Quentin looks at the dozen or so watches in the jeweler's window, "each with the same assertive and contradictory assurance that mine had, without any hands at all" (SF, 104). That each watch states that he is in a different moment of time establishes, for Quentin, the absurdity of making any statement whatsoever. At this point Quentin seems to be overwhelmed by empirical prescriptions. If science tells us that Jesus could not have walked on water, then the story is a lie. If the clocks, or whatever statements about reality we attempt, contradict each other, then the statements are absurd and meaning does not exist. Quentin does not realize that contradiction among timepieces or among any series of interpretations establishes only the inadequacy of any single interpretation of reality. A rigid doctrinaire statement may indeed be absurd with its assertive and contradictory assurance, but that is no reason to conclude, as Quentin does, that meaningful statement is therefore impossible.

Quentin is not like the big trout that delights in its life and puts its "nose into the current, wavering delicately to the motion of the water" (SF, 144); Quentin cannot move with any current. He would prefer to find shelter in a few rigid and clean concepts. Once forced, however, to admit the absurdity of those concepts, Quentin prefers death. His father says to him: "You cannot bear to think that someday it will no longer hurt you like this now were getting at it" (SF, 220). Quentin wants to isolate Caddy "out of the loud world" (SF, 220) or to abstract a single state out of the finite world and make it permanent. What he cannot bear is the suggestion ("now were getting at it") that his present anguish is only a temporary state.

The most appalling awareness forced upon Quentin is that in a mature and realistic world people often "cannot even remember tomorrow what seemed dreadful today" (SF, 98). In the penultimate paragraph in Quentin's section the phrase "and i temporary" occurs four times. Aghast over the suggestion that love and anguish will not last, Quentin keeps asking incredulously, "temporary [?]." Quentin is outraged over the evanescence of human affection, for his romanticism demands that states of the heart be absolute. Cleanth Brooks suggests that as the weeks passed after Caddy's marriage "perhaps Quentin did suspect that his anguish was diminishing and might finally become tolerable. Perhaps he killed himself for fear that if he waited longer, the staunchless wound would heal. Perhaps Quentin was really in love with his despair." ⁶ Only death, as Quentin sees it, can lift his anguish out of time so that it remains absolute, undiminished, and unscathed by flux. He thinks to himself: *"If it could just be a hell beyond that: the clean flame the two of us more than dead. Then you will have only me then only me then the two of us amid the pointing and the horror beyond the clean flame"* (SF, 144). In eternal torment, passion would remain unchanged and Quentin and Caddy would be *"more than dead."* Quentin feels the need for some imperishable bliss or, forsaking that, some imperishable torment. He wants to exclude major segments of existence and to lift a particular segment out of time so that it will remain forever. The novel establishes that Quentin deludes himself with such hopes and that his delusion is founded upon a configuration of reality which is mechanical rather than organic.

In an interview with Loic Bouvard, Faulkner insisted, "There isn't any time. . . . In fact I agree pretty much with Bergson's theory of the fluidity of time. There is only the present moment, in which I include both the past and the future, and that is eternity" (LG, 70). Faulkner's understanding of time is not to be confused with the mystic's refusal to distinguish between past, present, and future. It represents, instead, simply a refusal to divide time into mutually exclusive units and an insistence that past and future are immanent in the present. That is why

6 Brooks, *William Faulkner*, 333.

the disconcerting time shifts in his novels are crucial embodiments of Faulkner's sense of time.[7] Time for Faulkner is essentially a matter of consciousness. Any moment of consciousness
in the present includes both memory and tendency or the impact
of the past and the lure of the future. Man's mistake is to try
to deny that fact, to distort and falsify time with abstract configurations which fragment time into discrete units and which suggest
that man may disregard duration and choose to live in one
segment of time alone.

Clearly then, Quentin misconstrues actuality with a fixed,
mechanical notion of time. But the fixed concept is a distortion,
not just of time, but of quality as well, for any concept which
is lifted out of flux immediately becomes only a "fine dead
sound" (SF, 217). Quentin prefers such motionless dead sounds
because he can grasp them; they are almost tangible in comparison with the fluctuating, uncontainable experiential world. Thus
Quentin attempts to deal in a limited number of concepts which
are just as absolute, rigid, and quantitative as is his notion of
time.

Like his mother, Quentin has been "taught that there is no
halfway ground that a woman is either a lady or not" (SF, 127).
For Quentin, though, the definition of *lady* and with it that of
Compson honor become even narrower: to him a lady is a
virgin and Caddy's virginity is the equivalent of Compson honor.
Faulkner says of him in the appendix to *The Sound and the Fury*
that he "loved not his sister's body but some concept of Compson
honor precariously and (he knew well) only temporarily supported by the minute fragile membrane of her maidenhead"
(A to SF, 9). Quentin's father tries to tell him that virginity
is just a word (SF, 143), but to Quentin it is indeed a state
outside the flesh. That is why he is "incapable of love" (A to

7 Margaret Church, on the other hand, dismisses the import of these shifts
by describing them as mere gimmickery. See her *Time and Reality: Studies
in Contemporary Fiction* (Chapel Hill: University of North Carolina Press, 1963),
205.

SF, 10); he values in Caddy "not her but the virginity of which she was custodian and on which she placed no value whatever" (A to SF, 10). He loves the concept, not the person.

Quentin uses the concept of virginity and the lie about incest to isolate himself and Caddy from the terrible world of flux. To him the ultimate outrage is that "it [virginity] doesn't matter" (SF, 96). And he thinks of sex, "If it was that simple to do it wouldnt be anything and if it wasnt anything, what was I" (SF, 183). The loss of Caddy's virginity means nothing; it does not seem to matter; the world is not convulsed in a paroxysm of horror; events continue as before. Quentin is forced to see that he has spent his life in protection of a meaningless abstraction. Only his death will raise that abstraction out of flux so that it will finally matter after all.

Quentin's concern for concept rather than life is literally self-destructive. The fiction indicates, however, that self-destruction is inherent in devotion to any out-of-life abstraction. As Maggie Stevens Mallison remarks, referring to her brother Gavin's idealization of Eula Varner Snopes, " 'You don't marry Semiramis: you just commit some form of suicide for her' " (T, 50). Nevertheless, man makes a virtually suicidal attempt to wed himself to some absolute concept which he construes to be truth itself. Throughout the Faulkner canon and particularly in *Absalom, Absalom!* and *The Sound and the Fury,* truth is presented as elusive and multivalent. Therefore it is all the more appalling, as Michael Millgate points out, to see in those novels how "each man, apprehending some fragment of the truth, seizes upon that fragment as though it were the whole truth and elaborates it into a total vision of the world, rigidly exclusive and hence utterly fallacious." [8] Faulkner's perspective is, as Millgate points out, related to Sherwood Anderson's "theory of the grotesque," the idea being that when man appropriates a truth to himself he

8 Michael Millgate, *The Achievement of William Faulkner* (New York: Random House, 1965), 87.

becomes a grotesque and his truth becomes a falsehood. His willful single-mindedness then destroys or distorts both himself and his ideal.

The fiction records just how easy it is for even the most meaningful of concepts to be lifted out of flux and thereby to become falsehoods. Some obvious examples are the concepts of "nationalism" and "fatherland" in "Ad Astra" and *A Fable;* another is the insistence upon the sanctity of "private property" which determines the behavior of Jack Houston and the anonymous barn owner in *The Hamlet;* another is the talk of the "outrage" and "injustice" of slavery among those "females of both sexes," to whom, according to Isaac McCaslin, "the outrage and the injustice were as much abstractions as Tariff or Silver or Immortality" (GDM, 284). A national or personal or moral abstraction may then become only a "meaningless and verbose shibboleth" (WP, 24) when it is divorced from contingency.

In *The Hamlet,* for instance, the ideal of masculinity is defined in such narrow terms that it excludes the possibility of a relationship between a man and a woman based upon mutual respect and love.[9] Marriage, to most of the characters in *The Hamlet,* is simply a contest for dominance. That is how Jack Houston understands it. Therefore, when he has to admit that he cannot dominate Lucy Pate, Jack assumes that he must instead sacrifice all vestiges of masculinity when he marries her. That masculinity and femininity can survive and in fact deepen only through a mutual relationship founded on love, neither Jack nor Lucy will recognize. Each seems to feel that to show love means to admit one's need and thereby acknowledge one's weakness. And weakness, to the menfolk in *The Hamlet,* is incompatible with masculinity.

Mink Snopes too, though he is the only character in *The Hamlet* man enough to disregard social stigma and marry for

9 See my article, "Masculinity and Menfolk in *The Hamlet," Mississippi Quarterly,* III (Summer, 1969), 181–89, for further discussion of this point.

love, nevertheless feels an overriding compulsion to mask love as conquest; from his wife, he demands a signal of his ascendancy and "seal of [her] formal acquiescence" (H, 274). Despite his passion, Mink cannot forgive his wife for making him admit his need for her. Olga Vickery, Cleanth Brooks, and Warren Beck all discuss with some admiration Mink's code of honor to which he sacrifices all pragmatic and personal concerns. I suggest, however, that the novel implies that dehumanizing results accrue when a concept such as "honor" or "masculinity" is granted more validity than a human commitment. In *The Hamlet* the male identifies masculinity and honor with absolute self-sufficiency; thus he feels his masculinity threatened by human interdependence and by passion over which he has no control. Such a man as Mink would prefer to relegate women to the status of property and even to kill another man rather than admit his need.

Another example of a word which has been raised out of life into the status of shibboleth is "name." There is Jason Compson who insists that he cares only about his mother's good name. There is Goodhue Coldfield, who cares only about his own "reputation for probity" (AA, 60). There is Jody's concern for the Varner name, which cannot bear the disgrace of Eula's pregnancy. And there is even talk of the Snopes's good name which cannot bear association with stock diddling (H, 230). The word is made into a shibboleth; the dissidence between the ideal and the real is ignored. Among such characters the importance of good name is no longer even questioned, for "name" has become something more real and more crucial than people. Thus in *A Fable* General Gragnon would have gladly had the whole regiment executed to protect "the division's record and good name" (AF, 41).

The terrifying disregard for human lives Gragnon displays along with his fanatical insistence on the importance of "name" exemplifies what Whitehead calls the "intolerant use of abstrac-

tions [which] is the major vice of the intellect." [10] The overweening concern for an immobile abstraction like "name" is intolerant
because it is absolute; an intransigent devotion to the abstract
concept alone dissociates that concept from the human sphere
and therefore from the context of meaning and value. That is
what has happened to what Olga Vickery calls the "communal
mind and thought of the South." In the South, a complex of
concepts, such as "Calvinism, racial purity and white superiority,
Southern provincialism and insularity, [and] Civil War chauvin-
ism," [11] has been established with such unquestioning acceptance
that its reference to experiential realities has been utterly obscured. Consequently, almost no one, as Gavin Stevens remarks,
is able to "stand against the cold inflexible abstraction of a
long-suffering community's moral point of view" (T, 312). In
Knight's Gambit Captain Gualdres, the Latin suitor of the widowed
Mrs. Harriss, does challenge that "inflexible abstraction." We
are told that the townspeople "had foisted on, invested him
with a morality, a code which he had proved now was not his
either." They had tried to impose their presuppositions upon
the foreigner, but "they would never forgive him" (KG, 171)
because he did not fit the mold which the communal mind had
devised. The problem with such thinking, as Faulkner writes
in another context, is that with it "the body [is] capable of motion,
not the intellect" (WP, 13).

In *Go Down, Moses* he makes a rather explicit examination
of that communal mind which will not forgive differences or
move to incorporate them. In that novel the basis for the communal mind of the South is clearly the shibboleth of white superiority. Such racial presumption brought old Carothers McCaslin
to summon to his bed with impunity both the slave girl Eunice
and his own daughter Tomey and instigated the series of human

10 Alfred North Whitehead, *Science and the Modern World* (New York: Macmillan
   Company, 1925), 25.
11 Olga W. Vickery, *The Novels of William Faulkner: A Critical Interpretation* (Rev.
   ed.; Baton Rouge: Louisiana State University Press, 1964), 244.

catastrophes that followed. The assumption of racial superiority further explains old McCaslin's ultimate, terrifying "contempt for all his get" (GDM, 255). And it is this assumption that destroys two close foster brother relationships when one day the white brother orders the black one to sleep on the pallet. It is this assumption that gives Buck McCaslin the right to chase Tomey's Turl like an animal without giving him even the same respect accorded an animal quarry (FIU, 40).

But the specious notion of white superiority is compounded with another specious concept, that of "blood." Significantly these notions are so accepted and internalized that the Negro and the Indian accept their inferiority and even grant special distinction to a black man such as Lucas Beauchamp who bears McCaslin blood. Indeed, Lucas' specious notions of blood and ancestry are just as prideful, rigid, and absurd as those of Miss Sophonsiba. Lucas has utter contempt for George Wilkins, an "interloper without forebears" (GDM, 40), and almost equal contempt for the white sheriff who has no ancestry (GDM, 43). For Lucas considers blood the essential ingredient in quality. In fact, he defines his whole existence by the precept: "what Carothers McCaslin would have wanted me to do" (GDM, 53). Thus he stays in Mississippi, not because he has either material or moral shackles binding him there (GDM, 105), but because as "a McCaslin too and a man-made one" (GDM, 53) his specious consciousness of ancestry demands that he stay on the plantation where, despite his status as a Negro, his McCaslin blood is at least acknowledged. Old Carothers' blood does bestow genetically upon Lucas a number of McCaslin characteristics. In *The Reivers* Lucius Priest remembers that his great-grandmother had said Lucas "looked (and behaved: just as arrogant, just as ironheaded, just as intolerant) exactly like [old Carothers] except for color" (Rev., 229). Lucas did indeed inherit his looks from old Carothers, but he did not inherit arrogance. He acquired arrogance and intolerance through deference to the abstract concept of blood.

In one sense, Isaac McCaslin also accords tangible reality status to the concept of blood. Cass Edmonds accuses Ike of desiring simply to escape (GDM, 283). Isaac acknowledges that he is "repudiating and even hoping to escape [from] old Carothers' doomed and fatal blood" (GDM, 293). Understanding the vicious exclusion inherent in the idea of blood, Isaac nevertheless confers upon the concept the same measure of reality as does Lucas who defers to the concept. They both are then guilty of the intolerant use of abstractions.

So too is Sam Fathers, for, despite his independence of the McCaslins, his proficiency as a woodsman, and his priestlike function in the ritual hunt, Sam sacrifices integrity by allowing specious notions of blood to prescribe his existence. It is Sam's shame that *"for seventy years now he had had to be a negro"* (GDM, 215). Sam's own blood pride, not McCaslin prejudice, has kept him from entering the white man's world. As Cass says of Sam, " 'His cage aint McCaslins' " (GDM, 167). Cass could, of course, be referring to the taint of Negro blood as Sam's cage, but, as I read the passage, the usually astute Cass feels that Sam's cage is a state of mind. That is why Faulkner calls Sam "incredibly lost" (GDM, 172). He has identified only with his Indian heritage; thus when Jobaker, the last full-blooded Indian, dies, Sam feels no more responsibility to live among people. He soon pleads, "Let me go" (GDM, 173) and leaves Ike, preferring to live alone in the river bottom. Once Old Ben has been killed Sam seems to "just quit" (GDM, 248). Preferring to die rather than to witness the wilderness' destruction, Sam begs, " 'Let me out, master. . . . Let me go home' " (GDM, 245). Sam is an old man; his fatigue is understandable. He nevertheless seems to be another one of those characters who choose to stand still in the midst of motion and to face backwards toward a heritage already lost.

With such characters, tradition precludes participation and personal fulfillment; it becomes then a hindrance to living. Such traditions are founded upon pride which is "based not on any value" (GDM, 111) but on an abstraction as irrelevant as the "signed papers" which establish that men of Sutpen's kind are, Wash imagines, "among the first and foremost of the brave" (AA, 289). Such men possess only abstract qualifications. Their preeminence is established not by actual bravery or competence but rather has been dictated by a specious ideal like "class." And that, Faulkner writes, is one of the principal reasons the South lost the Civil War: "because of generals who should not have been generals, who were generals not through training in contemporary methods or aptitude for learning them, but by the divine right to say 'Go there' conferred upon them by an absolute caste system" (AA, 345). When the concept of class or caste conveys gratuitous, unexamined power to abuse others, corruption and decline inevitably result.

Horace Benbow is outraged to think of a person like Gowan Stevens "walking the earth with impunity just because he has a balloon-tailed suit and went through the astonishing experience of having attended Virginia" (San., 161). Gowan and Temple Drake both are like the callous college students Horace encounters on the train who brag of traveling " 'a thousand miles without a ticket' " and who block the aisles while "beyond the group a countrywoman with an infant in her arms stood braced against a seat. From time to time she looked back at the blocked aisle and the empty seats beyond" (San., 166). To the needs of others, these young people are crassly inattentive. From the privileges of money and education they derive only bravado. They, and Temple and Gowan too, are as callous as Wesley Snopes, who displays "a demagogue's capacity for using people to serve his own appetites" (T, 41), or as irresponsible as "one of the predators who debase police badges by using them as immunity to prey on [man's] helpless kind" (Rev., 176). Because these people enjoy privilege based not on any value but on an abstract artificial distinction, they debase the whole concept of "quality." They do not seem to realize, as Elnora says in "There Was a Queen," that "born Sartoris or born quality of any kind ain't *is*, it's *does*" (CS, 732).

Man prefers to deal with *is*, however, because *is* is a static condition. A state of being may, of course, be neatly labeled under such categories as "blood" or "quality"; static and fixed, the category does not then demand reexamining. Man's intellect, as Bergson explains, "takes up its position in ready-made concepts, and endeavors to catch in them, as in a net, something of the reality which passes." [12] Reality, however, is always a state of becoming, a matter of *doing*, and if the intellect remains locked in by a set of static concepts, reality eludes it altogether.

In a 1955 interview in Japan Faulkner remarked that "no matter how much they might want to, people simply won't fit into a mold or type" (LG, 159). Faulkner's novels establish the uncontainable and irrepressible nature of humanity, yet they reiterate how man, nevertheless, wants to mold or type his fellow human creatures. Upon women, for example, he imposes a "simple and erstwhile untroubled code in which females were ladies or whores or slaves" (AA, 114). But there is always the "incorrigibly individual woman" (U, 26) who survives despite even such a communal experience as the Civil War. In *The Unvanquished* young Bayard Sartoris thinks "how the War had tried to stamp all the women of [Drusilla's] generation and class in the South into a type and how it had failed" (U, 263). It failed because, despite environment, tradition, and the conditioning that may be a part of any group experience, human beings are still incorrigibly resilient and individual.

Man nevertheless wants to establish a country "all divided and fixed and neat with a people living on it all divided and fixed and neat because of what color their skins happened to be and what they happened to own" (AA, 221). He retains an unrestrained magical belief in labels which are invoked in order to fix existence into a state of being known and controlled by

12 Bergson, *An Introduction to Metaphysics*, 50.

a linguistic category. He so desires the security and certainty of a fixed category that, like the boys in *The Sound and the Fury* who hope for a twenty-five-dollar fishing prize, man makes "of unreality a possibility, then a probability, then an incontrovertible fact, as people will when their desires become words" (SF, 145). When used to obscure actuality, words then may fix and finalize reality into unreality, truth into falsehood. For the word itself carries more than naming power. Dawson Fairchild talks of man's " 'childlike faith in the efficacy of words . . . a kind of belief that circumstance somehow will invest the veriest platitude with magic' " (Mos., 249). And even Byron Bunch becomes philosophical enough to think "how a man's name, which is supposed to be just the sound for who he is, can be somehow an augur of what he will do" (LA, 29). In *Mosquitoes* we see Pat Robyn speaking the phrase Jenny Steinbauer has traded her as if it were an object (Mos., 271) and Josh Robyn using sailing lingo as an entree with the captain (Mos., 77). Along with the other characters in *Mosquitoes*, Pat and Josh do indeed display a childlike faith in the magical power of words. Such a faith seems innocent enough in *Mosquitoes;* in *The Sound and the Fury,* however, it becomes absurd, as with Mrs. Compson who does not want her brother's name borne by an idiot. She apparently even deludes herself into believing that she can remove idiocy from the family by changing her last-born child's name from Maury to Benjamin and that she can eradicate disgrace by forbidding the mention of Caddy's name.

Such confidence in words is both absurd and sophistic in *As I Lay Dying* where it offers a release from consciousness for Anse Bundren who wants neither to think nor to feel. As Olga Vickery remarks, "At the first sign of difficulty [Anse] falls back on his inexhaustible stock of moral platitudes to isolate himself effectively from the horrors of the journey, to avoid any exertion on his part, and to maneuver others into acting for him." [13] Anse's ready platitudes, like those of I. O. Snopes, are a device for

13 Vickery, *The Novels of William Faulkner,* 56.

extricating himself from existence. Anse can talk glibly about his "given promise" (AILD, 119); he can speak about his "regard for what folks say about my flesh and blood" (AILD, 99). He can rationalize any experience, remembering that "there is a reward for us above" (AILD, 104) and that "I am chosen of the Lord, for who He loveth, so doeth He chastiseth." [14] These are comforting words, though even Anse cannot but wonder, "I be durn if He don't take some curious ways to show it, seems like" (AILD, 105) and seek more solid comfort in the prospect of new teeth.

In her days as a schoolteacher Addie Bundren had desired some bodily contact with her pupils because "we had had to use one another by words" (AILD, 164). Words to Addie are irrelevant and empty; they "dont ever fit even what they are trying to say at" (AILD, 163). Addie has listened too long to Cora Tull and Anse whose words do not even attempt to fit what they are "trying to say at." Cora and Anse, in fact, manage so to use words that they express the exact opposite of their literal meaning. Questioning God, Cora says, "It is not my place to question His decree" (AILD, 8). Expecting credit, she says, "Not that I deserve credit for it" (AILD, 21). Irritated to be out in the rain, Anse insists, "I don't begrudge her the wetting" (AILD, 74). Annoyed by a potential doctor's fee, he says, " 'Hit aint begrudgin the money' " (AILD, 43). And inconvenienced by the wake ritual, he declares, "I can set up with her. I don't begrudge her it" (AILD, 110). The fact that he mentions it seems to indicate that he does begrudge Addie even the wetting. Such pronouncements represent a fine balance between dramatic irony (Anse being unconscious of the ironic implications of his statements) and conscious sophism (Anse being conscious of his word choice and hoping, indeed, that someone will insist that he does, for instance, "deserve credit").

14 "Anse's garbling of case and verb form suggests his garbling of meaning (as well as the attempt to sound the way Whitfield does)." Joseph L. Blotner to the author, March 1, 1971.

With Anse the word is indeed "just a shape to fill a lack" (AILD, 164). And Addie has encountered too many people like Anse and Cora who use a word like *love* or *duty* instead of showing love or performing a duty. Their distorted approach to existence is best exemplified by the behavior of Preacher Whitfield who does not confess when he discovers that Addie has died without revealing their secret. Although Whitfield has framed in his mind the words of a confession, he assures himself that the Lord "will accept the will for the deed" (AILD, 171) and feels no longer any obligation to confess to Anse. Dealing only with such people who use words in place of deeds, Addie could not but think that talking and doing are utterly disparate activities: "And so when Cora Tull would tell me I was not a true mother, I would think how words go straight up in a thin line, quick and harmless, and how terribly doing goes along the earth, clinging to it, so that after a while the two lines are too far apart for the same person to straddle from one to the other; and that sin and love and fear are just sounds that people who never sinned nor loved nor feared have for what they never had and cannot have until they forget the words" (AILD, 165–66).

Addie cannot imagine having an experience until she forgets the words. Her problem, though, is that she has only known the sort of verbiage that comes glibly to an Anse or a Cora or a Whitfield. These people's ideas and the words they use to express them float, in Bergson's terms, "on the surface, like dead leaves on the water of a pond: the mind, when it thinks them over and over again, finds them ever the same, as if they were external to it. Among these are the ideas which we receive ready made, and which remain in us without ever being properly assimilated, or again the ideas which we have omitted to cherish and which have withered in neglect." [15] The sameness of these concepts and of our stale terms for them typifies what Henry Adams calls "thought-inertia" or what old Doc Peabody has

---

15 Bergson, *Time and Free Will*, 135–36.

in mind when he ·says, "When I was young I believed death to be a phenomenon of the body; now I know it to be merely a function of the mind" (AILD, 42).

The later fiction further establishes just how insidious such mental deadness or thought-inertia may be. The results are terrifying when man may be irrevocably judged and irreparably placed by a few ready linguistic handles such as *white, nigger, quality, trash, lady, whore, South, North, American,* or *foreigner.* The most horrendous example of the power of a label is the word *nigger.* That word attempts to fix a man's behavior and to dictate his interests, his feelings, and even his aspirations. As Olga Vickery explains: "What starts as a verbal pattern of classification thus becomes a social order not to be challenged or changed. And what starts as a category becomes a myth, for certainly the word 'Negro' is a compressed myth just as the stock response to that word is a compressed ritual." [16] In *Go Down, Moses,* for example, the pattern of "what niggers do" is considered set and established. The assumption is that "them damn niggers . . . aint human" (GDM, 154). Thus to Buck and Buddy McCaslin it was incredible to think of a black woman's feeling enough grief and anguish to commit suicide; Buck wrote in the ledger, *"Who in hell ever heard of a niger* [sic] *drownding him self"* (GDM, 267). Similarly, in "That Evening Sun" when Nancy Mannigoe tries to commit suicide, the jailer theorizes that "no nigger would try to commit suicide unless he was full of cocaine, because a nigger full of cocaine wasn't a nigger any longer" (CS, 291). This kind of thinking unavoidably creeps into the consciousness of Negro as well as white. Nancy tells Quentin Compson, " 'I aint nothing but a nigger. . . . It ain't none of my fault' " (CS, 293). And Lucas Beauchamp finds it necessary to assert, " 'I'm a nigger. . . . But I'm a man too' " (GDM, 47).

Indeed, the label may carry with it such coercive power that some black men ·make no such assertion. Unlike Lucas, such

16 Vickery, *The Novels of William Faulkner,* 69.

a man simply patterns his behavior after the expectations inherent in the label. As Quentin comes to realize, "A nigger [then] is not a person so much as a form of behaviour; a sort of obverse reflection of the white people he lives among" (SF, 106). He is, in other words, an abstraction. Now Faulkner warns us, " 'Be careful of man in the abstract' " (LG, 72), for trouble accrues whenever the communal mind insists that a person mold himself according to its abstract concept of him. Such a demand reaches catastrophic proportions in the life of Charles Etienne de Saint Velery Bon who has known some abstractions, but those "were as purely rooted in the flesh's offices as the digestive processes" (AA, 199). The concept "Negro," on the other hand, is an abstraction divorced from the flesh, or so his mirror tells him. He keeps the shard of broken mirror hidden beneath his mattress: "who to know what hours of amazed and tearless grief he might have spent before it, examining himself in the delicate and outgrown tatters in which he perhaps could not even remember himself, with quiet and incredulous incomprehension" (AA, 199). He has been told by someone "that he was, must be, a negro" (AA, 198). Incredulous, he returns to the mirror to ask, "Why?" Like Joe Christmas, he fights first Negroes and then whites in a desperate attempt to establish his identity. In a knife fight his "sheer desperate will and imperviousness to the punishment" is "furious protest, [an] indictment of heaven's ordering" (AA, 202). He seems to seek a jail sentence in hopes that the sentence will decide his nature and therefore his future.

When General Compson interrupts the justice who has been talking to Charles Etienne Bon as to "a white man," the outraged justice cries, " 'What are you?' " (AA, 203). Bon cannot reply simply, "I am a man," for the communal mind demands that Charles Etienne Bon be either black or white, be something abstract and therefore less than human. When General Compson pays his fine and gives the young man money, he encourages him to leave, to go "among strangers, people who dont know you [where] you can be whatever you will" (AA, 204). This advice is essentially that given by Uncle Ike to the unnamed woman in "Delta Autumn"; the assumption is that strangers would not know that Bon and the woman were Negro. Perhaps also the advice given by General Compson and Isaac McCaslin involves a tacit recognition that "Negro" is only an abstraction located in space, for it would have no meaning elsewhere, and in time, for it would have no meaning in two thousand years (GDM, 361). Charles Etienne Bon, however, makes the abstraction concrete when he appears "with a coal black and ape-like woman and an authentic wedding license . . . [and rides] up to the house and apparently [flings] the wedding license in Judith's face with something of that invincible despair with which he had attacked the negroes in the dice game" (AA, 205).

Charles Etienne Bon declares his identity with the black race in the same manner his father Charles Bon declared his final identity with the octoroon mistress, Charles Etienne's mother: in defiance of those who would reject him for completely abstract and artificial reasons. The cruelty of such rejection is apparently what provokes General Compson to lament, *"Better that he were dead, better that he had never lived:* then thinking what vain and empty recapitulation that would be to [Judith] if he were to say it, who doubtless had already said it, thought it, changing only the person and the number" (AA, 205). In other words Judith too has wished, according to General Compson and his son, that "we" had never lived. When a word precipitates such a catastrophic sequence of rejections, one compounded upon another, as the word *Negro* does in *Absalom, Absalom!,* so that it would seem to be better if these people had not lived, then clearly man's concepts have tyrannized over his humanity.

It is true that, as even Rosa Coldfield realizes, *"there is some-thing in the touch of flesh with flesh which abrogates, cuts sharp and straight across the devious intricate channels of decorous ordering. . . . [Let] flesh touch with flesh, and watch the fall of all the eggshell shibboleth of caste and color too"* (AA, 139). But man prefers to avoid such contact. He deals in eggshell shibboleths rather than to encounter the immense variety and complexity of human existence. Labels are perfunctorily applied because it is easier to judge a man by color or lineage than to see him as a uniquely complex individual. Rather than encounter the complex, heterogeneous, and unpredictable, the "whole vast moil and seethe" (AF, 54) of humankind, man categorizes with a few worn-out labels. Gavin Stevens too falls into this trap of, in Bergson's terms, "giving the name of Idea to a certain settling down into easy intelligibility." [17] Trying to explain Joe Christmas' escape and then virtual self-immolation, Gavin talks in terms of blood: "Because the black blood drove him first to the negro cabin. And then the white blood drove him out of there, as it was the black blood which snatched up the pistol and the white blood which would not let him fire it" (LA, 424). Gavin concludes that it was Christmas' white blood that finally provoked him to "let them shoot him to death" (LA, 425). Gavin's explanation may make nice believing because it is so simple, but it is hardly worthy of a graduate of Harvard and Heidelberg. To equate, as several critics have, Stevens' point of view with Faulkner's is to disregard the rest of the novel altogether, for *Light in August* deals with nothing if not with the irrelevance of the abstract concepts and the disastrous consequences of thinking in such terms as *black blood*.

That novel explores in depth the horrendous ends that such concepts readily serve. The concept of *black blood* and the word *nigger* seem to guarantee certain stock responses. A devious and deranged character like Eupheus Hines depends upon these responses as he uses the word *nigger* to serve his own deliberate and demonic ends. Hines is acquitted of murdering Joe's father because, Mrs. Hines explains, " 'The circus owner come back and said how the man really was a part nigger instead of Mex-

17 Bergson, *An Introduction to Metaphysics*, 56.

ican' " (LA, 357). Hines wants to call Joe "nigger" to make Joe suffer for his mother's sin, although Hines ironically wants to interrupt the consequences of that word and keep Joe out of a Negro orphanage. The dietitian of course knows that by the word *Negro* alone she can have Joe not only removed, but "punished for having given her terror and worry" (LA, 121). And Joe himself even trades upon the stock reaction to the word *nigger*. He pays his women "when he had the money, and when he did not have it he bedded anyway and then told them that he was a negro" (LA, 211). Once when a women doesn't respond predictably by forgetting the money and chasing Joe out, he begins to beat her, viciously and horribly: "It took two policemen to subdue him. At first they thought that the woman was dead. He was sick after that. He did not know until then that there were white women who would take a man with a black skin. He stayed sick for two years. Sometimes he would remember how he had once tricked or teased white men into calling him a negro in order to fight them, to beat them or be beaten; now he fought the negro who called him white" (LA, 212). Like Charles Etienne Bon, Joe is testing the abstractions that pursue him. He is physically sick only when the certainty of linguistic categories breaks down.

Joe seeks frenetically to find a category that fits him. And the townspeople seek, almost as frenetically, to categorize Joe. They are angered, therefore, by Joe's ambiguous identity; we learn that Joe " 'never acted like either a nigger or a white man. That was it. That was what made the folks so mad' " (LA, 331). And Joanna Burden too feels an equally fanatic desire to *place* Joe. She wants to "make of him something between a hermit and a missionary to negroes" (LA, 257). She becomes "cold, remote, and fanatic. 'Do you realize,' she said, 'that you are wasting your life?' " (LA, 253). But above all, Joanna wants to place Joe Christmas as a black man. In their orgiastic sexual relationships there is always "her breathing: 'Negro! Negro! Negro!' " (LA, 245). She looks upon the prospect of bearing a

Negro child as a logical outcome of the stern New England prescription to " 'hate two things . . . hell and slaveholders' " (LA, 229). Thus when Joanna thinks she is pregnant she congratulates herself not on the fulfillment of love or on the renewal of life, but upon the fulfillment of an idea: " 'A full measure. Even to a bastard negro child. I would like to see father's and Calvin's faces" (LA, 251).

Joanna's father told her on an occasion which she remembered as the "only time I can remember him as somebody" (LA, 238) that her grandfather and brother were "murdered not by one white man but by the curse which God put on the whole race" (LA, 239). With the New England Burdens, whiteness is an abstract concept with just as odious a set of implications as those associated, for the southerner, with blackness. The habit of dealing in abstractions is readily compounded, and Joanna, after hearing of the white curse, comes to think of blackness too as an abstraction: "But after that I seemed to see them [Negroes] for the first time not as people, but as a thing, a shadow in which I lived, we lived, all white people, all other people. . . . And I seemed to see the black shadow in the shape of a cross" (LA, 239). This is the "bleak and bloodless logic" (LA, 229) of the New Englander; Faulkner is at some pains to imply that distance and dissociation increase the tendency to deal in abstractions. He describes the spectators at the fire as "casual Yankees and the poor whites and even the southerners who had lived for a while in the north, who believed aloud that it was an anonymous negro crime committed not by a negro but by Negro" (LA, 271). When Faulkner says that "even" southerners could make this mistake, he is not being chauvinistic. His point is simply that dissociation, whether physical or mental, from an actuality increases man's inclination to deal with that actuality as an abstraction.

Joe Christmas' problem is that he is himself only an abstraction with no real identity. At the orphanage Joe announces to a black man, " 'I aint a nigger,' " but the Negro replies, " 'You are worse than that. You dont know what you are. And more than that, you wont never know. You'll live and you'll die and you wont never know' " (LA, 363). To know what he is has been the compelling obsession in Joe's life. Alfred Kazin calls him "an abstraction seeking to become a human being." [18] Joe runs "for thirty years" in search of himself on "a paved street, where going should be fast," but the street "had made a circle and he is still inside of it" (LA, 321). When Joanna urges him to marry her Joe thinks, *"Why not? It would mean ease, security"* and yet he vehemently rejects the idea: " 'No. If I give in now, I will deny all the thirty years that I have lived to make me what I chose to be' " (LA, 250–51).

Whether or not Joe himself indeed chooses what he will be is a point upon which critics cannot always agree. Kazin feels that Joe does not choose, that he is "nothing but a victim." [19] But John L. Longley, Jr., insists that Joe does choose, that Christmas in fact bears comparison with Oedipus who "becomes tragic only because he does strive against the prediction." [20] Longley believes that Joe refuses to submit to conditioning: "All his life, people attempt to force him to be what they insist he must be. McEachern's beating him to inculcate worship of the Moloch-Jehovah; Mrs. McEachern's sickening attempts to make him as cringing as herself; Joanna Burden's final insistence that he 'become a nigger.' His method is active. . . . He will insist on his right to simply be; he has defined himself and has fought hard for the definition. The murder of Joanna Burden and his own death are the fruit of that insistence." [21] Longley, it seems, has to disregard considerable textual evidence in order to construe Joe as tragic hero. Joe, as we recall, finds respite in McEa-

18 Alfred Kazin, "The Stillness of *Light in August*" in Frederick J. Hoffman and Olga W. Vickery (eds.), *William Faulkner: Three Decades of Criticism* (New York: Harcourt, Brace, and World, 1963), 252.
19 *Ibid.,* 261.
20 John L. Longley, Jr., "Joe Christmas: The Hero in the Modern World," in Hoffman and Vickery (eds.), *William Faulkner,* 267.
21 *Ibid.,* 270.

chern's firmness; what he objects to is Mrs. McEachern's attempts to deal with him in sympathy as a human being. Similarly,
with Joanna, he does not object to her seeing him as "Negro!
Negro! Negro!"; what he does finally protest against is Joanna's
trying to pray over him, to call forth from him self-examination
and human remorse. Even while murdering Joanna, Joe excuses
himself by saying, *"I had to do it"* (LA, 264). Those are hardly
the words of a tragic hero. Nor is his reliance upon the label
"nigger" to pay his whorehouse bill exactly an example of
striving against the prediction. Indeed, what sickens Joe and
provokes that terrible beating he gives one woman is that she
did not react predictably. Sickened over the knowledge that
"there were white women who would take a man with a black
skin," Joe is thereafter ready to fight any "negro who called
him white" (LA, 212). In other words, Joe prefers the categories
to remain absolute. He cannot tolerate disregard for the color
barrier and would rather be black than identify himself with
whites who act as if color does not exist. Joanna's sexual relationship with Joe does not, of course, disregard color but is
instead founded upon it.[22]

22 It is not clear exactly when Joe tells Joanna about the possible Negro blood.
At the close of Chapter 11 (LA, 240), after Joanna has appeared in the cabin
and related to Joe the story of her father and grandfather, she asks Joe,
" 'You dont have any idea who your parents were?' " Joe replies, " 'Except
that one of them was part nigger. Like I told you before.' " As I read the
novel, he has seen her only three times before: on the first night when she
found him in her kitchen eating the field peas and molasses and later resisted
him sexually "fair, by the rules that decreed that upon a certain crisis one
was defeated" (LA, 222). Then on "the very next day" (LA, 222) he met
her again and "she did not resist at all" (LA, 223). And then on the "next
day" (LA, 223), *i.e.,* the third day, he goes again to the house and finds
all except the kitchen door locked. In the kitchen there is still warm food,
"set out," Joe thinks, *"for the nigger. For the nigger"* (LA, 224). Apparently, then,
Joe "told [her] before" about the Negro blood on either their first or second
meeting. I would assume it to have been after their first sexual experience
(when she resisted him) and that would explain her lack of resistance at
the second meeting. Certainly, at any rate, she does know about the Negro
blood after their discussion in the cabin. And it is after this that "the second
phase" begins, when Joanna wants, apparently, to live "not alone in sin but
in filth" (LA, 244). It seems legitimate, therefore, to assert that the intensity
of their sexual relationship is founded upon the breaking of the color barrier.

Indeed, rather than striving against an unambiguous system for categorizing people, Joe Christmas submits to such a system gladly. He admits, *"All I wanted was peace* thinking, 'She ought not to started praying over me'" (LA, 104), and "'That's all I wanted,' he thought. 'That dont seem like a whole lot to ask'" (LA, 108); later he becomes "one with loneliness and quiet that has never known fury or despair. 'That was all I wanted,' he thinks, in a quiet and slow amazement, 'That was all, for thirty years. That didn't seem to be a whole lot to ask in thirty years'" (LA, 313). The repetition of the phrase "That was all" seems to refer to the initial statement *"All I wanted was peace."* In the "peaceful" dawn (LA, 313) Joe remembers again how simple were the demands he made on existence.

Joe Christmas' problem has been that "in the quiet and empty corridor" of his abstraction-haunted existence "he was like a shadow" (LA, 111). Indeed, shadow imagery follows him throughout *Light in August.* He is described as "the shape, the shadow" which "faded on down the road" (LA, 177). After he escapes, the crowd remains around the jail " 'looking at the jail like it might have been just the nigger's shadow that had come out'" (LA, 338). And finally, as Percy Grimm castrates Joe, we are told that "the man on the floor had not moved. He just lay there, with his eyes open and empty of everything save consciousness, and with something, a shadow, about his mouth" (LA, 439).

Alfred Kazin refers to this final shadow as the "shadow thrown from the Cross of Christ." [23] I suggest, on the other hand, that this is the same shadow which has followed Joe Christmas throughout the novel and which has signified his lack of concrete identity. That it is diminished to linger only about the mouth may indicate now that only Joe's voice would question his iden-

23 Kazin, "The Stillness of *Light in August,*" 261. Kazin's remarks sound somewhat like those of Joanna Burden, who saw Negroes "not as people, but as a thing, a shadow. . . . the black shadow in the shape of a cross" (LA, 239).

tity. The last remnant of consciousness may be seeking once
again to formulate the words "But am I black?". Nevertheless,
in choosing to stand before Percy Grimm and not to shoot, Joe
has chosen in one sure act of free will to be himself. The shadow
only hovers momentarily now about his mouth. Though the
shadow lingers, Joe himself is no longer a shadow. Though he
has found respite in one shadow identity after another, at the
time of his death he ceases to be a shadow and becomes himself.
Only then does he at last discover, not what he is, but who
he is.

If Joe Christmas is an abstraction seeking to become a human
being, so are most of the characters in *Absalom, Absalom!*. It
is as if, in that novel, no one can exist in his own right but
only through someone else's concept of him. Charles Bon, like
Christmas, is " 'shadowy: a myth, a phantom: something which
they engendered and created whole themselves' " (AA, 104). He
is the man " 'on whom Henry foisted . . . the role of his sister's
intended' " (AA, 102). To Ellen Sutpen he is " 'almost baroque,
the almost epicene object d'art which with childlike voracity
she essayed to include in the furnishing and decoration of her
house' " (AA, 101). Shreve McCannon imagines that even to
his mother Bon was not a child: " 'It wasn't him at all she was
washing and feeding the candy and the fun to but it was a
man that hadn't even arrived yet' " (AA, 306).

Similarly Judith, according to Mr. Compson, " 'was just the
blank shape, the empty vessel in which each of them [Charles
and Henry] strove to preserve, not the illusion of himself nor
his illusion of the other but what each conceived the other to
believe him to be' " (AA, 119-20). Miss Rosa's shadelike existence surely results from her being to her spinster aunt "not
only a living and walking reproach to her father, but a breathing
indictment, ubiquitous and even transferable of the entire male
principle" (AA, 59-60). Thought to be only an abstraction, Miss
Rosa has trouble being any more than just that. She sees herself

and Clytie as only *"the two abstract contradictions which we actually were"* (AA, 138). And she sees Sutpen himself as just another abstraction. To her, Sutpen *"was not articulated in this world. He was a walking shadow. He was the light-blinded bat-like image of his own torment"* (AA, 171). These characters refuse to acknowledge their companions' living, breathing humanity. Like Gail Hightower who believed at once that the girl he married "was beautiful, because he had heard of her before he ever saw her and when he did see her he did not see her at all because of the face which he had already created in his mind" (LA, 454), these characters cannot see the human face for the abstract mask they have invented. They confront not the man but the abstraction, not an amorphous fluctuating personality, but a conveniently projected, fixed concept.

There is a curious passage in *Go Down, Moses* in which Faulkner says Isaac McCaslin was "taking with him" something of his "evil and unregenerate" grandfather (GDM, 294). What Isaac takes with him, apparently, is his grandfather's habit of confronting not the man but the abstraction. When he relinquishes the land, Isaac imagines that his might be a divinely ordained deed intended " 'to set at least some of His lowly people free' " (GDM, 259). Freeing the lowly is to Isaac, however, largely a matter of committing the "heresy" of saying that the Negroes are " 'better than we are' " (GDM, 294), as if, to expiate for centuries of treating Negroes as inferiors, all Isaac McCaslin has to do is call them superiors. When Faulkner writes that "even in escaping he was taking with him more of that evil and unregenerate old man . . . than even he had feared" (GDM, 294), he implies that both Isaac, who can say "They are better," and the old man his grandfather, who never questioned the Negro's inferiority, are dealing only with the abstraction "Negro."

With his pristine ideal of freedom for the Negroes Isaac makes little show of brotherhood. There is something of compulsion in the manner in which he dispenses the thousand dollars to each of his Negro cousins: to Lucas who banks it as symbol of his station and to Fonsiba who can only assert, " 'I'm free' " (GDM, 277–80), though she is also desperate, impoverished, and hungry. Isaac regrets that Tennie's Jim escapes on his twenty-first birthday before the thousand dollars can be passed on to him. His regret seems somehow more selfish and compulsive than not, as if he too wanted to make a payment, discharge a duty, and thereby be freed of an obligation. Isaac denies what Faulkner calls the necessarily "slow amortization" (GDM, 266) of injustice. Isaac's ultimate failure results from his encountering a "specific tragedy which had not been condoned and could never be amortized" (GDM, 266); Isaac, however, expects to write off the tragedy with a few words, a few dollars, and with one grand sacrifice: the relinquishment of the property which bears the curse.

Isaac makes his sacrifice in the name of freedom. Cass Edmonds has told him freedom will come " 'not now nor ever, we from them nor they from us' " (GDM, 299), and authorial comment insists that "no man is ever free" (GDM, 281), but Isaac nevertheless seeks for himself and the Negroes an impossible state idealized as "freedom." For himself, Isaac sees freedom in Sam's terms, which are those of isolation and dedication to a way of life which is no longer a viable choice in the twentieth century. But "adaptability in Faulkner," to quote Arthur Kinney, "presages the only meaningful liberty."[24] Isaac, however, is reluctant to adapt to motion and change. Kinney explains: "Ike is able to accommodate new meaning given the wilderness only until the death of Old Ben; at that point his definition is fixed: Ike freezes his picture of the woods in memory willed kinetic; he simultaneously turns a solitary moment of wilderness existence into an external refuge, a personal and private sanctuary."[25]

Indeed, Isaac's life has been "drawing inward" (GDM, 335)

24 Arthur F. Kinney, "Faulkner and the Possibilities for Heroism" *Southern Review*, n.s., VI (Autumn, 1970), 1119.
25 *Ibid.*, 1118.

ever since his sixteenth year. The inwardness of his life is signified by his childlessness. Isaac's attempt has been to repudiate "that same wrong and shame [his grandfather's] from whose regret and grief he would at least save and free his son and, saving and freeing his son, lost him" (GDM, 351). But there is a sense in which Isaac has, in fact, repeated the sin of old Carothers McCaslin, who with a "contempt for all his get" (GDM, 255) disdained obligation for his descendants. Isaac has no son, and, though he may be "uncle to a half a county" (GDM, 3), he seems to have been unable to pass on any of his code of honor even to his kinsman Roth Edmonds. In "Delta Autumn" he is seen as an old man who has done little since his sixteenth year: he seems only to have "lived so long and forgotten so much that [he doesn't] remember anything [he] ever knew or felt or even heard about love" (GDM, 363). Isaac, as an old man, even ceases to care that the wilderness is vanishing since there is "just exactly enough" to last his lifetime (GDM, 354).

Freedom, to Isaac, is not what it is to Thucydus who insists on working out his freedom (GDM, 266), or to Old Ben who puts his freedom in jeopardy (GDM, 295). It is more like the freedom applauded in "warm and air-proof" (GDM, 283) legislative halls, a freedom assumed to have been accomplished by the Emancipation Proclamation. In other words, Isaac looks upon freedom as a state of being, accomplished by proclamation or thousand-dollar payment or by relinquishment. For him, the concept becomes another refuge from the flood.

Ike then is no different from Fonsiba and her husband who also grant magical status to the mere concept of freedom. Fonsiba keeps repeating, "I'm free," as if in her situation freedom makes any difference. It does not. "Freedom" is just an empty word that avails nothing, when on her Arkansas farm there are no crops, no stock, and only a meager and insufficient pension and when her husband only repeats the empty politicians' words about an era dedicated to freedom. Ike sees all this as the "rank stink of baseless and imbecile delusion," meaning only freedom from work, but still Fonsiba asserts, " 'I'm free' " (GDM, 277–80). Just afterwards Faulkner juxtaposes Ike's assertion that he himself is "repudiated denied and free" (GDM, 281). Doubtless the irresponsibility, the empty words, the inertia of the Arkansas Negro are to be compared with Ike's escape under the guise of the word *freedom*. As Ike continues to insist, " 'I am free' " (GDM, 299) and " 'Sam Fathers set me free' " (GDM, 300), it becomes apparent that Isaac, like Fonsiba and her husband, has also endowed the concept itself with the magical power.

So too do Harry and Charlotte in "Wild Palms" endow the concept with magical properties. Harry says that he had once looked *"upon love with the same boundless faith that it will clothe and feed me as the Mississippi or Louisiana countryman, converted last week at a camp-meeting revival, looks upon religion"* (WP, 85). For Harry, the ideal of love has acquired a hyperreality which overbalances life; even love then becomes only another "complete immobile abstraction" (WP, 5). It is not that the ideals of "freedom" or "love" are necessarily hollow; it is just that invoked as a cure-all for human anguish, the ideal becomes as absurdly inadequate a gesture toward reality as Flem Snopes's hat or Thomas Sutpen's design.

So used, the ideal is an evasion. Charlotte and Harry, of course, consider themselves to be seeking and embracing experience at its utmost intensity. But the juxtaposition of their quest for love and the convict's quest for peace implies that each is in flight. In *Flags in the Dust* Faulkner for the first time worked out such a comparison, revealing similarity beneath apparent dissimilarity. He writes that Narcissa Benbow regards the Sartoris twins with "shrinking, fascinated distaste" and thinks "of them only to remember Horace and his fine and electric delicacy, and to thank her gods he was not as they" (FD, 65). But Faulkner ironically implies that both the Sartoris twins and Horace are in reality making similar evasions. Bayard Sartoris returns from the war seeking, like Charlotte in "Wild Palms," adventure, the more dangerous and foolhardy the better, while Horace Benbow returns seeking, like the convict in "Old Man," a quiet dull peace. The implication is that either quest is in reality a romantic flight from the entanglements and caprices of the human community.

In "Wild Palms" Charlotte and Harry seem to be not so much in love as in love with an idea, the *"idea of illicit love"* (WP, 82). They cannot bear to think that there is a *"routine even of sinning"* (WP, 126), and they keep running to find some place, even Utah, where dull sameness cannot tarnish their love. Charlotte is in some respects like Addie Bundren to whom adultery with a man of God seems a compounding of sins, more intense because of its effrontery to God. Addie and Charlotte both yearn for experience which, in its intensity, is more alive and more real. Their romanticism is rather like that of Gavin Stevens, who understands "how much effort a man will make and trouble he will invent to guard and defend himself from the boredom of peace of mind" (T, 135). Charlotte invents trouble by breaking whatever pattern her life begins to settle into. She feels that only when life is perpetually new and only when it includes suffering can it be alive.

In *Love in the Western World* Denis de Rougemont writes that Western man "reaches self-awareness and tests himself only by risking his life—in suffering and on the verge of death" and that this "repressed longing for death, for self-experience at the utmost" manifests itself not only in our ideals of love but also of war.[26] Harry associates Charlotte's death with the waste of human life in the war to make the world safe for democracy, a war aimed at *"preserving nations and justifying mottoes"* (WP, 316). As Edmond Volpe comments, 'This strange and startling reference to the war to end all wars, to the war that revealed to

26 Denis de Rougemont, *Love in the Western World* (New York: Pantheon Books, 1956), 5.

a generation the hollowness of its ideals, places Charlotte's death
on a par with the death of those who died in vain." [27] Faulkner's
point, though, is not just that Charlotte dies in vain but that
her ideals too are hollow and death oriented. For Charlotte has
insisted that "love and suffering are the same thing and that
the value of love is the sum of what you have to pay for it
and any time you get it cheap you have cheated yourself" (WP,
48). Charlotte's ideal of pristine freedom, her longing for intense
experience at its utmost, is, as de Rougemont verifies, as unrea-
listic and death oriented as the most naïve war slogan and
as inhuman, as literally life denying, as Quentin Compson's
vision of Caddy's virginity.

Indeed, Charlotte bears further comparison with Quentin.
When she first meets Harry, she describes the artwork around
them as the "Might-just-as-well-not-have-been" (WP, 41). Her
sculpting, on the other hand, is to be tangible and permanent.
Quentin too wants to make his ideals tangible and permanent.
His ultimate notion of horror is a vision of the "might-just-as-
well-not-have-been," a vision in which "all stable things had
become shadowy paradoxical all I had done shadows all I had
felt suffered taking visible form antic and perverse mocking
without relevance inherent themselves with the denial of the
significance they should have affirmed thinking I was I was not
who was not was not who" (SF, 211). Quentin sees his concrete
identity crumbling about him because he has established it upon
the ephemeral standard of an abstraction which he has tried
to construct into a permanent and inviolable shape. Charlotte
too wants to make the amorphous and unconstricted quality
of "love" into an *idée fixe* as concrete and inviolable as her
sculpture.

In the process of evading such shibboleths as "respectability,"
Charlotte and Harry manage instead to make a shibboleth out

27 Edmond L. Volpe, *A Reader's Guide to William Faulkner* (New York: Noonday
Press, 1964), 229.

of love. The result is inherent in any attempt to make a tangible and permanent refuge out of a concept; for, as Dawson Fairchild remarks in *Mosquitoes,* " 'When you've made a form of behavior out of an ideal, it's not an ideal any longer' " (Mos., 39); it is only a lifeless concept. Therefore Charlotte's decree that " 'it's got to be all honeymoon, always. . . . Either heaven, or hell, no comfortable safe peaceful purgatory between for you and me" (WP, 83) becomes as rigid and life denying as any traditional concept she rejects. Isaac and Harry and Charlotte are all aware of the dangers of using abstractions. But, with each of them, there is a fundamental discrepancy between the professed and the achieved. They try to do without abstractions, but they end by committing the very error they intended to escape. As they invest an ideal, whether freedom or love, with magical properties, they have raised it to the place of an absolute and have thereby devitalized the ideal and themselves as well.

Whenever human life is sacrificed to an abstract ideal, man's deference to concepts becomes indeed pernicious. When Charlotte refuses to have a child, the lifelessness of her ideal is established. The same implications are made in *The Unvanquished* when Drusilla insists, " 'There are not many dreams in the world, but there are a lot of human lives' " (U, 257). We see throughout the Snopes trilogy, in which Flem sacrifices wife and family for the ideal of respectability, how insidious man's concern with concepts may be. We even see it in *The Mansion* with Gavin Stevens, who doesn't marry Linda Snopes because "he had his own prognosis to defend, make his own words good no matter who anguished and suffered" (Man., 219), and with Linda who "bulled right ahead with her idea" (Man., 223). Emphatically, no idea can retain its validity when it is used to usurp or deny life.

Too often man intends to invoke the fixed and therefore invalid idea precisely because he wishes to deny or evade life. As Faulkner said in a 1955 interview, man tries "to use all sorts of shabby and shoddy means and methods to assuage himself" (LG, 102), and the ready abstraction is a convenient means for assuaging the self and excluding contingency. Numbers of characters, for example, avoid introspection or concern for the future simply by relying upon some facile notion of their own imperviousness. Dewey Dell Bundren cannot believe that she would have the bad luck to become pregnant (AILD, 39); Thomas Sutpen cannot believe that his design is fallible; the sentry in *A Fable* cannot believe that death could come to him; he cries, " 'No! Not to us!' " and insists, " 'They cant kill us! They cant! Not dare not: they cant!' " (AF, 321–22). But they do.

Few of Faulkner's characters can cope with the fact of injustice. Most of them prefer to posit an ontology in which right prevails, in which accident and injustice have no place. If everything that *is* is right and whatever happens is for the best, there is no need to interfere. That is why Mrs. Compson insists that no one can "flout God's laws with impunity" (SF, 247). Such a statement, as a defense against despair, is consoling; but it is further a defense against any kind of personal action since, assuming that God will right all wrongs, Mrs. Compson absolves herself of responsibility for dealing with wrong; her passivity is sanctioned by her abstract faith in the right order of the world. Mrs. Compson envisions, of course, the order of the universe as simply an extension and reinforcement of her own private vision. She seeks to impose on the world her own limited understanding of purpose and justice. But human beings cannot dictate to the universe. It is exceedingly nearsighted and decidedly presumptuous of man to demand that his codes and formulas be underwritten by divine law. It is consoling to believe "that decency and right and personal liberty [will] prevail simply because they [are] decent and right" (Man., 302). But such a belief is remote from reality. Such blindness to actuality explains, we learn in *Mosquitoes*, the inadequacies of Dawson Fairchild's (and by implication Sherwood Anderson's) writing. For Fairchild's " 'writing seems fumbling, not because life is unclear to him, but because of his innate humorless belief that, though it bewilder him at times, life at bottom is sound and admirable and fine' " (Mos., 242). Such a belief is as naïve as Horace Benbow's assumption that God is a gentlemen (San., 273), who would not allow injustice to persist. Horace urges Lee Goodwin to testify against Popeye Vitelli, insisting, " 'You've got the law, justice, civilization' " (San., 127) on your side. But neither law nor God intervenes to stop the lynching of the innocent man.

Lee's name is pointedly ironic, for neither in *Sanctuary* nor in the rest of Faulkner's fiction do the good win out. Robert Jacobs writes that in the Faulkner canon "to the genuinely humble and the genuinely proud . . . providence generally provides." [28] The characters certainly expect providence to provide and protect; Mrs. Compson insists, " Whoever God is, He would not permit that. I'm a lady' " (SF, 374); but the evidence of the fiction is that God does permit almost anything. He does not provide for such characters as Lee Goodwin or Joe Christmas or Judith Sutpen or Dilsey. Only in the case of Mink Snopes, who makes a contract with God to take care of Stillwell (the man who would murder Mink) and who is rewarded almost ludicrously by having a church fall on Stillwell (Man., 101), does God seem actively to intervene in human affairs.

To be sure, Faulkner's villains usually come to no good end. But, with the exception of Popeye who sees a *deus ex machina* in his arraignment for the wrong crime and therefore submits passively to an absurdly inappropriate death sentence, Faulkner's villains bring about their own destruction. No *deus ex machina* (again with the possible exception of Popeye) accomplishes their demise in the name of justice. In *As I Lay Dying* Vernon Tull examines man's habit of reading providential significance into

28 Robert D. Jacobs, "Faulkner's Tragedy of Isolation," in Louis D. Rubin, Jr., and Robert D. Jacobs (eds.), *Southern Renascence: The Literature of the Modern South* (Baltimore: Johns Hopkins Press, 1953), 173.

catastrophes entirely of his own making and concludes, "If it's a judgment, it aint right. Because the Lord's got more to do than that" (AILD, 70). Most of Faulkner's characters, however, reject the notion that God might have more to do than to wrestle daily circumstance about into a continuous sequence of judgments and rewards. These characters expect a *deus ex machina*. Jewel Bundren protests, "If there is a God what the hell is He for" (AILD, 15). He would, like Mink Snopes, demand that life show him something before he believes. Mink even vows to disbelieve in God because "he had seen too much in his time that, if any old Moster existed, with eyes as sharp and power as strong as was claimed He had, He would have done something about" (Man., 5). The expectation that God will do something about injustice is mistaken because it is founded upon stubborn blindness to reality. It is mistaken, furthermore, because it encourages passivity, as with Wash Jones who assumes that the godlike Sutpen " 'will make hit right' " (AA, 284) or with Lena Grove who waits until the ninth month of her pregnancy to start looking for the father of her child, saying all the while, "I reckon the Lord will see to that" (LA, 18). We admire Lena precisely because she does not leave to the Lord the restoration of her family but instead tries to see to it herself.

The tendency with most Faulkner characters is, however, to slough off the human responsibility for seeing to things themselves. We see the debilitating effects of such irresponsibility in Anse Bundren who insists that " 'there is Christians enough to help you' " (AILD, 49) and that there isn't "any luck living on a road" (AILD, 34); for the Lord "aimed for [men] to stay put like a tree or a stand of corn. Because if He'd a aimed for man to be always a-moving and going somewheres else, wouldn't He a put him longways on his belly, like a snake? It stands to reason He would" (AILD, 35). Anse's incredibly sophistic logic is used to endorse the status quo and justify passivity. So too is Cora Tull's hand-of-God theory. And at the catastrophe when Darl sees a log, which *"surged up out of the water and stood for an instant upright upon that surging and heaving desolation like Christ"* (AILD, 141), he too seems to be reading fate into events. For the log is like Christ not because it walks upon water but because it portends the Bundrens' fate: " 'Log, fiddlesticks,' Cora said. 'It was the hand of God' " (AILD, 145). Such a belief in portents or fate or supernatural intervention is harmful because it offers another refuge from the flood and it encourages, as we have seen, passivity.[29]

Like Henry Sutpen and Charles Bon, who have decided that " 'maybe the war will settle [our dilemma] and we wont need to [take action ourselves]!' " (AA, 342), many of Faulkner's characters rely on an abstraction to settle their difficulties for them. Such evasion tactics are a family habit with the Compsons. Mrs. Compson resigns herself to disaster exclaiming, "Who can fight against bad blood" (SF, 128). Mr. Compson interprets all circumstance to be the working of inexorable fate. And even Jason finds pleasure in the conviction that the disasters which beset him are not of his own doing but rather the workings of a malevolent fate. Getting "actual pleasure out of his outrage and impotence" (SF, 378), Jason seeks the sense of being helpless before circumstance. Chasing his niece and the man with the red tie, Jason thinks "with a sort of triumph" of himself "stalled somewhere miles from town" (SF, 380). Jason's willingness to

29 In *Sanctuary*, Popeye's passive acceptance of the death sentence is decidedly enigmatic. A conjectural reading of the closing pages of that novel suggests, however, that here we may have another example of a sense of fate accomplishing only inertia. That Popeye is to be executed for a murder he did not commit does indeed make "justice a laughing stock" (San., 304), but the irony is double-edged, for Popeye can establish his innocence only by acknowledging that on June 17 he was actually somewhere else committing another murder. Apparently to Popeye the irrationality of being jailed for the wrong June 17 murder is more than coincidence. Exclaiming "for Christ's sake" (an expression new to him) four times in jail, he apparently sees the hand of God in his arrest and conviction and feels helpless to protest. I suggest that Popeye's acquiescence directly results from his seeing the "hand of God" in circumstance and that, no matter how welcome is Popeye's end, the point remains that a belief in fate results in passive acquiescence.

see himself as victim, as an object in the universe, is perfectly consistent with his eagerness to victimize others. Erich Fromm insists that the two impulses are inextricably related and that together they constitute an "escape from freedom." Fromm writes that the authoritarian character "loves being submitted to fate" and explains that "the feature common to all authoritarian thinking is the conviction that life is determined by forces outside of man's own self, his interests, his wishes." [30]

There is indeed with Jason a sadomasochistic desire to see himself as victim of external forces that have the magical power to disrupt and destroy his best-laid plans. Jason's father also attributes to fate a magical power, but with Mr. Compson the pattern of sadomasochism is not evident; Mr. Compson shows no compulsion to victimize others. He is resigned to seeing himself as victim of fate only because he would prefer to evade the blame for his family's disintegration and the responsibility for taking action against specific wrongs. Indeed, the authoritarian impulse is seen only in Jason. The other Compsons wish to rely upon fate simply to excuse themselves, for it is the Compson family trait to say, as Quentin does, "theres a curse on us its not our fault" (SF, 196), though only Quentin would also have asked, "is it our fault[?]" (SF, 196).

Faulkner insists that "it" is indeed man's fault. To blame "it" upon something foreign is only a pathetically absurd attempt to invent alibis and to evade responsibility. The absurdity of such an evasion is perhaps best exemplified in the cotton-picking scene in *As I Lay Dying*. Dewey Dell there determines to leave her seduction to "fate": "because I said if the sack is full when we get to the woods it wont be me. I said if it dont mean for me to do it the sack will not be full and I will turn up the next row but if the sack is full, I cannot help it. . . . I said 'What are you doing?' and he said 'I am picking into your sack.' And so it was full when we came to the end of the row and

---

30 Erich Fromm, *Escape from Freedom* (New York: Rinehart and Co., 1941), 170–71.

I could not help it" (AILD, 26). As Robert Jacobs says, fate to
Faulkner is "a matter of human contrivance, not divine." [31]

Man bears absolute responsibility for his own deeds and
for all human error as well. That is why man cannot justify
passivity, as long as evil exists, by saying, as Horace Benbow
does, "Ah, well, we all respond to strings" (FD, 344), or by
concluding that " 'it aint none of our business' " (H, 81). That
is why man must not posit a teleology by which, in Sartre's
terms, "the universe no longer requires anything of us." [32] For
a faith in and expectation of "simple fundamental justice and
equity in human affairs" (Man., 6) tends to compound with
passivity and inertia or what V. K. Ratliff calls simply "laziness."
Ratliff may theorize, " 'I've heard laziness called bad luck so
much that maybe it is' " (H, 358), but he knows that it is just
simple laziness. He understands how "men have done learned
how to forget quick what they aint brave enough to try to cure"
(H, 99). They can blind themselves to it or forget it, according
to the "fatalism of [their] nature" (FD, 194) by expecting luck
or fate or "simple fundamental justice" to take care of it for
them, but they accomplish in their passivity their servitude. Free
and courageous persons, on the other hand, should try to live
independently of such abstractions as luck, fate, or justice,
whatever evil "it" may embody. As Harry Wilbourne in "Wild
Palms" realizes, courage simply amounts to "a sincere disbelief
in good luck" (WP, 134). It is the willingness to choose the
self rather than to depend upon luck or something outside the
self.

It is not to be supposed, however, that if passivity is an
escape from freedom, then action is an acceptance of freedom.
Motion, it must be reiterated, is not an ultimate value with
Faulkner. The fiction is full of characters who are committed

---

31 Jacobs, "Faulkner's Tragedy of Isolation," 179.
32 Jean-Paul Sartre, *The Emotions: Outline of a Theory* (New York: Philosophical Library, 1948), 65.

to action but who are nevertheless shielding themselves from awareness and responsibility and are therefore denying their freedom. For man may act with great vigor and stamina, but he does so in utter servitude whenever he performs in a make-believe realm or whenever he sees himself as acting as an agent. Fromm sees the impulse to see the self as agent of another as an evasion of responsibility and a masochistic attempt "to become a part of a bigger and more powerful whole outside of oneself, to submerge and participate in it."

This power can be a person, an institution, God, the nation, conscience, or a psychic compulsion. By becoming part of a power which is felt as unshakably strong, eternal, and glamorous, one participates in its strength and glory. One surrenders one's own self and renounces all strength and pride connected with it, one loses one's integrity as an individual and surrenders freedom; but one gains a new security and a new pride in the participation in the power in which one submerges. One gains also security against the torture of doubt. The masochistic person, whether his master is an authority outside of himself or whether he has internalized the master as conscience or a psychic compulsion, is saved from making decisions, saved from the final responsibility for the fate of his self, and thereby saved from the doubt of what decision to make. He is also saved from the doubt of what the meaning of his life is or who "he" is.[33]

When the women of Jefferson persecute Ruby Lamar, they seem to exempt themselves from doubt and responsibility, for they act in the name of "righteousness." Now righteousness is precisely the "bigger and more powerful whole" that Fromm discusses, for it is a cause in whose service they appear to be mere instruments without volition or responsibility. Similarly, the paraphernalia of office, authority, or legality offers an "unshakably strong, eternal, and glamourous" alibi for action. The opening pages of *A Fable* tell of a sergeant, who in donning his uniform has relinquished "volition and the fear of hunger and decision," but in so doing he has erected an "insuperable

33 Fromm, *Escape from Freedom,* 155–56.

barrier of . . . vocation" between himself and "the whole human race." Indeed this sergeant, in seeking "the isolation, insulation, of that unchallengeable immunity" which he assumed upon becoming one with the military, has denied his humanity. Faulkner makes the point unmistakably clear: "in return for the right and the chance to wear on the battle-soiled breast of his coat the battle-grimed symbolical candy-stripes of valor and endurance and fidelity and physical anguish and sacrifice, he had sold his birthright in the race of man" (AF, 9–10). When a man allows himself to become no more than an agent of God or an appendix of the military, the church, the community, or any other institution, he enslaves the self to the not-self and ceases to function as a man. Rather than resenting the encroachments of institutions, however, man willingly, often eagerly, abandons his individuality to them; for he deludes himself into believing that when he functions officially he is relieved of accountability for his own behavior.

With Faulkner, who says the one issue he would preach against is the individual's relinquishing his selfhood to groups (FIU, 269), such fusion of the self with an outside power is humanly disastrous. He considers it "true slavery," [34] defined as "the will of the enslaved [to be] assimilated" (H, 237). He presents it as a dominating compulsion in *Light in August*, where character after character construes his own actions to be guided and controlled by some supernatural power. These characters commit deeds with incredible certitude, the "cold and implacable and undeviating conviction of both omnipotence and clairvoyance" (LA, 190), because they act not as individual men. Hines feels himself guided by "God Almighty" (LA, 354), though his wife says, " 'It was the devil that guided him' " (LA, 355).

34 George Bedell associates such slavery with Kierkegaard's aesthetic stage, for the aesthetic " 'abandons himself to lay hold of something great outside himself' such as Hegel's Idea or a similar abstraction." *Kierkegaard and Faulkner: Modalities of Existence* (Baton Rouge: Louisiana State University Press, 1972), 91.

At any rate, with his sense of mission Hines managed to chase down his daughter as she was eloping: "he took the only short cut he could possibly have taken, choosing it in the dark, out of a half a dozen of them, that would ever have caught up with them. And yet it wasn't any possible way that he could have known which road they had taken. But he did" (LA, 355). Hines's willful fanaticism does indeed seem to lend the man a peculiar power. So too with McEachern who also appropriates holiness to himself, acting "in that same pure and impersonal outrage, as if he believed so that he would be guided by some greater and purer outrage [so] that he would not even need to doubt personal faculties" (LA, 189). McEachern perhaps believes that he "had been guided and were now being propelled by some militant Michael Himself." (LA, 190). Therefore, as the "actual representative of the wrathful and retributive Throne" (LA, 191), he seeks Joe and with amazing surety finds him at a dance with the "harlot" Bobbie. McEachern confronts "Satan" with the "dreamlike exaltation of a martyr," and Joe, after bashing the old man over the head with a chair, runs to the exact spot where the horse is tied (LA, 191-94). Faulkner is at some pains to point out that Joe is propelled just as Hines and McEachern were: "He could not have known where McEachern had left the horse, nor for certain if it was even there. Yet he ran straight to it, with something of his adopted father's complete faith in an infallibility in events" (LA, 193-94).

Such confidence does tend to grant man an infallibility, as we see most clearly in the case of Percy Grimm who chases Joe on a bicycle. Faulkner writes that "the bicycle possessed neither horn nor bell. Yet they sensed him somehow and made way; in this too he seemed to be served by certitude, the blind and untroubled faith in the rightness and infallibility of his actions" (LA, 434). Grimm proceeds down an alley and turns into the very lane Christmas had turned into. Grimm pedals "with the delicate swiftness of an apparition, the implacable undeviation of Juggernaut or Fate" (LA, 435). His face "rocklike, calm, still bright with that expression of fulfillment" (LA, 436), Grimm chases Christmas around a Negro cabin with undeviating certitude: "Above the blunt, cold rake of the automatic his face had that serene, unearthly luminousness of angels in church windows. He was moving again almost before he had stopped, with that lean, swift, blind obedience to whatever Player moved him on the Board. . . . He seemed indefatigable, not flesh and blood, as if the Player who moved him for pawn likewise found him breath" (LA, 437).

Throughout this sequence, Faulkner uses the conditionals "as if" and "as though" to refer to the Player. But the final paragraph of Chapter 19, which includes the castration scene, begins, "But the Player was not done yet" (LA, 439); here Faulkner uses no conditional qualifier. He describes the Player almost as Thomas Hardy might, as a suprahuman force easily and perhaps malevolently manipulating human affairs. Faulkner's ambivalence here is not easily explained. Throughout the fiction there is implicit condemnation of those characters who expect God or the Player or fate to intervene in their lives; yet here and occasionally elsewhere Faulkner implies that a Power does intervene, manipulating events and lending "unfailing certitude" (LA, 439) to those characters who believe in the Power. The infallibility of Hines, McEachern, and Grimm defies rational explanation, but it may be attributed to the purely psychological phenomenon which Norman Cohn describes as the "personal magnetism" of eschatological saviors. In his historical study, *The Pursuit of the Millennium,* Cohn discusses the appearance in the medieval world of self-appointed saviors whose paranoid megalomania "contributed more than anything else to their success"; these men saw the world convulsed in evil and were willing to accept the projection of savior for they "passionately desired to be seen as infallible, wonder-working saviors." There were, furthermore, others who attached themselves to the savior and thereby "partook in that power and thereby became more than human. . . . Their final triumph was decreed from all eternity; and meanwhile their every deed, though it were robbery or rape or massacre, not only was guiltless but was a holy act." [35]

Cohn might well be describing any one of the characters in *Light in August* who imagines himself to be acting in fulfillment of God's will. Such characters direct, in the name of God, appallingly cruel deeds at a scapegoat who is construed to be a demonic Antichrist. To combat demonry and rid the earth of the scourge of evil, cruelty seems necessary, even hallowed. For Hines and McEachern the scapegoat is all womankind with its " 'bitchery and abomination! Abomination and bitchery' " (LA, 341). For Percy Grimm the scapegoat is Joe Christmas as Negro. They are each subject to a paranoid fantasy in which evil can be located and isolated and purged from the earth by the man of God. Each is deluded in his neat division of good and evil; each is deluded in thinking himself the agent of some supernatural power; but *Light in August* does imply that a very real power accrues to each character who indulges in such a fantasy. This power may be explained, not rationally, but mythically. For the mythic consciousness breaks away from the merely pragmatic and rational. It presupposes liberation from the limitations of a finite existence, and, unhampered by the skepticism of a rational mind, it makes of power an actuality, for the human consciousness does carry within it the potential to shape reality into congruence with its will. And when human consciousness, being intentionalistic, becomes public, then intent may become actuality, the possible real, and the "as if" may become "is"; thinking, then, may make it so. In *Requiem for a Nun* and *A Fable* such a mode of thought is presented as the ideal but difficult belief that transcends reason. In *Light in August* that same mode is, however, presented as a decided perversion of consciousness.

35 Norman Cohn, *The Pursuit of the Millennium* (Fairlawn, N.J.: Essential Books, 1957), 70, 71.

The differing points of view may not be explained by any sort of "conversion" to mysticism on Faulkner's part after 1950, but rather by his lifelong insistence upon the necessity of maintaining absolute responsibility and total commitment to the human community. In *Light in August* a mythic mode of thought is used to divide man against man and to transfer to some power outside the human sphere the responsibility for man's own acts. Even Joe Christmas, who denies belief in any such power, tries to construe his murder of Joanna as determined by God's will. Faulkner writes that Joe "believed with calm paradox that he was the volitionless servant of the fatality in which he believed that he did not believe" (LA, 264). With Faulkner such a belief, whether or not it carries with it any sort of mythic power, is pernicious; for, even though it results in action rather than passivity, it nevertheless accomplishes man's servitude. For it projects upon a man the role, not of a subject, but of an object which has no free will and thus is not responsible.

Concepts such as fate or God's will obviously deprive man of volition and accountability and awareness. Paradoxically, however, such deprivation often seems desirable. For, as Nietzsche explains, man often prefers to follow his "instinct for self-preservation that teaches [him] to take things lightly, to skim over the surface, to be false." [36] Or, as Darl Bundren phrases it, "All people are cowards and naturally prefer any kind of treachery because it has a bland outside" (AILD, 127).

Abstract concepts do have an especially bland outside. When existence seems indigestible, the abstraction remains preeminently bland and palatable. And so man creates configurations of reality which ignore reality. They seem to offer a sanctuary from the flood and therefore they make nice believing. Contracting rather than expanding existence, however, such fine dead sounds mock the vital, properly used abstraction.

36 Frederick Nietzsche, *Beyond Good and Evil*, trans. Marianne Cowan (Chicago: Henry Rernery Company, 1955), 65.

Man must deal in abstract concepts in order to know when to plant and when to reap, in order to know what to expect from existence and certainly in order to improve that existence. Man must not, then, fear abstract concepts. Henri Bergson acknowledges that "certainly, concepts are necessary," [37] but man must try nevertheless to free the mind, in Bergson's terms, "from rigid and ready-made concepts in order to create a kind very different from those which we habitually use; I mean supple, mobile, and almost fluid representations, always ready to mold themselves on the fleeting forms of intuition." [38] Faulkner's fiction attests to the necessity of man's freeing himself from the grip of rigid concepts; it testifies, however, to the extreme difficulty of doing so.

37 Bergson, *An Introduction to Metaphysics,* 20.
38 *Ibid.,* 30.

Abstraction
and Authenticity

AUTHENTICITY
You Would Not Escape
Even If You Had the Choice

IN TIMES such as our own, chaos and disruption are no longer the exception but the rule. The pace of change, as Henry Adams predicted, has accelerated rather like a geometric progression, and human existence seems undermined by the very terms it has created for itself. In such a world the center cannot hold. Future shock threatens and human beings are becoming increasingly alienated. Individual man seems no more than a cog in the machine, a usable tool, a "natural resource," [1] or a "manipulable *it*." [2] Depersonalization has become so normative that modern man is almost inured to it. In the latter half of the twentieth century the novelist consequently has resorted increasingly to hyperbolic, exaggerated, distorted, violent means merely in order to show us *how it is* (as Samuel Beckett entitles his very blank

---

1 Ralph Ellison, *Invisible Man* (New York: Modern Library, 1952), 230.
2 William V. Spanos, *A Casebook on Existentialism* (New York: Thomas Y. Crowell Company, 1966), 3. In a letter to this author dated March 5, 1974, Spanos explains these terms: "The *'it'* is Buber's; the *'manipulable'* is mine. The point is that the transformation of a subjectivity—which is always threatening in this unpredictability—into an *it* makes that subjectivity, the nothing, some *thing* that you can *take hold of,* as the etymology suggests. In other words, the phrase is a kind of conflation of all existential philosophy (but especially Heidegger's) which interprets *inauthenticity* as the *objectification* of Nothing for the sake of neutralizing anxiety or dread."

161

and bleak antinovel). Apparently, modern man is in, such a catatonic state that only a sort of literary shock treatment can startle him into consciousness. As Flannery O'Connor writes, "For the hard of hearing you shout; for the nearly blind you draw large and startling pictures." [3]

O'Connor writes to expose the villainy of an age in which persons become so well adjusted that they no longer have to think. Similarly, Ralph Ellison depicts social adjustment as the ultimate sacrifice of individuality; in *The Invisible Man* the individual is threatened with castration and lobotomy; in a surrealistic sequence he is recycled and reassembled by a machine in order to fit society's specifications. In Joseph Heller's view of the modern age the individual is only government issue; he can claim neither his mind nor his body as his own. The system is thus, both literally and metaphorically, out to kill the individual. And from Ken Kesey's perspective the system is a vast combine controlled by the insane in order to annihilate the sane.

Such fiction draws a vividly bleak and terrifying picture of reality. Its violent denunciation and distorted presentation are designed to shock us out of our complacency, to force upon us awareness of the insidious but commonplace threats to our humanity, and to startle us into a determination to preserve or reclaim and reassert our humanity. Yet such fiction remains rather vague about possible means for reclaiming humanity. O'Connor's Hazel Motes blinds himself with lime, wears barbed wire around his chest, and fills his shoes with broken glass. Ellison's invisible man retreats to hibernate underground. In Kesey's *One Flew Over the Cuckoo's Nest* McMurphy's humanity is destroyed by shock treatment and lobotomy; the narrator can only perform euthanasia and escape; he does of course write (as does the invisible man) to tell us how it is. Heller's Yossarian deserts and sets out in the Mediterranean rowing to Sweden.

3 Flannery O'Connor, "The Fiction Writer and His Country," *Mystery and Manners*, ed. Robert and Sally Fitzgerald (New York: Farrar, Straus, and Giroux, 1969), 34.

But even Heller acknowledges that "he's not going to get there, he knows that." [4] None of these books, then, present especially viable or specific alternatives to a deranged modern world. Such random examples indicate that in the latter half of the twentieth century inauthenticity is more than amply documented. Our contemporary writers, however, are rather vague about authenticity.

Heller's *Catch-22* offers the caveat that if people are to be more than garbage (guts, tools, cogs, computer print-outs, natural resources, robots, or government issue) they must reclaim their spirit. Actively resisting the system and finally deserting, as Yossarian does, are assertions of the spirit. Nevertheless, like lighting out for the territory, it is based on the ultimately naïve hypothesis that place can redeem, that the good life can be achieved elsewhere.

Faulkner subscribes to no such naïve hypothesis. His heroes who try to get away from it all find it all following them wherever they go (witness Charlotte and Harry's flight to Utah). In Faulkner, there is no escape. Furthermore, although Faulkner is a supremely individualistic writer who perhaps posits individual freedom as the one absolute,[5] he never suggests that retreating within is any more satisfactory than escaping without. Since the beginning of the twentieth century, many writers tend to suggest that individual consciousness is the primal and the only reality. They then substitute the inscape for the landscape; that is, they imply that since the objective realm has decayed, only the subjective remains. Virginia Woolf certainly does so, and to some extent later introspective writers like Carson McCullers, James Agee, and perhaps even Walker Percy also suggest that consciousness of dehumanization is sufficient defense against

4 Joseph Heller, interview in Robert M. Scotto (ed.), *Joseph Heller's "Catch-22": A Critical Edition* (New York: Dell Publishing Co., 1973), 473.
5 During one of his interviews in Japan Faulkner insisted upon the "fact that man has got to accept freedom or accept servitude—one of the two completely, that there cannot be degrees of human freedom" (LG, 114).

it. To Faulkner, on the other hand, consciousness alone is insufficient as defense and as refuge. It invites a dangerous solipsism, if it allows a man such as Hightower to divorce himself from actuality and to insist with satisfaction and apparently conviction as well: " 'I am not in life anymore' " (LA, 284).

Although twentieth-century art has from its beginnings exposed inauthenticity, the exposures seem to be becoming more and more strident with the passage of time. Faulkner too is amazingly prolific in inventing and animating characters of different sexes, races, ages, and classes who are nevertheless alike in their preference for and compulsion toward inauthenticity. By far the majority of the persons who people Faulkner's fiction seek "to live unconfused by reality, impervious to it" (CS, 898). They prefer, in short, to live inauthentically. Their minds refuse to harbor experiential reality, and so they retreat, finding specious comfort in the abstract symbols, codes, and concepts which deny that such a reality exists.

Such inauthentic responses do predominate in Faulkner's fiction, as they typify our times, yet they do not monopolize it. Faulkner does present some few specific examples of achieved authenticity; a very few of his characters do manage to encounter a chaotic world and to surmount it. Rather than writing only to expose how bad it is, Faulkner does then indicate how it might be better. His evidence seems far more persuasive (aesthetically as well as ethically) than the various vague protests, retreats, denials, and despairing deaths that typify much later twentieth-century fiction.

The Faulknerian hero entertains no illusion that he may escape the world's troubles either by seeking a better place to live or by retreating inward. His affirmation of spirit and humanity in fact is contingent upon his remaining in the "sorry shabby world." Such affirmations may be rare in the fiction, yet they are there. And they are not vaguely implied but rather are portrayed and actualized.

Authenticity is vital, eclectic, unstructured, and therefore difficult to categorize. Faulkner has little faith in patterns and categories and formulas; with Harry Wilbourne he acknowledges, "They cant tell you, forewarn you, what to do in order to survive" (WP, 137). And Faulkner has little interest in the "good and shining angel" (FIU, 2). Yet he does present instances of heroic authenticity about which it is possible to generalize. I suggest that there are three very broad aspects of that authenticity. They are awareness, acceptance, and affirmation. None of these positive expressions is sufficient or meaningful alone, but the three in combination constitute the essence of authenticity.

The first term, awareness, means full consciousness not only of all that is good but also of all that is grievous in human affairs. Particularly does such awareness necessitate acknowledgment of the irrationality of happenstance and the inefficacy of formulas. It means recognition of, in Bergson's terms, the *"depressing margin of the unexpected between the initiative taken and the effect desired,"* [6] or in Mr. Compson's words, the "curious lack of economy between cause and effect" (AA, 119). Such recognition is to Mr. Compson's way of thinking "hard believing" (SF, 221); yet it is necessary believing, for Faulkner's fiction repeatedly establishes how uncontainable, unaccommodating, and inaccessible to rational precept is actuality. At Virginia he says that this "universe is not a very rational one"; in fact it is a "ramshackle universe . . . all irrational" (FIU, 267). To pretend otherwise would be to delude the self. To be aware of the recalcitrance of existence is, on the other hand, in some sense to surmount it.

In these terms, man must acknowledge the existence of evil; for evil exists, first of all, as testimony to recalcitrance, as irrefutable evidence that existence does not conform to man's concepts of goodness and justice. Evil in one sense, then, establishes the

6 Henri Bergson, *The Two Sources of Morality and Religion,* trans. R. Ashley Andra and Cloudesley Brereton (New York: Henry Holt and Co., 1935), 130.

irrelevance and inefficacy of such concepts. Yet evil and goodness are at the same time contingencies of each other, for goodness could not exist except through conflict with its opposite. As the old Negro preacher tells the runner in *A Fable:* " 'Evil is a part of man, evil and sin and cowardice, the same as repentance and being brave. You got to believe in all of them, or believe in none of them. Believe that man is capable of all of them, or he aint capable of none' " (AF, 203). The runner comes to recognize that good requires evil just as much as evil requires good. His awareness of both is the initial step toward the authentic heroism which he clearly exemplifies at the novel's close.

In *The Reivers* the young hero Lucius Priest too is forced to recognize that evil "not only was, but must be, had to be if living was to continue and mankind be a part of it" (Rev., 174). Horace Benbow comes face-to-face with evil in *Sanctuary,* and he finds it not so much in the derelicts from society as in the custodians of order, propriety, and justice; he even finds it in his sister.[7] Horace, however, flees the encounter, rejects the awareness. Lucius Priest, on the other hand, is not defeated by awareness. He resists, as most of Faulkner's characters do not, the impulse for sanctuary from such a disturbing revelation. He has progressed terribly fast "in weary unillusion" (Rev., 228), yet knows he cannot go back. He explains, "I was just eleven, remember. There are things, circumstances, conditions in the world which should not be there but are, and you cant escape them and indeed, you would not escape them even if you had the choice, since they too are a part of Motion, or participating

7 On the day that Narcissa asks him for the district attorney's name, Horace packs up his suitcase (San., 29). Apparently, then, he does realize that Narcissa has betrayed him in the interests of respectability. Recognizing the affinity for evil in such respectable women as Narcissa Benbow, little Belle Mitchell, and Temple Drake and faced with inefficacy of the shibboleths of law and civilization, Horace abandons his Quixotic attempt to combat injustice and to be his own man. When he packs his suitcase and returns to Belle's home and the humiliating routine of picking up each Friday's shipment of shrimp for her, we see only a capitulation.

in life, being alive" (Rev., 155). Though only eleven, Lucius already knows what few other Faulknerian characters can accept: that "you would not escape . . . even if you had the choice." Lucius realizes that he lacks a "receptacle, pigeonhole" (Rev., 155) in which to relegate evil without pain and laceration. What he lacks, in other words, is the habit of evading reality by forcing it into conformity with a few Procrustean abstractions.

Lucius is deeply troubled over the mistreatment of the black man Uncle Possum (Parsham Hood) and the prostitute Everbe. He finds it very hard to acknowledge "that such not only was, but must be" (Rev., 174). But it is even harder for Lucius to acknowledge that he too is implicated in evil and injustice. He acknowledges a knack for deceit "so fast had I progressed in evil" (Rev., 66); yet Lucius is disconcerted to hear that his misdeeds are not to be dismissed with a perfunctory whipping (as they were for Joe Christmas) and that instead he must live with the past and all of his mistakes. Lucius queries, " 'Live with it? You mean, forever? For the rest of my life? Not ever to get rid of it? Never? I cant. Dont you see I cant?' " and yet his grandfather insists, " 'Yes you can. . . . You will. A gentleman always does' " (Rev., 302). Lucius, furthermore, is forced to recognize that his irresponsibility has in some way contributed to the impunity with which the sadist Butch misuses the law. His grandfather tells him that " 'a gentleman accepts the responsibility of his actions and bears the burden of their consequences, even when he did not himself instigate them but only acquiesced to them, didn't say No though he knew he should' " (Rev., 302). It is necessary not only to recognize that evil does exist but to acknowledge that tacit approval is tantamount to complicity. In *The Reivers* such complicity is rather overtly established, but it is implied, though less directly, in the earlier fiction: in, for instance, *As I Lay Dying* Cash recognizes that because he too considered burning the barn, he too is implicated in Darl's guilt.

While recognition of evil is difficult, acknowledgment of complicity in that evil is grievous indeed. Nevertheless, authenticity is predicated upon such a shattering awareness and acknowledgment. In *Mosquitoes*, Gordon explains that " 'only an idiot has no grief; only a fool would forget it. What else is there in this world sharp enough to stick to your guts?' " (Mos., 329). Faulkner's fiction is full of fools who want only to pigeonhole trouble and to forget grief, but Faulkner reiterates that "between grief and nothing only the coward takes nothing" (AF, 399). These lines call to mind Cass Edmonds' statement in "The Old People": " 'Even suffering and grieving is better than nothing' " (GDM, 186). They suggest also the choice Harry Wilbourne makes at the end of "Wild Palms" when, through acceptance of grief and responsibility, Harry asserts his own being.

Harry has been an essentially passive character engulfed and uprooted like the convict in the yellow flood of Charlotte's "yellow stare" (WP, 108). He has exhibited a faith in love which seemed to justify carelessness about the future. Faulkner explains that Harry's faith was not "the Micawber-like faith of the inert in tomorrow" but instead "it was a profound faith in her. Not in them, in her. *God wont let her starve, he thought. She's too valuable. He did too well with her. Even the one who made everything must fancy some of it enough to want to keep it*" (WP, 93–94). Harry's faith lacks the self-congratulation of Charles Dickens' Micawber, but it manifests itself in a similar passivity, a similarly irresponsible confidence that God will take care even when man does not. There is some truth in McCord's accusation, " 'You haven't even got the courage of your fornications' " (WP, 101).

Harry's faith in love has encouraged a passivity which denies his full humanity. He emerges from that passivity, however, when he refuses for a time to commit the abortion. It is not an "obsession" on Harry's part, though Joseph J. Moldenhauer insists it is,[8] that Harry wishes to see the child born. It is instead

8 Joseph J. Moldenhauer, "Unity of Structure and Theme in *The Wild Palms*," in Frederick J. Hoffman and Olga W. Vickery (eds.), *William Faulkner: Three Decades of Criticism* (New York: Harcourt, Brace, and World, 1963), 312.

a Faulknerian awareness of responsibility to the future. Harry, however, capitulates and agrees to perform the abortion. Like young Bayard Sartoris, whose reckless driving has caused his grandfather's death, Harry too is "afraid to face the consequences of [his] own acts" (FD, 306). Harry agrees with Charlotte to seek to evade the consequences of their passion and to deny responsibility for their freedom.

That Harry bungles the abortion may be taken as evidence of an unconscious death wish, but I think Harry's conscious explanation of the abortion itself must hold: " 'Then how do you account for this failure?' He could have answered that: *I loved her*. He could have said it: *A miser would probably bungle the blowing of his own safe too. Should have called in a professional, a cracksman who didn't care, didn't love the very iron flanks that held the money*" (WP, 297). But caring deeply, Harry cannot be rational, cold, objective. If, like the doctor that the convict met on the boat, he could perform the operation with "nothing in the world in [his eyes] but complete impersonal interest" (WP, 242), if he could be "as dispassionate as ice" (WP, 246), then no doubt his hand would not have failed him. That it does is irrational and tragic, but it is also an indication of Harry's humanity. The original title for the novel, "If I Forget Thee, Jerusalem," was taken from Psalm 137, verse 5: "If I forget thee O Jerusalem, let my right hand forget its cunning." Harry does deviate from the acceptance of death inherent in Charlotte's rigid ideal. He bungles the abortion; his hand forgets its cunning because he feels human pity and terror over his own deed. That Harry lacks both the tall convict's primitive ability to cope with circumstance and his "clean steady hand" (WP, 265) indicates Harry's fuller humanity, his deeper suffering.

Harry then reveals his greater humanity in his reluctance to perform the abortion and then in his inability to perform it with detachment. And he reveals it finally and conclusively in his refusal to jump bail or to take the cyanide. The abortion was a denial of human responsibility to the future and a refusal to face the consequences of love; remaining in prison is all Harry can do to efface that denial. The Harry Wilbourne we see at the book's close achieves heroic stature because he acknowledges guilt and no longer wants to escape accountability. In Faulkner's scheme of things, suicide would be not a free act but instead only an evasion. Harry's choice *"between grief and nothing"* (WP, 324) recalls the admonitions in *Mosquitoes, Go Down, Moses,* and *A Fable* that only fools or cowards would prefer nothing; by inversion, the suggestion is that to choose to live with grief is courageous.

That Harry's decision to remain in prison is termed courageous while the convict's decision to return to prison is termed cowardly may appear to be inconsistent. The judgments, however, conform to a single principle of accountability: the acceptance of full human responsibility for one's own acts and for their consequences. Such an acceptance of responsibility is the second qualification of an authentic existence. For Faulkner holds considerable contempt for whatever would blind us to experiential realities, and he holds perhaps even more contempt for all of the "abstractions . . . which take all the shame out of irresponsibility" (FIU, 242). Sheltering him from awareness and responsibility, man's lifeless abstractions insulate him from flux and deprive him, as Faulkner sees it, of the human freedom to act as a subject, not an object.

A further comparison of the tall convict and Harry Wilbourne may help to clarify the importance, for Faulkner, of both awareness and acceptance as indices of authenticity. Both men are caught in the "yellow tide" (WP, 315) of catastrophe; both feel the "force and power of blind and risible Motion" (WP, 335) against them; and both make an "ultimate acquiescence to desperate and furious motion" (WP, 157), Harry by choice, the convict by necessity. The adventitious disasters that besiege the convict cannot be rationally explained. They are a "gambit which he had not elected" (WP, 266). With Vernon Tull in *As I Lay*

Dying, he might well have complained, *"It's a fact. A fellow wouldn't mind seeing [his crops] washed up if he could just turn on the rain himself"* (AILD, 85). But the convict has neither brought on the floods himself nor provoked the Lord to do so. That he is nevertheless besieged by disaster cannot be explained; there is no meaning, purpose, or design in the troubles he encounters. The convict is forced to recognize that the world is neither admirable nor fine, but the recognition is too much for him and so he (and with him most of mankind) seeks shelter.

While disaster for the tall convict is unprovoked, with Harry and Charlotte it is entirely a matter of their own contrivance. Faulkner is at some pains to show that their failure cannot be blamed on some arbitrary quirk of circumstance or on some malevolent power above. Charlotte and Harry act entirely as free agents; the convict does not. But Charlotte, along with the convict, complains that circumstance has denied her when she asked so little. All the convict wanted was to earn money in peace: "just permission to endure and endure to buy air to feel and sun to drink" (WP, 256), but when he is evicted from the Cajun's cabin he assumes that even that little bit has been denied him. The convict "wanted so little" (WP, 161), but he had to face the "intolerable fact not that he had been refused but that he had been refused so little" (WP, 169). And Charlotte insists that all she likes is "bitching, and making things" (WP, 287) and that "it seemed so little, so little to want, to ask" (WP, 324). Faulkner feels that man really has no basis for asking and expecting anything of the universe, even so little. For disaster may or may not be provoked, but man should not complain or excuse himself. The tall convict and Charlotte both complain, insisting that they have not merited such injustice.

Harry, though, does not protest. He had once looked *"upon love with the same boundless faith that it will clothe and feed me as the Mississippi or Louisiana countryman, converted last week at a camp-meeting revival, looks upon religion"* (WP, 85); but he comes to realize that courage involves simply "a sincere disbelief in good luck" (WP, 134): a refusal, in other words, to be passive before circumstance. Thus he makes no demands upon the universe; grateful for his brief "bright wild passion" (WP, 279), Harry can accept and endure whatever befalls him. And finally he arrives, through suffering, at the sort of impregnability the middle-aged doctor senses in him: *"There are rules! Limits! . . . To that of love and passion and tragedy which is allowed to anyone lest he become as God Who has suffered likewise all that Satan can have known"* (WP, 280). In accepting grief and suffering, Harry may not become godlike, but he does approach heroic stature.

In *The Wild Palms* both protagonists are initiated into the nature of experience. "Old Man" serves as a fable recording how man, after withstanding ultimate trials, finally allowed himself to be defeated by the inexplicable, the unprovoked, and how he has retreated from the full expression of his humanity. "Wild Palms," on the other hand, tells the story of a single finite being whose first vital human relationship so touches the fabric of his being that he has no desire to retreat into the safe or the comfortable. Accepting full responsibility for the accidental death of his beloved, he seeks no absolution from guilt, no escape from despair. At the book's beginning, Harry is an essentially passive character. At its end, he is a man of courage, possessing the will to endure and affirming his final heroic stature. The profound intensity of his last words reminds us of the grandeur of human commitment: *"Because if memory exists outside of the flesh it wont be memory because it wont know what it remembers so when she became not then half of memory became not and if I become not then all of remembering will cease to be.—Yes,* he thought, *between grief and nothing I will take grief"* (WP, 324). He will not attempt to escape or to insulate himself; Harry will accept responsibility for his deeds and cling to whatever of living remains.

Like Jean-Paul Sartre, Faulkner feels that each man should acknowledge and bear the "absolute responsibility" which is

the "logical requirement of the consequences of our freedom."
As Hightower realizes at the end of *Light in August,* " 'After all,
there must be some things for which God cannot be accused
by man and held responsible. There must be' " (LA, 462). There
are, of course. All history is humanly contrived and man must
accept responsibility for it. Yet Faulkner, even while implying
that man must bear "absolute responsibility," nevertheless evidences far more compassion than Sartre for man's attempts to
slough that burden. Maurice Friedman says of Sartre: "He admits
of no conditioning by society that could excuse one's conform-
ing." [10] To Sartre, no excuse is excusable. In his essay "Freedom
and Responsibility" he maintains that "nothing foreign has decided what we feel, what we live, or what we are." [11] Faulkner
is more inclined than Sartre to acknowledge that things foreign,
like society's prescriptions about black blood, may indeed make
it very difficult for a man to feel and live and be on his own
terms, but Faulkner would nevertheless insist with Sartre that
no man can excuse himself from responsibility by blaming
circumstance. Byron Bunch defines that unavoidable responsibility as the price a good man must pay. He says to Hightower:
" 'I mind how I said to you once that there is a price for being
good the same as for being bad; a cost to pay. And it's the
good men that cant deny the bill when it comes around' " (LA,
369). Young Bayard Sartoris, Temple Drake, Charlotte Ritten-
meyer, and any number of other Faulkner characters have all
tried to deny the bill, to evade the consequences of their own
acts. But with Faulkner you cannot "repair your mistakes [or
anyone else's for that matter] by turning your back on them
and running" (AA, 27). Man must admit his mistakes as part
of himself before he can surmount them.

9 Jean-Paul Sartre, *Existentialism and Human Emotions* (New York: Philosophical
   Library, 1957), 53.
10 Maurice Friedman, *To Deny Our Nothingness: Contemporary Images of Man* (New
   York: Delacorte Press, 1967), 251.
11 Sartre, *Existentialism,* 53.

Man's proclivity for reliving his mistakes in dreams baffled Sigmund Freud for much of his career. He finally realized, however, as he explained in *Beyond the Pleasure Principle,* that man may establish self-esteem by acknowledging error. Thus reliving a failure again and again in a dream is explained as an attempt "at restoring control of the stimuli by developing apprehension." [12] To apprehend is to become fully aware of an experience as an irrevocable part of one's past. Only with such an acceptance can the experience ever be mastered. That is why Mrs. Wallstreet Panic Snopes does not want her husband to change his name, no matter how much she hates " 'them goddamn Snopes' " (T, 149). As V. K. Ratliff explains, " 'She dont want to change it [the name]. She jest wants to live it down. She aint trying to drag him by the hair out of Snopes, to escape from Snopes. She's got to purify Snopes itself' " (T, 149). To change the name would be to grant, with Mrs. Compson, magical power to the word itself and, therefore, to render the self an object of the word. To "purify" the name, meaning to live with it and work against whatever it connotes, on the other hand, is to master the word and to return it to its object status.

The human position in the world should be that of subject not of object. Man is completely free and may not excuse himself from the burden of freedom by blindness, irresponsibility, or passivity. In the Faulknerian scheme of things, a man must be fully aware of the inscrutable elusiveness of flux—its defiance of all the precepts and concepts which would contain it; he must accept responsibility for his own deeds and their consequences and for his complicity in human error; and he must resist the evil he sees around him. The necessity of struggling against evil is the third aspect of human freedom presented in the Faulkner canon. Alfred Kazin finds this theme emerging in the fiction only after 1950. Before that time he insists that "endurance" is "the key word in Faulkner's system of values"; from

12 Sigmund Freud, *Beyond the Pleasure-Principle* (London: Hogarth Press, 1948), 37.

Kazin's vantage point only with *A Fable* does the virtue of prevailing take precedence over that of enduring. But Faulkner himself saw his values more affirmatively. In 1941, he wrote to Warren Beck: " 'I have been writing all the time about honor, truth, pity, consideration, the capacity to endure well grief and misfortune and injustice and then endure again, in terms of individuals who observed and adhered to them not for reward but for virtue's own sake, not even merely because they are admirable in themselves, but in order to live with oneself and die peacefully with oneself when the time comes.' " [13] Implying that Faulkner felt only after 1950 that man must try to struggle against evil, Kazin has, however, disregarded a great deal of the fiction.

The difference between enduring and prevailing appears, in fact, even as early as *Soldier's Pay.* There Cecily and Emmy and Margaret present the three possible reactions to trauma which Faulkner later, talking of *Go Down, Moses* and *A Fable*, differentiated among. At Virginia he called it: "the trilogy of man's conscience [which in *A Fable* is] represented by the young British Pilot Officer, the Runner, and the Quartermaster General. The one that said, This is dreadful, terrible, and I won't face it even at the cost of my life—that was the British aviator. The Old General who said, This is terrible but we can bear it. The third one, the battalion Runner who said, This is dreadful, I won't stand it, I'll do something about it" (FIU, 62).[14] Faulkner, of course, endorses the decision not just to endure or bear it but to prevail or do something about it. In *Soldier's Pay* his trilogy of the conscience clearly distinguishes among Cecily who literally runs away, Emmy who endures, and Margaret who tries to ameliorate. Faulkner himself explained: "In my books . . . I hoped [I]

---

13 Alfred Kazin, "The Stillness of *Light in August,*" in Hoffman and Vickery (eds.), *William Faulkner,* 257; Joseph L. Blotner, *Faulkner: A Biography* (New York: Random House, 1974), II, 1081.

14 Faulkner originally explained the "trinity of man's conscience" in a gloss written for *A Fable.* See Blotner, *Faulkner: A Biography,* II, 1494–95.

showed that injustice must exist and you can't just accept it, you got to do something about it. That when you are brave you may not get the reward for it, but the bravery is its own reward" (LG, 125). Faulkner made that statement in 1955 but he refers to all his books; for throughout the canon, awareness and acceptance are necessary, but they are not enough. The courage to struggle against injustice is, on the other hand, enough; it is its own reward. Such courage is man's way of prevailing in the universe. Ruby Lamar cannot understand that " 'a man might do something just because he knew it was right' " (San., 268), and Temple Drake Stevens cannot understand "why they don't stink—what reason they would have for not stinking" (Req., 65); neither Ruby nor Temple can understand the courage to sacrifice self-interest to do good for its own sake. Faulkner insists, however, that the good deed is humanly valuable only when it is performed for its own sake.

In *The Emotions* Sartre discusses the behavior of a sick person who "had delivered herself from the painful feeling that the act was in her power, that she was free to do it or not. Here the emotional crisis is the abandoning of responsibility. There is magical exaggeration of the difficulties of the world." [15] In these terms even characters so astutely conscious of human motive and human error as Mr. Compson and Darl Bundren have performed a magical exaggeration of the world's difficulties. They have allowed awareness to defeat and debilitate them because they too wish to retreat from human responsibility. The manuscript of *As I Lay Dying* includes a statement which Faulkner deleted from the typescript apparently because it was too obvious. Faulkner cut "It's because he thinks he cannot bear it, O gods. Darl thinks he cannot bear it," [16] but the book establishes that Darl's problem remains his inability to bear absurdity.

15 Jean-Paul Sartre, *The Emotions: Outline of a Theory* (New York: Philosophical Library, 1948), 67.

16 These two sentences are part of a long paragraph in the manuscript of *As I Lay Dying* which was entirely deleted from the typescript. In the paragraph Darl is clearly overwhelmed, unequivocably insane. The deletion seems to have been made so that Darl's insanity or sanity would remain problematic:

Cleanth Brooks explains that Darl is paralyzed by too much truth: "But Darl's truth is corrosive and antiheroic, and in its logic perhaps finally inhuman. Does he really grieve for his mother at all? It would be hard to say. In a sense, he knows too much about her and too much about the absurdity of reality to have any emotional commitment." [17]

It should be reiterated that awareness of absurdity need not obviate commitment, as it does with Darl. Faulkner's heroic characters are always those who have seen how ultimately inaccessible to reason is existence; yet they are not paralyzed by the sight. They indeed exemplify what Paul Tillich calls a "courage to be" in the face of despair. Tillich writes: "Even in the despair about meaning being affirms itself through us. The act of accepting meaninglessness is in itself a meaningful act. It is an act of faith." [18] In the *Sound and the Fury* Dilsey makes such an act of faith. Though she may say, " 'I done stood all I kin' " (SF, 357), she continues to try to ameliorate. She endures pettiness, injustice, and indifference. She can accept her nothingness in the Compson world and can experience human disaster without herself ever being hardened or becoming vindictive or morose. Because it is a part of living, Dilsey accepts grief; because she accepts it and does what she can to minimize it, she surmounts it.

In *Absalom, Absalom!* Faulkner seems to see in man's very indefatigability another such act of faith. Judith Sutpen wisely acknowledges that "it cant matter, you know that, or the Ones that set up the loom would have arranged things a little better, and yet it must matter because you keep on trying" (AA, 127). [19]

Nevertheless, that Darl "cannot bear it" remains the crux of his problem. William Faulkner, "As I Lay Dying" (MS in Alderman Library, University of Virginia, Charlottesville).

17 Cleanth Brooks, *William Faulkner: The Yoknapatawpha Country* (New Haven: Yale University Press, 1963), 146.

18 Paul Tillich, *The Courage to Be* (New Haven: Yale University Press, 1952), 176.

19 Mr. Compson is repeating the conversation between Judith and his mother, repeated to him by his mother. The statement then is not a matter of conjecture but is to be taken as Judith's own.

Judith herself does keep on trying, though to her events are as meaningless as they are tragic, for Judith does not know why Henry shot Charles. She remarks to Mrs. Compson that the war will be over soon " 'since they have begun to shoot one another now' " (AA, 128). That her brother has shot her fiancé and vanished is to Judith inexplicable, yet she perseveres stoically among gratuitous violence and hardship. That Judith can close the door on Charles Bon's dead body and immediately order in one breath cooking and coffinmaking, that she can hold her tears until Sutpen returns, that she can extricate her father's coffin from a ditch and bury him herself do not necessarily imply that Judith is unfeeling. Perhaps *"she had no time to mourn"* (AA, 186), but probably, as the tears indicate, her anguish is so profound that acknowledging it would break her. Like Dilsey, Judith Sutpen endures. And she acts. Surely Judith's adoption of Bon's illegitimate son and certainly her willingness to nurse him through a treacherous yellow fever attack which finally kills them both testify to her active commitment; while Miss Rosa feels that *"there are some things which happen to us which the intelligence and the sense refuse"* (AA, 151), Judith seems to refuse nothing.

Prevailing amongst meaninglessness, Judith exemplifies mankind's capacity for courage. But it is Henry Sutpen who explains, rather as Tillich does, assertion of being as an act of faith, a conquest of meaninglessness: *"and so if you dont have God and you dont need food and clothes and shelter, there isn't anything for honor and pride to climb on and hold to and flourish. And if you haven't got honor and pride, then nothing matters. Only there is something in you that doesn't care about honor and pride yet that lives, that even walks backward for a whole year just to live; that probably even when this is over and there is not even defeat left, will still decline to sit in the sun and die"* (AA, 349). With Faulkner, that man considers himself to be without God or any sure signposts of meaning and yet still declines just to sit in the sun and die is itself an affirmation of monumental stature.

Recognizing on the one hand that "all truth is unbearable" (SP, 318), man must, in Faulkner's view, on the other hand attempt to bear it. In *A Fable* the runner comes at last to understand how man can do both. He concludes that " 'man can bear. anything, provided he has something left, a little something left: his integrity as a creature tough and enduring enough not only to hope but not even to believe in it and not even to miss its lack' " (AF, 203). In other words, the fact that man can exhibit courage or integrity, while accepting the possibility that such virtues may indeed be meaningless, is in itself a guarantee of meaning.

In Japan, Faulkner insisted that "to theorize about an evil is not enough. Someone, somewhere, must do something about it" (LG, 142). It is not enough to become aware of evil and to theorize about it. Nor is it enough to dissociate oneself from it. Isaac McCaslin says only, 'This is bad, and I will withdraw from it" (FIU, 246). The same is true of the Subadar in "Ad Astra" who refuses to return to India. Bland accuses him of " 'clear[ing] out and let[ting] foreigners who will treat the people like oxen or rabbits come in and take it' "; but the Subadar rests easy in the confidence that " 'by removing myself I undid in one day what it took two thousand years to do. Is not that something?' " (CS, 427). To Faulkner, such a negative act may be "something," but it is not much: "What we need are people who will say, This is bad and I'm going to do something about it, I'm going to change it" (FIU, 246). Isaac and the Subadar do very little. Their confidence in their own righteousness is based upon the assumption that evil may be contravened by a few painless gestures. And it offers another example of the way in which man relates to the world by magical action. Mr. Compson and Darl exaggerate the difficulties of the world; Isaac and the Subadar belittle them. All four use the magical shape they place upon existence to deny the further need for their involvement and struggle.

V. K. Ratliff, on the other hand, is not overwhelmed by injustice. He possesses a sort of "moral [or] spiritual eupepsia" (FIU, 253) which enables him to taste it but not to tolerate it, for Ratliff is willing to struggle against injustice. Vernon Tull admits that Flem Snopes's cheating black people " 'aint right. But it aint none of our business' "; but Ratliff insists, " 'I believe I would think of something if I lived there' " (H, 81). Perhaps he would. Certainly he closes the peep show and goes to some expense and trouble to be kind to the helpless wives of Mink Snopes and Henry Armstid. Ratliff says of himself that he is " 'not righter. Not any better, maybe. But just stronger' " (H, 227), but he does admit that maybe all he cares about is "just to have been righteouser" so that his "conscience is clear" (H, 227). Ratliff is an extremely honest man. He realizes that virtue may be, in Robert Penn Warren's terms, a defect of desire, that even the most apparently generous deed may be performed for selfish reasons. And Ratliff is willing to accuse himself of such selfishness. His kindnesses to the helpless seem, nevertheless, generous deeds, as free from self-interest as man's acts can be. Ratliff does, however, tire of his struggle against evil. Crying, " 'I could do more, but I wont. I wont, I tell you!' " (H, 367), in *The Hamlet* Ratliff finally retreats from commitment and the strenuous demands his conscience makes. An older Ratliff says, " 'When you are young enough and brave enough at the same time, you can hate intolerance and believe in hope and, if you are sho enough brave, act on it. . . . I wish it was me,' I says" (Man., 161). Ratliff is often brave enough to act, but not always. But then perhaps no human being ever is consistently brave enough.

Ratliff says he could do more but won't. Similarly, when asked to provide an alibi for Joe Christmas, Gail Hightower cries: " 'It's not because I cant, dont dare to. . . . it's because I wont! I wont! do you hear?' " (LA, 370). But Hightower does make a last-minute effort to save Joe Christmas. Though the attempt is futile, Hightower has aligned himself once again with the living world. Later he presides triumphantly at the birth of Lena Grove's child and tells Byron that he has been "restored" to life (LA, 392). When he acts, Gail Hightower does cease to be a shadow; he is restored to the world of men. For men must, as Gavin Stevens explains, act: " 'Just to hate evil is not enough. You—somebody—has got to do something about it' " (Man., 307). Chick Mallison does something, a great deal in fact. He makes an indefatigable, hair-raising, and ultimately successful attempt to establish the innocence of Lucas Beauchamp and thus prevent a lynching. He does so in fact in direct defiance of wise and cautious and practical adults. Lucius Priest too learns that he must do something about evil and injustice. We can understand and sympathize with eleven-year-old Lucius' desire to abandon his free will and "to return, relinquish, be secure, safe from . . . decisions and deciding" (Rev., 66), but such an option is not open to the mature human being, and it is proof of Lucius' stature that he does not accept that option either. He has come to know that there are times and instances of evil "that all you can do about it is not quit" (Rev., 251).

In *The Mansion* Chick Mallison explains that "what you need is to learn how to trust in God without depending on Him. In fact, we need to fix things so He can depend on us for a while" (Man., 321). A few characters in Faulkner manage to so fix things: Lucius, Chick, and the runner are among them. They are dependable and courageous precisely because they do not depend upon anything foreign to themselves; they may trust, that is, but they do not depend; thus they manage not just to endure, but also to prevail.

That distinction between trust and dependence is crucial in Faulkner. Perhaps it further explains his ambivalence about fate or the Player: there may well be a Player in control of events, but it is nevertheless disastrous to expect and depend upon the Player's intervention. To *depend* upon God or upon any abstraction is humanly debilitating; for whenever he turns to something outside the self for absolution from difficulty, man abandons his responsibility for self-determination. Retreating behind a framework of specious abstractions, he decides on the nonhuman whenever, as Sartre writes in *The Emotions*, his "system is *called* upon to mask, substitute for, and reject behavior that one cannot or does not want to maintain. [It represents] a peculiar subterfuge, a special trick, each [type of abstraction] being a different means of evading a difficulty." [20] Sartre is speaking of a system of emotions, but his observations hold true and are especially applicable to a system of abstractions which man uses to so restructure and pigeonhole a difficult existence that it does not touch him vitally; his imperviousness seems then established, his complacency endorsed.

What the Faulknerian hero should do is to cut himself loose from whatever would desensitize or insulate or assure, from whatever would hold him outside of flux. To do so, he must dismiss all the rigid abstractions by which he has distanced himself from reality. He cannot allow a belief in the right order of the world to justify his passivity, nor can he allow a confidence in supernatural guidance to deny his own accountability. He cannot so objectify, codify, or conceptualize life that it demands nothing from him. For existence demands that man be aware of all it offers: that man acknowledge the impossibility of predicting, categorizing, controlling, or exhausting experience and that he accept grief, suffering, and injustice and nevertheless struggle to do whatever he can to cure them. To do so, he must abandon all the precepts and concepts he has used to restructure actuality into something fixed and certain and manageable. He must strip himself of whatever barriers stand between himself and reality. He must abandon the impulse for sanctuary and involve himself in the actuality of flux. Instead of playing a role or following a code in order to render himself "impervious to actuality," man must be himself and "just do the best [he] can" (Man., 429). As Eula Varner Snopes explains, "You just are . . . and so you do" (T, 94).

20 Sartre, *The Emotions*, 32.

Charles Bon writes to Judith Sutpen that his faith in humanity has been restored because of man's refusal to *"become inured to hardship and privation"* (AA, 130). In other words, authentic man never quite acquiesces; he resists or, according to Bon, at least his body does. And Bon too determines to resist, to act at last. That same letter announces Bon's decision to disregard stigma and marry Judith. As Bon's letter declares, it is because old shibboleths are dead and irrelevant that he and Judith now may, indeed must, act: *"We have waited long enough. . . . Because what WAS is one thing, and now it is not because it is dead, it died in 1861"* (AA, 131). Rather than being mere products of a tradition or mere lifeless abstractions, *"just illusions that [Henry] begot"* (AA, 348), Charles Bon and Judith can now be living human beings. Through their *"hurdling of iron old traditions"* (AA, 207) they have the option to live. Of Bon's decision to marry Judith, *"Henry said 'Thank God. Thank God,' not for the incest of course but because at last they were going to do something, at last he could be something even though that something was the irrevocable repudiation of the old heredity and training and the acceptance of eternal damnation"* (AA, 347). The Sutpens had at this point, Henry felt,[21] the chance of *being* something; but it was not "even though" they repudiated the sterile abstractions of training but actually because they were to repudiate what was no longer valid in tradition that they might at last have been and done something. To disregard whatever is defunct in tradition and training and "be something," on one's own terms, is to act in good faith, to achieve authenticity.

Such authenticity is precisely what Charlotte and Harry in "Wild Palms" strive to achieve. They have been essentially

21 As I read the novel, the entire section in italics, pp. 346–58, is not supposition but historical actuality, given validity by the paragraph on p. 355 which begins, "Nor did Henry ever say. . . ." In other words, the section in italics is Henry's memory of his meeting with his father when Sutpen did play the "last trump" and of his conversation with Bon which ends, *'You will have to stop me, Henry.'* Quentin heard these things from Henry on the September night in 1909 and, like Henry, *"remembers all of it"* (AA, 355).

rebelling against what authorial comment describes as the existence of the "old married," typified by "baseless assurance and hope and incredible insensitivity and insulation from tomorrow" (WP, 254). Yet their faith in love, though hardly insensitive, involves just as much "baseless assurance and . . . insulation from tommorow." They deny their responsibility for the future and for struggling, as at the Utah mines, against evil. They too even come to make a pattern out of love.

Seeking all that is vital and intensely alive in a human relationship, these two lovers make a grand and desperate attempt to break from the devitalized, insular, patterned society most other characters covet. They have realized how debilitating symbols, codes, and concepts may be, yet in breaking away from such prescriptive abstractions, they fail to live in good faith. Faulkner's sympathy is obviously with these two lovers, yet he allows their quest to end in total debacle. He does so not to punish them or to imply that an authentic vital relationship is an unattainable ideal; rather Faulkner depicts the failure of their love in order to indicate instead how very easy it is for man to solidify even the best of dreams and ideals into props of inauthenticity, tokens of bad faith.

Harry prevails over tragedy only when he ceases to run and takes upon himself the burden of human responsibility. He has awakened, only belatedly, to the baselessness of his assurance, the selfishness of his tomorrowless days, and the irresponsibility of his solipsism. It is too late for Harry to "do something" about evil, but at least he has experienced an awakening and has accepted accountability. Only at the novel's end does Harry come to live in good faith and to make an affirmation in the midst of despair.

In *A Fable* the runner too undergoes an initiation into experience. He comes to see the recalcitrance of actuality and he too comes to replace irresponsibility with responsibility. He had relied upon, "in place of the harassing ordeal of thought[,] a fragment out of the old time:"

lo, I have committed fornication.
But that was in another country; and besides,
the wench is dead. (AF, 70)

The denial of responsibility in the quotation from Marlowe has offered another shelter from existence. But the runner no longer wants to escape the ordeals of either thinking or acting. He becomes willing to accept his involvement with all mankind, even though that involvement means suffering and death. Such involvement is an act of love and commitment. In affirms that man is not garbage but rather a unique being possessed of a soul. It challenges paradise (AF, 153). The garden world was well lost because its very insularity, though safe and secure, was a limitation. Faulkner suggests, "Maybe there's no such thing as peace, that it is a negative quality" and "Maybe peace is not is, but was" (FIU, 67). His characters who live authentically then do not seek peace or sanctuary. Instead they encounter the "living and fluid world" which is neither safe nor secure; it is not even rational or just. They assert themselves in hopes of improving the quality of that living world.

Faulkner's vision of that living, fluid world is no more palliative than that of the generations of fiction writers who follow him. The avarice, cruelty, and injustice he depicts convince us that this is indeed a "ramshackle universe" (FIU, 267) and that "all truth is unbearable" (SP, 318). Yet paradoxically the fiction also convincingly affirms that man may bear the unbearable. Even Hightower recognizes, "Man performs, engenders, so much more than he can or should have to bear. That's how he finds that he can bear anything" (LA, 262). Faulkner writes of course about a great many characters who try to bear nothing. They retreat from this irrational world by using abstractions to create an intentionally Edenic but actually insipid and illusory sanctuary. Faulkner does depict, as we have seen in this chapter, some few other characters who are willing to encounter actuality face-to-face and who can sustain the experience. These characters do surmount the flood and manage to prevail in the universe.

ABSTRACTION
Shapes and Sounds
as Means to Truth

IN AN AGE when empiricism, generally considered a panacea, nevertheless is so woefully incapable of curing our troubles, it is tempting to confuse cure with symptom; thus there is a certain rather modish tendency today to blame empirical methodology not only for the inefficacy of its solutions but also for the problems of modernity itself. According to this line of thinking, man's reason is progenitor of all his problems. Twentieth-century romantics, artists and critics alike, lament our loss of emotion, intuition, sensitivity, and love, our respect for reason alone. They regret the disease of civilization and speak of art as if all it should do is to reinstate within us the primacy of the instincts and reclaim for us contact with the physical world. According to Ihab Hassan, the logic of such an argument, following Sigmund Freud and Norman O. Brown, is that "repression begets civilization, civilization begets more repression, more repression begets abstraction, and abstraction begets death." [1] The implication is that abstract thinking will dehumanize humanity.

1 Ihab Hassan, *The Literature of Silence: Henry Miller and Samuel Beckett* (New York: Alfred A. Knopf, 1967), 25.

186

That, at any rate, is the antiintellectual position paradoxically adopted by a great many very intellectual persons today. Such people assume, with D. H. Lawrence, that the real job for the scientist or artist is at last "to free us from the most hateful of all shackles, the shackles of ideas and ideals." [2] Such a reaction unfortunately counters one extreme with another and results in severe fragmentation. It involves, furthermore, a distortion of the Lawrentian point of view, for even D. H. Lawrence insisted that he emphasized the body more than the mind only to right the balance in an age which had lost touch with the physical. Today, however, many pseudoromantics and self-proclaimed disciples of Lawrence seize upon only a part of Lawrence's message, ignoring his overall intent. Thus they would discard mental consciousness altogether and be true only to the blood. Or so they say. The irony lies in the highly intellectual nature of their arguments against the intellect and the naïveté of their assumption about the "natural"; the implication is that a man's brain is not natural to him. [3]

Such a modish stance prods all too many Faulkner critics into romanticizing his idiots, denouncing his intellectuals. Faulkner does exhibit, of course, how very often simple people have retained virtues like compassion and pity while their more cerebral contemporaries have not. The idiot Ike Snopes is a prime example. Of all the menfolk in *The Hamlet* only Ike seems to intuit that there is "something in passion . . . which cares for its own" (H, 221). Only Ike can love without greed, bloodthirst, ego assertion, or conscience, yet his remains a mindless love squandered on a mindless beast. Ike's passion may ironically be purer than most other people's, but the irony serves to expose

2 D. H. Lawrence, *Psychoanalysis and the Unconscious* and *Fantasia of the Unconscious* (New York: Viking Press, 1960), 35.

3 A flagrant example of this sort of argument may be found in *Faulkner's Women: Characterization and Meaning* (Deland, Fla.: Everett-Edwards, 1973), 164–65. There Sally R. Page argues that "in real life man is simply incapable of submitting himself completely to woman and to nature as the idiot can submit himself to the cow. Man is not natural; he is human and fallen."

inadequacies elsewhere, not to imply that the idiot and the cow have an ideal relationship. The tale is a *mock* idyll.

Quite a few Faulknerian critics, however, would idealize relationships almost in direct proportion to their mindlessness. Such critics recognize some of the distortions accomplished by abstract thinking and hypothesize therefore that in Faulkner's world man would be better off if he could not think at all. They assume that only the spontaneous, intuitive, physical reaction has validity. For them any matter of conscience, any abstract question of right or wrong, is merely (as Mr. Compson imagines it is for Charles Bon) "a fetish-ridden moral blundering" (AA, 93). Like Cora Tull they mistakenly sentimentalize inarticulateness or unresponsiveness as proof of a "heart too full for words" (AILD, 24). They therefore discuss Jewel Bundren, the tall convict, Lena Grove, Monk and Fentry in *Knight's Gambit,* and even Ike Snopes and Benjy Compson as Faulknerian heroes.

Those critics who would idealize the preabstracting state of a Benjy Compson or an Ike Snopes have surely misconstrued the fiction, for Faulkner never sets up mindlessness as an ideal. It is not an achievement but a liability that Benjy cannot comprehend such an abstraction as time and that, therefore being "timeless," he loses nothing (A to SF, 4). Three years after Caddy's marriage, girls passing the house with their booksatchels still to Benjy signal Caddy's return. As T. P. says, *"He think if he down to the gate, Miss Caddy come back"* (SF, 63). Benjy's simplified existence is rigid, closed, frozen in time. Caddy, who smells like trees, cannot be herself with perfume. Benjy's "graveyard" must have its blue bottles at either end of the mound.

Benjy's rigid insistence upon the details of order is similar to that which, according to Ernst Cassirer, typifies brain-damaged patients: "Having lost their grip on universals, they stick to the immediate facts, to concrete situations." [4] Such tenacious atten-

4 Ernst Cassirer, *An Essay on Man: An Introduction to a Philosophy of Human Culture* (New Haven: Yale University Press, 1944), 41.

tion to the predictables of existence—concrete details and the certainty of routine—signifies total inability to cope with flux and the indeterminacy of human existence. Although Lawrance Thompson may consider Benjy's role at the novel's end to be a reestablishment of "the ritual of orderly return" and Benjy himself to represent "the human power to create order," [5] common sense should indicate just how absurd it would be to accept Benjy as an ideal. For Benjy's sense of order does not shape human flux; it is simply incapable of assimilating or comprehending it. Like the brain-damaged patients Cassirer describes, Benjy demands that which is rigid, mechanical, unchanging, only because he is incapable of accepting that which changes. That Benjy with his "tranquil and empty" (SF, 354) mind can accept no change in the rigid order of things, that a change in scent or the removal of a bottle or a reversal of direction can send him into an "unbelievable crescendo" (SF, 400) of howling outrage, indicates just how subhuman is preabstracting rigidity.

Furthermore, although Benjy may indeed serve "as a kind of moral mirror" [6] in which the other characters' humanity or lack of it is reflected, he himself is not a moral character. Morality is impossible without consciousness, and Benjy is not even conscious of his own connections with his hands or with his voice, much less with his actions. He may have, as Thompson insists, "the instinctive and intuitive power to differentiate between objects or actions which are life-encouraging and others which are life-injuring," [7] but so does a dog love what is good to it. Benjy loves three things: the pasture, Caddy, and firelight. Caddy is simply one of the things in his life; like the red-yellow cushion and the satin slipper, she is a security object. Ben is outside human relations because no one, not even Caddy, can

5 Lawrance Thompson, "Mirror Analogues in *The Sound and the Fury*," in Frederick J. Hoffman and Olga W. Vickery (eds.), *William Faulkner: Three Decades of Criticism* (New York: Harcourt, Brace, and World, 1963), 223.
6 *Ibid.*, 215.
7 *Ibid.*, 214.

make demands upon him. And he is immune to human vicissi-tudes because, timeless, he loses nothing. Rather than being a symbol of human value as Peter Swiggart,[8] among others, sug-gests, Benjy serves instead as an emblem of subhumanity.

Benjy's subhumanity is established precisely because he is unable to abstract any details from the shifting welter of day-to-day experience. His mind works only mechanically. Entire in-cidents from his past are preserved intact to be called forth by the proper association, as automatically as a coin in a jukebox produces a tune. The complete objectivity of his recollections indicates that, with Benjy, the imagination exerts no shaping influence. Rather than being a participant in its own experience, Benjy's consciousness is passive, mechanical. A single sound can trigger only one response with Benjy. He is incapable of dissociating the golfer's call "caddie" from recollections of his sister. The uniquely human achievement of considering a sound apart from its meaning or of accepting a sound as capable of two totally disparate meanings is beyond Benjy. That Benjy's mind functions only by Hartleian association is in itself a guar-antee that Benjy is immune to the agony of consciousness and totally immune, as Olga Vickery says of another character, "to the uncertainties and anguish which even a limited ability to abstract and generalize can engender." [9] In his 1955 interview with Jean Stein of the *Paris Review*, Faulkner said, "The only emotion I can have for Benjy is grief and pity for all mankind. You can't feel anything for Benjy because he doesn't feel any-thing. . . . Benjy is incapable of good and evil because he had no knowledge of good and evil. . . . Benjy wasn't rational enough even to be selfish. He was an animal" (LG, 245–46). Faulkner's remarks indicate how absurd it would be to idealize the subrational existence which is free from the distorting power

8 Peter Swiggart, "Time in Faulkner," *Modern Fiction Studies*, I (May, 1955), 26.
9 Olga W. Vickery, *The Novels of William Faulkner: A Critical Interpretation* (Rev. ed.; Baton Rouge: Louisiana State University Press, 1964), 10–11.

of abstractions. The character Benjy, who bears some resemblance to a "big foolish dog" (SF, 371), in fact epitomizes a
reductio ad absurdum of the "ideals" of objectivity and primitivism.
As Cleanth Brooks astutely observes, "Evil for Faulkner, then,
involves a violation of nature and runs counter to the natural
appetites and affections. And yet . . . the converse is not true;
Faulkner does not consider the natural and instinctive and im-
pulsive as automatically and necessarily good." [10]

Faulkner may write quite a bit about the simple people, and
the critics may sentimentalize them even more. The fiction,
however, makes no such facile distinction between superior
primitives and inferior cerebrals. Nor does it imply that, because
abstractions are so frequently misused, we should manage to
do without them. No matter how corrupt the abstracting process
may become, Faulkner's fiction offers no justification either for
idealizing Benjy's incapacity for abstraction or for approving
Addie Bundren's rejection of abstraction.

Addie's assumption is that all abstractions are invalid, irrelevant, life denying. She characterizes abstractions as words which
are "no good," for words "dont ever fit even what they are
trying to say at" (AILD, 163). Language has been so misused
by husband, father, lover, neighbor, that we sympathize with
Addie's hostility toward words and understand her determination
to live without words for the touch of flesh on flesh alone.
Nevertheless, the novel itself forces us to acknowledge that Addie
misdirects her hostilities and furthermore that she deludes herself
in assuming that she has been true to the "terrible blood" (AILD,
167) alone.

Even in her passionate affair with the Reverend Mr. Whitfield, Addie never really abandons words for blood, flesh, or
life; for it is the concept rather than the flesh which determines
the affair's intensity. Addie sees their sin as "more utter and

10 Cleanth Brooks, *The Hidden God: Studies in Hemingway, Faulkner, Yeats, Eliot,
and Warren* (New Haven: Yale University Press, 1963), 29–30.

terrible since [Whitfield] was the instrument ordained by God" (AILD, 166). Even this affair of the flesh is determined by a word, for Addie says that she wished to "shape and coerce the terrible blood to the forlorn echo of the dead word high in the air" (AILD, 167). In other words, she is making the deed fit the specifications of the word. Furthermore, in trying to make the affair more horrific, Addie makes tacit acknowledgment that the touch of flesh on flesh is not adequate. She needs the concept of sin to make even sex more intense.

Addie's delusion is further compounded by her concept of "housecleaning." When, in the interests of cleaning house, she tallies up her children, giving Anse two more to compensate for one sin of commission, one of omission, clearly she sacrifices humanity to concept. In fact, Addie's subsequent rejection of those children she considers Anse's alone is as specious an example as any in the canon of deference to an empty abstraction.

Addie deludes herself in thinking that she can do without words and concepts. She cannot do so, nor should she wish to, for no matter how often it is so used (or misused), language is not just a shape to fill a lack. The abstraction which is language in fact is a fulfillment, not an evasion, of existence. Properly used language affirms being. Thus it is only when Addie's eldest son Cash begins to use words to express doubt, concern, pleasure that we are assured of his full humanity.

Because we are probably most familiar with the ways in which it may be either fixed or flexible, in touch or out of touch, language in fact serves as an especially clear example of the way abstractions function. Language is extremely volatile; it has enormous and easily recognized power to reshape experiential reality. Just as honor defended "was whether or not" (A to SF, 4), the spoken word *is*, whether or not. It creates, in other words, its own reality. Thus Quentin Compson wants to make Caddy *"say we did"* (SF, 185) because the word *incest* will create the sin whether or not they have actually committed it. And in *As*

I Lay Dying Darl Bundren says to Dewey Dell, " 'The reason you will not say it is, when you say it, even to yourself, you will know it is true: is that it?' " (AILD, 39). The power of the word is so immense that Dewey Dell apparently feels that only when the word is spoken will the pregnancy be actualized.

Words have power to create reality, but they also have the potential to displace or to destroy it. In *The Town* Gavin Stevens thinks about Linda Snopes's "good name" and hypothesizes that such words destroy the very qualities they are intended to represent: "You see? That was it: the very words *reputation* and *good name*. Merely to say them, speak them aloud, give their existence vocal recognition, would irrevocably soil and besmirch them, would destroy the immunity of the very things they represented, leaving them not just vulnerable but already doomed; from the inviolable and proud integrity of principles they would become, reduce to, the ephemeral and already doomed and damned fragility of human conditions" (T, 202). Such a point of view seems curious for such a verbose intellectual as Gavin. Certainly for him language is part of reality, yet he poses as a man who distrusts words altogether. Perhaps, like Addie, he sees only how open they are to abuse, yet unlike Addie, he does not pretend to do without them. At any rate, perhaps we might say to Gavin, as Julius Kauffman says to Dawson Fairchild: you are " 'a funny sort to disparage words; you, a member of that species all of whose actions are controlled by words. It's the word that overturns thrones and political parties and instigates vice crusades, not things: the Thing is merely the symbol for the Word' " (Mos., 130).

Indeed the word is such a volatile catalyst that it may, as Julius suggests, change the course of history. Yet Gavin's fear that the word will doom the principle is realized only when the word is used as surrogate for the principle (the word may be often so misused, but it need not be so). The word does have power to destroy as well as create—Gavin recognizes the power of *"one bald unlovely"* word [apparently "fuck"] to dispel *"all that magic passion excitement"* (Man., 239)—but its positive or negative effect is determined by its human use.

Nevertheless, some Faulkner critics too attack the word itself. And they also are "a funny sort to disparage words." Eric Larsen, for instance, in an article on Faulkner's language writes that words are necessarily "a barrier to truth." [11] But Larsen is puzzled to explain how words, if they are a barrier to truth, may create truth. He concludes that they do so in Faulkner's fiction but considers that fact most ironical.

That words may create truth is neither ironical nor paradoxical, however, if language and art are properly understood. It is true that language may be as irrelevant to experience as Maury Compson's new name; as Dilsey says, *"Name aint going to help him. Hurt him, neither"* (SF, 71). A word may be only a "fine dead sound" (SF, 217) or a shape to fill a lack or to guard against truth; but it may, on the other hand, be a vital part of human experience with power to shape and to heighten human experience. Similarly, all abstractions may be shapes and sounds to guard against truth, or they may be shapes and sounds to enhance truth. They may impede or further the motion which is life, and they may also diminish or enrich the quality of that motion.

Thus we need to reexamine the concept of good faith discussed in the previous chapter in order to determine whether or not abstractions play any part in it. Often of course affirmations of good faith are contingent upon rejection of abstract tradition. Finally Colonel John Sartoris and then his son Bayard resist the traditional code of violence. In *The Unvanquished* we see that each of them becomes truly heroic only when he acts "in the face [or against the face] of blood and raising and background" (U, 249). And the boy named Colonel Sartoris Snopes, who has been brought up to believe "you got to learn to stick

11 Eric Larsen, "The Barrier of Language: The Irony of Language in Faulkner," *Modern Fiction Studies*, XIII (Spring, 1967), 30.

to your own blood or you ain't going to have any blood to stick to you" (CS, 8), also rejects "the old habit, the old blood which he had not been permitted to choose for himself" (CS, 21); he tries to warn Major de Spain that his father Ab is going to burn the barn. After that deed he cannot return home. Both Bayard Sartoris and Sarty Snopes reject an empty tradition and a meaningless code. They do so in order, however, to follow a higher principle of honor. Each has rejected a meaningless abstraction for a meaningful one.

Similarly, Eula Varner Snopes seems to have totally emancipated herself from meaningless tradition. Her love for Manfred de Spain is more important to her than her marriage bond to Flem Snopes. She establishes her superiority and her authenticity by just being herself. As she explains to Gavin Stevens, "You just are, and you need, and you must, and so you do" (T, 94). And so Eula disregards what Gavin calls the "damned female instinct for uxorious and rigid respectability" (T, 182). But the point is that Eula can "just be" because she has risen above irrelevant abstractions, not because she has dismissed abstract thinking altogether. She danced with Manfred de Spain "that way in public, simply because she was alive and not ashamed of it"; she dances then in "splendid unshame" (T, 75). Yet being so abundantly alive does not mean that she disregards loyalty, pity, or concern for her child's future. In other words, meaningful abstractions frame even her splendid vitality.

In the course of *Light in August* Byron Bunch develops from an inauthentic to an authentic existence. That development was alluded to in Chapter VII, but should be examined here because it most clearly exemplifies that there is a difference between the inert and the vital abstraction. To a large extent Byron's development hinges upon his willingness to violate the old inert precepts by which he has lived. He loves Lena Grove *despite* "all the tradition of his austere and jealous country raising which demands in the object physical inviolability" (LA, 44). And he tells Gail Hightower, " 'There are secret things a man can do without being evil, Reverend. No matter how they might look to folks' " (LA, 289). He obeys love rather than precept, need rather than appearance.

Hightower seems to feel that such inner direction is extremely presumptuous. He asks, " 'But are you going to undertake to say just how far evil extends into the appearance of evil? just where between doing and appearing evil stops?' " Byron replies that he is not, but then he speaks "as if he too were waking: 'I hope not. I reckon I am trying to do the right thing by my lights' " (LA, 289). Although Byron will not verbalize the difference between appearance and actuality, he is willing now to reevaluate appearance. He knows that "public talking" does not make truth (LA, 344). And "as if he too were waking," he develops trust in his own judgment. At last he is mature and independent enough to act "by [his] lights"; that is, he can reevaluate prescribed notions of right and wrong, and he can act according to his own understanding of right.

The Reverend Mr. Hightower, of course, suspects that Byron is acting selfishly, not rightly; he even accuses Byron of being helped " 'by the devil' " (LA, 291). But Byron's actions clearly are motivated simply by a strong desire to see right (as he knows it to be) prevail. Byron's concern to find the father of the child because " 'that baby never done the choosing' " (LA, 297) certainly seems unselfish. Furthermore, he seeks to help Joe Christmas for the sake of Joe's grandparents; Joe himself means nothing to him. And Byron fights Lucas Burch because " 'you've done throwed away twice inside of nine months what I aint had in thirtyfive years. And now I'm going to get the hell beat out of me and I dont care about that, neither' " (LA, 415). These deeds hardly seem an attempt to ingratiate himself with Lena. Instead they represent a determined and desperate effort in the interests of justice and decency. Hightower may attack Byron's motives, but he actually objects not to the motives but to the confidence with which Byron discards received morality and obeys his own self-derived standards.

To a certain extent, Byron's actions seem uncerebral, " 'like a fellow running from or toward a gun aint got time to worry whether the word for what he is doing is courage or cowardice' " (LA, 371), yet in a larger sense they are highly rationalized deeds motivated by some concept of right and wrong, some determination to do the best by his light. His code is not received but rather independently derived. He has rethought tradition, but he has not jettisoned it altogether. Before the birth of Lena's baby, Byron pitches a tent by her cabin so that he can be near if she needs him. He knows how irrelevant questions of appearance may be, yet he still defers enough to propriety (out of concern for Lena's "reputation") to put a lock on her door and place himself at some distance from the cabin. And in his involvement with Lucas Burch and Joe Christmas' grandparents, Byron does become in a sense " 'the guardian of public weal and morality' " (LA, 344). In other words, he is concerned about such abstractions as propriety and justice and he understands that inconvenience is the price a good man must pay (LA, 369). Byron begins as an escapist, but at the close of *Light in August* he is " 'desperated up to risking all' " (LA, 475). His development hinges upon awareness, acceptance, and affirmation and further exemplifies that, to lead an authentic existence in Faulkner's scheme of things, it is necessary to go beyond the empty precept, but not to discard the vital abstraction.

The point is that abstractions per se are neither good nor bad; they are volatile and therefore open to abuse. If they become Procrustean distortions of existence used to evade awareness of an irrational world, to deny the need to struggle against evil, or to avoid accepting complete responsibility for human error, then their effect is disastrous. The heroic affirmations discussed in Chapter VII involved no such distortion or evasion. To a considerable degree those affirmations take place precisely be-

cause these characters allow no Procrustean abstraction to intervene between themselves and existence. And yet it would be
naïve to assume that such persons dispense with abstractions
altogether. Their lives, like that of Byron Bunch, are not constricted by rigid abstractions but neither are they so unrestricted
that relevant abstractions such as justice, loyalty, and responsibility do not pertain. Their authenticity testifies that there is
no need to regress to a preabstractive state in order to live in
good faith.

In *Mosquitoes* Dawson Fairchild talks of the difference between people who "destroy life by making it a ritual" and those
who "put life into ritual by making conventions a living part
of life" (Mos., 117). That distinction was important to Faulkner
throughout his career; for no matter how extensive is his disclo-
sure of the life-denying use of abstractions, his awareness that
abstractions may also be life fulfilling remains intact. In
Faulkner's view of things, abstractions may be used to embrace
and enhance life so long as they remain "rooted in the flesh"
(AA, 199). That is, they remain meaningful and vital when they
retain their relations to concrete reality and are not used to
replace or misplace that reality. Harry Wilbourne realizes that
"*if memory exists outside of the flesh it wont be memory*" (WP, 324);
it would be empty, devitalized abstraction. Conversely, if the
flesh exists, as with Benjy, without memory or mental recol-
lection, then it will not be human, for the mind and the body
should exist in conjunction. The abstract creations of the mind
lose their meaning when they lose their connections with the
flesh. Ideally, flesh and spirit, body and mind, feeling
and thought, concrete and abstract should interpenetrate and
amplify each other. The concrete must be impregnated with the
abstract, the abstract embodied in the concrete. Mental constructs
may then expand the depth and range of the physical while
the physical assures the vitality of the mental.

That is why Whitehead talks of the need for a "renewal

of connection" [12] between the abstract and the concrete. In this respect he differs radically from Bergson who assumes that the abstraction, by definition, is divorced from the concrete. With Bergson, the intuition is true and the creations of the intellect are therefore false.[13] And with Bergson reality is flux and the fixed abstraction therefore is unreal. In his book *To Deny Our Nothingness* Maurice Friedman discusses Bergson as an example of a modern vitalist and points out the inadequacies in Bergson's endorsement of simple flux itself: "Understandable as a reaction against the sterile abstractions of philosophical idealism and rationalism, Bergson's vitalism falls into the trap of an identification of energy with ultimate reality and of a relativism in which all movement, of whatever nature, is equally good so long as its flow is not staunched. That Bergson himself would have been the first to be horrified by the Nazi conversion of vitalism into unlimited demonry only shows that he had other values that found no explicit place in his philosophy." [14] Faulkner too may be termed a modern vitalist, but he may not be accused of such relativism. For although Faulkner agrees "pretty much" (LG, 70) with Bergson that reality is flux and insists that "the only alternative to life is immobility, which is death" (FIU, 271), to him flux is simply the nature of things; nowhere does he suggest that mobility itself is an absolute value or that abstractions are necessarily immobile, inert, life denying.

Faulkner does copiously detail negative uses of abstractions. Perhaps he assumed, throughout much of his career, that their positive use is an acknowledged fact. In *Requiem for a Nun*, however, he is explicitly concerned to illustrate that abstractions

---

12 Alfred North Whitehead, *Modes of Thought* (New York: Free Press, 1968), 124.

13 Bergson does speak in *An Introduction to Metaphysics*, trans. T. E. Hulme (Indianapolis: Bobbs-Merrill, 1955), 30, of our need for supple abstractions. Nevertheless, the bulk of his writing seems to imply that a flexible abstraction is a contradiction in terms.

14 Maurice Friedman, *To Deny Our Nothingness: Contemporary Images of Man* (New York: Delacorte Press, 1967), 72.

need not be disastrous, disruptive, or dehumanizing. In the first section of that novel entitled "The Courthouse (A Name for the City)," the physical courthouse of brick and board is presented as symbol of the idea of *community*. Building the courthouse is a community effort which transforms the amorphous frontier settlement into a community of men. Faulkner describes the builders working "as one because it was theirs, bigger than any because it was the sum of all and, being the sum of all, it must raise all of their hopes and aspirations level with its own aspirant and soaring cupola, so that, sweating and tireless and unflagging, they would look about at one another a little shyly, a little amazed, with something like humility too, as if they were realizing, or were for a moment at least capable of believing, that men, all men, including themselves, were a little better, purer maybe even, than they had thought, expected, or even needed to be" (Req., 42–43). Through the symbol, the community experiences a sort of transubstantiation in which the whole becomes more than the sum of its parts.

Requiem's second section is entitled "The Golden Dome." Like the county courthouse, the dome of the state capitol symbolizes a lawful and orderly confederation of men. Representing "the gilded crumb of man's eternal aspiration" (Req., 100), the symbol is "beacon focus and lodestar" (Req., 223) for them to establish "in the wilderness a point for men to rally to in conscience and free will" (Req., 105); the golden dome is "more durable than the ice and the pre-night cold, soaring, hanging as one blinding spheroid above the center of the Commonwealth, incapable of being either looked full or evaded, peremptory, irrefragible [sic], and reassuring" (Req., 110). The dome is durable, not because it is gilded in gold, but because it is a symbol. In *A Fable* Faulkner makes the same point about the unknown soldier monument: "invincible and impervious, to endure forever not because it was stone or even because of its rhythm and symmetry but because of its symbolism" (AF, 434). Marvelous and inexplicable, the symbol is an essential part of civilized existence. As Whitehead writes: "No elaborate community of elaborate organisms could exist unless its systems of symbolism were in general successful. Codes, rules of behavior, canons of art, are attempts to impose systematic action which on the whole will promote favourable symbolic interconnections." [15] The symbol is, however, more than just an efficient device for imposing order. It embodies our immortality, our "universal need," as Robert Jay Lifton phrases it, "for imagery extending beyond the individual life span." [16] As such, the symbol contains a mystical but very real power, for when the pioneers conceived the ideal of *commonwealth* "something happened to them" (Req., 30). Making a lawful confederation is for the pioneers a spiritual experience which confirms the importance of the symbol.

It is through the idea of commonwealth, the concept of cooperation without coercion, and the dome which expresses these ideas that man elevates his existence above the animal level. That complete cooperation in freedom is an unattainable ideal is beside the point. Man works through symbols of an ideal which, though never achieved, are valuable precisely because as utopian ideal they are always above and beyond man's aspiration. Ernst Cassirer in *An Essay on Man* explains: "The great mission of the Utopia is to make room for the possible as opposed to a passive acquiescence in the present actual state of affairs. It is symbolic thought which overcomes the natural inertia of man and endows him with a new ability, the ability constantly to reshape his human universe." [17] The important point with Faulkner is not that Jackson, Mississippi, represents a vulgarization of the ideal of commonwealth, but that because of the ideal something happened to the pioneers: while building

15 Alfred North Whitehead, *Symbolism: Its Meaning and Effect* (New York: Capricorn Books, 1959), 87–88.
16 Robert Jay Lifton, *Boundaries: Psychological Man in Revolution* (New York: Vintage Books, 1970), 61.
17 Cassirer, *An Essay on Man*, 62.

a courthouse, which was symbol more than building, they were transformed.

Faulkner does then explicitly, at least in *Requiem for a Nun*, clarify the importance of abstract concepts and the tangible objects that symbolize them.[18] He does, furthermore, assume that codes are modes of abstraction with enormous potential for value. In "The Bear" it is the ritualized nature of the hunt that keeps the affair from disintegrating into a meaningless animal slaughter and ennobles it into a "yearly pageant-rite" (GDM, 194).[19] And in *The Reivers* too the value of codes and rituals is rather explicitly asserted. At the livery stable, for example, "the mutual gentlemen's assumption was that no one on the staff of the establishment even owned a firearm from the time he came on duty until he went back home, let alone brought one to work with him" (Rev., 6). Yet John Powell's "pistol was the living symbol of his manhood . . . [and] he must have it with him; he would no more have left the pistol at home . . . than he would have left his manhood in a distant closet or drawer when he came to work" (Rev., 7). And, as Lucius Priest explains, "So Father's moral problem was exactly the same as John Powell's, and both of them knew it and handled it as mutual gentlemen must and should" (Rev., 8). In other words they both appear to follow the externals of a code; one pretends to enforce the decree, the other to obey it. They manage thereby to keep the business running and their relationship harmonious.

That incident is accorded substantial attention in the novel, not because it has any essential relevance to the plot, but because it is thematically related to the entire novel's emphasis on the

18 My article *"Requiem for a Nun:* No Part in Rationality," *Southern Review,* n.s., VIII (Autumn, 1972), 749–62, further develops this point.
19 I do not find any irony in Faulkner's referring to the hunt as pageant, rite, or ceremony. In "The Bear" the ceremonial aspect of the hunt is not an evasion of brutality but rather an ordering of man's right relation to the animal kingdom. Through ritual, the hunt has meaning and value. In "Delta Autumn" it is precisely because ritual is no longer valued that the hunt disintegrates into only a meaningless exhibition of man's mastery over nature.

value of codes. Grandfather and Boon Hogganbeck make
their disagreement over whether the new automobile is to be
stored or used "a full-scale action . . . logistics came into it,
and terrain; feint thrust and parry, deception; but most of all,
patience, the long view" (Rev., 32). The form of their almost
military confrontation is enjoyed for its own sake. Similarly,
form is important and valued when Lucius "makes his manners."
Always there is an "unspoken gentlemen's ground" (Rev., 37)
which demands that codes be honored. Thus when Miss Reba
says of Boon, " 'At least you got to admire him for it,' " Lucius
questions, " 'For what?' " and Miss Reba rejoins, " 'You think
that still trying to tear that . . . Butch's head off before they
even let him out of jail, aint nothing?' " and Lucius answers,
" 'He had to do that' " (Rev., 277). The gentleman's code demands
defending women. As Faulkner said at the University of Virginia,
'It's a very fine quality in human nature. I hope it will always
endure" (FIU, 141). Defending women is an obligation that the
gentleman has no choice but to fulfill. In *The Reivers* at least
the code can no more be set aside than that pistol, as symbol
of manhood, could be left behind.

Faulkner's awareness of the positive uses of abstractions
seems to increase with the passage of time, but nowhere in the
fiction is there a denial that the process of abstracting is an
imperative of human existence. We learn in *Go Down, Moses*
that objects may be "insignificant to sight but actually of profound meaning" (GDM, 135). A further dimension of meaning
is added to the relationship of Rider and Mannie by the fire
on the hearth which has burned ever since their wedding night;
the fire symbolizes the permanence of their love; it is extin-
guished only when Mannie dies. It is not intended to stand
in place of love but rather as symbol to intensify it.

Codes too may certainly retain significance. In *The Hamlet*
Ratliff is "moved by his itinerary . . . the pleasure of retaining
it. . . . It was absolutely rigid, flexible only within itself" (H,

62). With Ratliff and characters who are not trying to evade life, order may in itself afford very real pleasure. Codes then are not necessarily evasions. A code of honor prevented Labove from unrestrained stealing of the cleated football shoes; as Will Varner admiringly realizes, he " 'never taken a pair except when [his team] beat' " (H, 124). And it is Mink Snopes's honor which prevents him from stealing even when he has been robbed. Such characters are admirable, while Flem Snopes is despicable, precisely to the degree that they have some codes and principles while he has none and to the degree that the codes are used to enhance, not to evade, ethical responsibility.

Concepts also may be meaningful forces in shaping human actuality, rather than merely "ordered certitudes long divorced from reality" (SF, 155). In *Mosquitoes* Julius Kauffman remarks rather cynically that "man is not only nourished by convictions, he is nourished by any conviction" (Mos., 131). There is indeed a mysterious ineradicable human need to believe in something. Ideally, of course, man continues to believe in universals, what Faulkner calls the "old verities." These verities seem in themselves to possess considerable shaping power. Mr. Compson realizes as much when, thinking of Judith Sutpen, he asks: "Have you noticed how so often when we try to reconstruct the causes which lead up to the actions of men and women, how with a sort of astonishment we find ourselves now and then reduced to the belief, the only possible belief, that they stemmed from some of the old virtues?" (AA, 121).

In the Virginia classroom sessions Faulkner clearly stated that man's survival is contingent upon his ability to conceptualize the ideal: "Without those verities [man] would have vanished, just like the mastodon and the other ephemeral phenomena of nature have come and gone in the history of the world. Man has endured despite his frailty because he accepts and believes in those verities" (FIU, 133). Similarly, Whitehead insists that human existence is distinguished by the ability to abstract. If man's abstractions too often tend to constrict existence, therefore, he must not cease to abstract but rather should revise the "*modes of abstractions*"[20] he depends upon. Whitehead would apparently recommend our use of subtle, fluid abstractions which do not fix but rather expand existence. And Faulkner seems, particularly in the later fiction, to suggest just such a use of abstractions. The verities he speaks of may be the ancient ones, but they retain significance only through flexible contact with a world constantly renewing itself. Instead of being outside of life and offering a shield against it, abstract symbols, codes, and concepts may intensify and transfigure life.

Like Bergson, Faulkner seems to think there are two ways by which we may get outside ourselves: we may move down to homogeneity, repetition, materiality, stasis or we may move up to a "living moving eternity."[21] Apparently the vast pattern of modern life represents, to Faulkner, a downward step. *Requiem for a Nun* especially, however, reflects Faulkner's increasing faith that it is possible to transcend the homogeneous, the material, the rational, and the static and to move upward to a "living moving eternity." Like Whitehead, but unlike Bergson, Faulkner sees in the vital abstraction a means to such a transcendence.

In *Requiem for a Nun* the stories of Cecilia Farmer and Nancy Mannigoe, which have between them "no part in rationality" (Req., 231), exemplify that transcendence. Like a symbolic lodestar, Cecilia draws "the substance—the will and hope and dream and imagination—of all men" (Req., 260) throughout all time. Her face at a window draws a husband out of the "fury and pell mell of battle" (Req., 232) to return, a year later, against all probabilities to marry the unknown girl. The story evidences how a dream has "ever been immune to the ephemerae of facts" (Req., 235). And one hundred years later, Cecilia's name

20 Alfred North Whitehead, *Science and the Modern World* (New York: Macmillan Company, 1925), 82.
21 Bergson, *An Introduction to Metaphysics*, 49.

scratched on the windowpane speaks out of the past to "a stranger, an outlander" (Req., 252), murmuring "from the long long time ago: 'Listen, stranger: this was myself: this was I' " (Req., 262). The experience illustrates Bergson's intuition or White-head's prehension. It is akin to two mystical experiences in *Go Down, Moses,* when Rider sees Mannie, just after her death " 'wawkin yit' " (GDM, 136, 140–41) and when Sam and Ike alone see the magnificent buck Sam addresses as " 'Oleh, Chief. . . . Grandfather' " (GDM, 184). To Faulkner such experiences remain inexplicable, but they do evidence how vast, how "limitless in capacity is man's imagination to disperse and burn away the rubble-dross of fact and probability, leaving only truth and dream" (Req., 261). Having "no part in rationality," the Cecilia Farmer story prepares us for Nancy Mannigoe's story, which is to be approached only after a suspension of rational disbelief.

Just as, in the prose preamble to the last act, Cecilia Farmer's just *being* burst the confines of time, space, and logic, so in Act III, Nancy's just *believing* bursts the structures of law and reason. Her behavior presents a challenge to Temple Drake Stevens to break from that rational-empiric mode, from merely doing her "best . . . according to [a] code" (Req., 54) to accepting a mystical involvement with God and the whole race of men throughout all time. Temple must accept full responsibility for living in time; she must acknowledge accountability and recognize, as Olga Vickery explains, that "man's ethical responsibility is a necessity and not a contingency."[22] To do so she must adopt something of the suprarational faith of Nancy who instructs her just to "believe" (Req., 283). She must adopt, in short, a mode of thought which, like Nancy's, is mythic, not rational; for, being the nun of the title (FIU, 196), Nancy is here presented as possessor of an ideal but difficult belief that transcends reason.[23]

22 Vickery, *The Novels of William Faulkner,* 123.
23 In an article on Faulkner and the question of social commitment, Walter Taylor makes no effort to understand this belief. He dismisses both *Requiem*

Such a belief is what Kierkegaard means by the "leap of faith." It is the "will to believe" not in William James's pragmatic terms but a "will to faith," which demands no empirical substantiation. Temple is reluctant, probably unable, to make this leap because she wants empirical evidence and guaranteed results. She questions Nancy, "And suppose tomorrow and tomorrow, and then nobody there, nobody waiting to forgive me—." Nancy answers simply, "Believe." But again Temple queries, "Believe what, Nancy? Tell me." And again as she exists, Nancy answers, "Believe" (Req., 283).

The play and the book end with this challenge to transcend a pragmatic and rational but limited and insulatory scheme of thinking. Significantly, Nancy cannot detail any one belief which Temple must cling to, for such specificity would limit and fix; nevertheless, the act of hoping or dreaming or believing implies the mental ability to project beyond *what is* with some concept of what *might be*. The distinction is akin to that made in "Carcassonne" between the body which lies "beneath an unrolled strip of tarred roofing made of paper" and "that part [of him] which suffered neither insects nor temperature and which galloped unflagging on the destinationless pony, up a piled silver hill of cumulae where no hoof echoed nor left print, toward the blue precipice never gained. This part was neither flesh nor unflesh" (CS, 895). In other words, Faulkner distinguishes between the body and the mind, the literal and the imaginative. It is the mental and imaginative that project *what might be;* yet, while not of the flesh, they nevertheless retain connection with the flesh.

Although it may sometimes seem that "the body [is] capable of motion, not the intellect" (WP, 13), it is not necessarily so. The mind of Byron Bunch moves, as do those of Eula Varner

---

for *a Nun* and *Intruder in the Dust* by saying that in neither was the author able "to portray heroism except in terms of fantasy and sensationalism." Walter Taylor, "Faulkner: Social Commitment and the Artistic Temperament," *Southern Review,* n.s., VI (Autumn, 1970), 1092.

Snopes, Lucius Priest, the runner, and all the other characters in the fiction who achieve some measure of authenticity. The intellect then need not be suspect. As Karl Jaspers writes, "To protect itself against the absolutization of limited, empirical things in the world, the known and investigable, to hold itself free for Transcendence, and to preserve itself from the empty understanding and the endless formalization of speech which no longer comprehends, thought . . . must always reason in order to perceive that which is more than reason." ²⁴ Man must use his ability to abstract, to conjoin, and finally surmount flux, not to limit or insulate. He is to adopt a sense of being which is beyond reason and which is itself confirmation of meaning in the universe. As Judith Sutpen says, "It must matter because you keep on trying" (AA, 127).

It is Faulkner's final faith in man's power " 'to believe and to hope' " (AF, 203) that perhaps justifies Walter Slatoff's terming Faulkner a "nonrationalist," ²⁵ though Faulkner himself would not be typed by any label but "humanist" (LG, 141). Faulkner holds no contempt for reason. He deplores, however, our restricting the reason to the analysis of finite entities, when man's mental powers are capable of comprehending realities which transcend the finite. He deplores the fact that we have made our symbols and codes and concepts only meaningless shibboleths, emblems "rock-fixed, of things as they are" (Man., 222) rather than means to a "living moving eternity."

Toward the end of *Light in August* Gail Hightower observes that "ingenuity was apparently given man in order that he may supply himself in crises with shapes and sounds with which to guard himself from truth" (LA, 453). Such shapes and sounds are the inert abstractions most of Faulkner's characters use to

---

24 Karl Jaspers, *Reason and Existenz*, trans. William Earle (New York: Noonday Press, 1955), 126.
25 Walter Slatoff, "The Edge of Order: The Pattern of Faulkner's Rhetoric," in Hoffman and Vickery (eds.), *William Faulkner*, 197.

fabricate a sort of sieve interposed between themselves and actuality. The sieve allows them to encounter only that part of experience from which heterogeneity and complexity have been sifted, which is then simplified into congruence with their presuppositions and diminished accordingly. Used thus as a barrier against, a belittlement of, or a refuge from actuality, abstractions are pernicious indeed. Faulkner's fiction also testifies that abstractions may be vital rather than inert. Some few of his characters do manage to keep their abstractions flexible, alive, in touch with actuality. Their example affirms that abstractions need not guard against truth but rather may be a means to a more complete truth.

All literature is itself an abstraction from experiential reality, and it too may be misused to insulate man from life or rightly used to fulfill life. Literature may be just another shape or sound with which man guards himself from truth; it may be just a shape to fill a lack. Or it may pretend to be experience itself accurately reproduced; in that case it may be immediate and concrete, but it remains an emblem "rock-fixed of things as they are." For unless matter is imbued with meaning, it remains merely an assemblage of data, not art. Art, on the other hand, may exist as a vital abstraction whose connections with the "motion, which is life" are never severed. Such literature is as alive, but as difficult and disturbing, as life itself. Fiction which is alive is not to be used in place of the harassing ordeal of thought, for it demands thinking, acceptance, and involvement. It places the full burden of his humanity on man himself. Rather than insulating him, it challenges him, and as it does so it may sublimate not just circumstantial actuality but all humankind.

Modern literature offers us easier reading than the fiction of William Faulkner. It presents us with pleasant and saccharine pictures of ourselves which do indeed make nice believing. But like the vital abstraction, which does not insulate man from flux but rather involves him in a living and fluid world,

Faulkner's fiction replenishes our existence. It renews our connections with actuality and enables us to transcend "things as they are." Faulkner's intention has been "sublimating the actual into [the] apocryphal" (LG, 255). Though difficult and disturbing, his fiction belongs to that body of literature that lives because it is, in Faulkner's sense of the term, apocryphal. As it demands of man an attempt to apprehend the motion which is life, Faulkner's fiction offers man a means for sublimating himself and for prevailing over existence.

Index